Leadership
Coaching

Leadership
Coaching

Working with leaders
to develop elite performance

Edited by
Jonathan Passmore

LONDON PHILADELPHIA NEW DELHI

First published in Great Britain and the United States in 2010 by Kogan Page Limited
Reprinted 2010

120 Pentonville Road	525 South 4th Street, #241	4737/23 Ansari Road
London N1 9JN	Philadelphia PA 19147	Daryaganj
United Kingdom	USA	New Delhi 110002
www.koganpage.com		India

© Association for Coaching, 2010

The right of the Association for Coaching to be identified as the author of this work has been asserted by them in accordance with the Copyright, Designs and Patents Act 1988.

ISBN   978 0 7494 5532 3
E-ISBN 978 0 7494 5902 4

British Library Cataloguing-in-Publication Data

A CIP record for this book is available from the British Library.

Library of Congress Cataloging-in-Publication Data

Leadership coaching : working with leaders to develop elite performance / [edited by] Jonathan Passmore.
    p. cm.
  Includes index.
  ISBN 978-0-7494-5532-3 — ISBN 978-0-7494-5902-4 (ebook) 1. Leadership.
2. Executives—Training of. 3. Mentoring in business. 4. Executive
ability. I. Passmore, Jonathan.
  HD57.7.L4322 2010
  658.4'092--dc22
                                      2009037005

Typeset by JS Typesetting Ltd
Printed and bound in India by Replika Press Pvt Ltd

This book is dedicated to Beatrice.

Contents

Acknowledgements

I would like to thank a host of people for their assistance with this book, not least the authors who gave their time in writing and editing these chapters without remuneration. All the proceeds for this book go to the Association for Coaching to enable them to take forward their work. I particularly appreciate the positive way that all of the authors responded to requests for redrafts and to suggested changes that I as the editor made. I hope they feel the result was a worthwhile effort.

I would also like to thank the people at Kogan Page, Hannah Berry and her team, for their work on bringing this fourth book in this series into print.

I would also like to acknowledge the work of colleagues at the Association for Coaching, which is an excellent partner for this series. Their commitment to the initial project of *Excellence in Coaching* has built and allowed this series to develop.

Finally I would like to thank my wife, Katharine, and our daughter, who arrived during the writing of this book, for accepting the time commitment that developing a proposal, identifying authors, commissioning authors, editing chapters, and managing the project involves.

About the contributors

THE EDITOR

Dr Jonathan Passmore

Jonathan Passmore is one of the UK's leading coaches. He is a chartered occupational psychologist, an accredited AC coach, a coaching supervisor and fellow of the CIPD. He has wide business consulting experience, having worked for PricewaterhouseCoopers, IBM Business Consulting and OPM, and as a chief executive and company chairman in the sports and leisure sector. He is based at the School of Psychology, University of East London, and is Director for the Coaching and Coaching Psychology programmes. He is the author of several books including works on the psychology of social networking and on organizational change, as well as three previous books in this series: *Excellence in coaching, Psychometrics in Coaching* and *Diversity in Coaching*. He can be contacted at: jonathancpassmore@yahoo.co.uk.

ABOUT THE CONTRIBUTORS

Juliette Alban-Metcalfe

Juliette Alban-Metcalfe is an organizational psychologist and Managing Director at Real World Group. She has a particular interest in leadership, equality and diversity, and engagement for sustainable organizations. She has worked across the public sector and in the private sector as an

OD consultant and researcher and has co-authored various psychometric instruments to assess leadership and organizational culture.

Professor Reuven Bar-On

Reuven is a professor of psychology at the University of Texas. He is a pioneer in emotional intelligence (EI) and has been involved in defining, measuring and applying this construct since 1980. He coined the term 'EQ' and has authored 40 publications, including four measures of emotional intelligence. Reuven can be contacted via his website www. ReuvenBarOn.org.

Dr Peter Clough

Peter is Head of Psychology at the University of Hull. He is a chartered occupational and chartered sports psychologist with a particular interest in performance enhancement in stressful environments. He developed the Mental Toughness model and questionnaire (2003) and supervised the development of the Integrated Leadership model and measure. He has wide experience of line management and consultancy in the occupational world. Contact via p.j.clough@hull.ac.uk.

Stuart Duff

Stuart is a partner and Head of Development at Pearn Kandola. He is a chartered occupational psychologist with a background in management development, leadership and coaching. Stuart specializes in identifying leadership talent, developing potential through one-to-one coaching and designing innovative development methodologies. He is the Occupational Editor for the BPS journal *Assessment and Development Matters* and regularly contributes commentary to the national press.

Martin Egan

Martin Egan has operated as an organizational development and coaching consultant across a range of organizations since 2004. He is also an accredited psychotherapist working in an Integral way from a Jungian core. In 2006 Martin established New Direction Consulting to provide integrally informed support for individuals and organizations. He combines scientifically robust approaches to performance and business with insights from Jungian psychology. Martin works internationally with global executives to develop their leadership ability and performance, most recently as Principal Consultant with Axialent Inc. Supporting leaders to create enlivening and effective work cultures is his special interest. He enjoys lecturing and speaking engagements. He is a graduate of the Integral Leadership programme from the Integral Institute Business Centre in Colorado. He holds certification in Conscious Business philosophy and Conscious Business Application Coaching.

Gerard Fitzsimmons

Gerard is head of coaching services at Hay Group in the UK. He spent 2003–06 at the Hay Group McClelland Center for Research and Innovation in Boston and specializes in leadership and organizational effectiveness. Gerard has extensive international and multicultural experience in designing and leading development and coaching programmes across a wide range of business sectors. Gerard can be contacted at: Gerard_Fitzsimmons@haygroup.com.

Professor Adrian Furnham

Adrian is a professor of psychology at the University of London, a fellow of the British Psychological Society and is among the most productive psychologists in the world. He was educated at the London School of Economics and holds four degrees, three at doctoral level. He has written over 700 scientific papers and 57 books. In addition to his role in London he is Visiting Professor of Management at Henley Management College and Adjunct Professor of Management at the Norwegian School of Management.

Dr Marshall Goldsmith

Marshall is a *NYT* best-selling author and editor. His recent book, *What Got You Here Won't Get You There,* is a *WSJ* #1 business best-seller and Harold Longman Award winner for Best Business Book of the Year. Dr Goldsmith is one of the few executive advisors who has been asked to work with over 100 major CEOs and their management teams. He has been recognized as one of the world's top executive educators and coaches by the American Management Association, *Business Week, Fast Company, Forbes, Economist* and *The Wall Street Journal.* His material is available online at www.MarshallGoldsmithLibrary.com.

Samantha Guise

Samantha Guise is a writer and product developer. Her role is to make Hay Group offerings – development materials, e-learning content and feedback reports – engaging and accessible. She works with colleagues and draws on her consulting experience to help clients to get what they need from Hay Group's insights and research.

Professor Jean Hartley

Jean Hartley is Professor of Organizational Analysis at the Institute of Governance and Public Management at Warwick Business School, University of Warwick. Her research interests are in public leadership, and she has been active in both research and development work with local and national politicians, across all parties and with independents, in three of the four nations of the UK. She can be contacted on Jean.Hartley@warwick.ac.uk.

Dr Nollaig Heffernan

Nollaig is a psychologist and consultant specializing in leadership and team building. She gained her PhD for her work on the development of the Integrated Leadership Model (2008). Nollaig can be contacted at nollaig.heffernan@consultant.com.

Dr Ho Law

Ho is a chartered occupational psychologist, chartered scientist, fellow of the Royal Society of Medicine, a founding member of Association for Coaching, Society for Coaching Psychology (Honorary Treasurer), British Psychological Society's Special Group in Coaching Psychology (Chair 2010), and the President of Empsy® Network for coaching (www.empsy.com). He is an international practitioner in psychology, coaching, mentoring and psychotherapy. He is the principal author of *The Psychology of Coaching, Mentoring & Learning* (John Wiley, 2007). He is also a senior lecturer at the University of East London Coaching Psychology Unit, where he teaches on the Masters in Coaching Psychology.

Graham Lee

Graham Lee is Managing Director of The Thinking Partnership, a leadership consultancy specializing in enabling senior managers to express their character strengths authentically within their complex roles. He seeks to integrate learning from business and psychotherapy, and is well known for his influential book, *Leadership Coaching: From personal insight to organizational performance* (CIPD, 2006).

Glenn Mead

Glenn Mead is a full-time coaching consultant with Real World Group and an occupational psychologist in training. He has broad experience of practical leadership development and executive coaching of both individuals and groups in various organizations in the public, private and not-for-profit sectors, including as an officer in the British Army.

Judith Okonkwo

Judith Okonkwo is a business psychologist with a background in human performance. She has worked in Africa, Asia and Europe, and currently practices at the University of Westminster's Business Psychology Centre, where she is also pursuing a PhD. Her research interests include leadership, personality and the transcultural application of business psychology.

Barry Oshry

Barry's work spans a half-century, beginning in 1960 with his selection to National Training Laboratories' first Applied Behavioral Science Intern Program, which introduced him to what he experienced as the magic and power of experiential education. His mission ever since has been to use experiential education as a means of illuminating and empowering people in all the social systems of their lives. Barry is the author of several best-selling books including *Seeing Systems: Unlocking the Mysteries of Organizational Life* and *Leading Systems: Lessons from the Power Lab*. He and his wife – Karen Ellis Oshry – are co-directors of Power + Systems, Inc. www.powerandsystems.com.

Jonathan Perks MBE

Jonathan is Penna's Managing Director of Board and Executive Coaching; a passionate board level leadership coach and inspirational speaker who challenges, supports and inspires leaders to make a positive difference in the world. HM The Queen awarded him the MBE for leadership and he has an MA, MBA, and FRSA. He is an ICF and AC accredited coach. He is a popular speaker and writer and can be contacted at jonathan.perks@penna.com.

Kate Pinder

Kate Pinder is a senior associate with Warwick University and other national organizations, with a background in local government in personnel and education. She is an established national coach and development specialist at chief executive level, working with members and officers. She uses a number of diagnostic tools, is an accredited mediator, and facilitates action-learning sets.

Ian Roberts

Ian is a principal with The Thinking Partnership, an innovative business psychology consultancy which focuses on the character of leaders. His work focuses on the assessment and development of senior leadership talent. Ian is an experienced coach of senior and high potential leaders within the private and public sectors. In the early stages of his career he was in the music industry, then moving into a career as a university lecturer.

Ceri Roderick

Ceri is a partner and leads the Assessment business at Pearn Kandola with over 20 years experience in assessment, management development, coaching, facilitation and organizational learning. Ceri's driving interest is what makes individuals, teams and businesses tick. His work focuses on the pragmatics of making people and businesses perform better. Ceri is a regular press commentator and writes/presents regularly on assessment and leadership issues.

Doug Strycharczyk

Doug is MD for AQR Ltd, which he founded in 1989 and which has since developed into a highly innovative test publisher, working in more than 30 countries. AQR focuses its attention on individual and organizational performance. Doug collaborated with Dr Peter Clough, Head of Psychology at Hull University, to develop the Mental Toughness Questionnaire (MTQ48) and the Integrated Leadership Measure (ILM72), which are distributed through AQR Ltd. Contact via doug@aqr.co.uk.

Katharine Tulpa

Katherine is Co-CEO of Wisdom8, an international coaching firm specializing in board/top-team development, and Chair and co-founder of the Association for Coaching®. She is also a sought-after CEO/global coach, author, keynote speaker, visiting lecturer at the University of East London, and coach mentor. Recipient of a number of awards, including 'Coaching Mentoring/Person of the Year' by Coaching at Work, Katherine is passionate about raising the bar of coaching and stretching global leaders, wholly and authentically, so that they make a positive impact in the world. She can be contacted at ktulpa@wisdom8.com.

Declan Woods

Declan is a board and executive level leadership coach, business psychologist and management developer with a 20-year track record delivering sustainable people-based change. He works with experienced leaders, identified by their organizations as highly talented, to help them reach their maximum potential. After working in corporate performance and post-merger integration, Declan worked as a strategy consultant with Accenture, helping organizations produce and implement corporate strategies. As well as holding an Executive MBA (Warwick) specializing in strategy development, he is accredited as an executive coach with Ashridge and the Association for Coaching (AC). Declan is Penna plc's Director of Public Sector Board and Executive Coaching and coaches leaders across the private and public sectors. He can be contacted at declan.woods@penna.com.

Georgina Woudstra

Georgina is Co-CEO of Wisdom8, an international firm specializing in board/top-team development, Georgina is a strong and experienced coach. She has worked with CEOs and C-suite executives and their teams for over 15 years on achieving greater results, legacy and fulfilment. She can be contacted at georgina@wisdom8.com.

Foreword: The inner game of coaching

This book is filled with useful models, insights, and profound thinking that can serve any serious coach.

Yet from my perspective no model is really useful unless the reader remembers that coaching is fundamentally about facilitating learning and unlearning in the coachee. It is not the problem, the task, or even the fulfillment of a dream that is the coach's primary focus. Coaching is about changes that take place *within* the person being coached. This means that the coach is interacting in a territory that belongs to another person. It is a *sacred* territory precisely because it is *inner*, touching upon on the personal thinking, feeling, and intention of another human being.

There is one law that governs the domain of the inner that must be observed. Because it *belongs* to the one being coached, the person in whom the change is to take place must remain in charge. Nothing can be imposed without the explicit or implied permission of the coachee. Thus the coach is not the boss. This is perhaps the most important understanding for the manager or leader who seeks to coach effectively.

The abilities to learn and unlearn are amongst the most powerful evolutionary forces within each individual or group of individuals. At the same time they are powerful, they are also very delicate. They don't like being tampered with without extreme care. Most adult human beings feel their most vulnerable when in the position of the learner. Learning involves stepping into the unknown and invites a very natural fear. Unlearning, is perhaps an even more difficult and important kind of learning in an age of change because it involves not only confronting the new, but admitting that one's accustomed ways of thinking and feeling may no longer be useful, or at least not useful in the given circumstance.

Thus, unless the coaches have become comfortable negotiating the fears and doubts that accompany learning, they will no doubt invite resistance to the very learning they are attempting to evoke. The coachee that feels judged inevitably shuts down to real learning and reverts to rote learning, lip service, or blind compliance. To overcome this latent resistance, there is no more important skill than non-judgmental awareness.

The challenge of increasing non-judgmental awareness of *what is* requires that a suspension of judgment not only by the coach but by the coachee as well. It is fear of judgment in the eyes of others and oneself that creates resistance to natural learning and inhibits truth from emerging. Creating an environment that minimizes judgment is one of the central attributes of successful coaching. Because coaching takes place in the domain of the inner, the unique human gifts of compassion, kindness, and clarity are required in greater degrees than are normally expected in the fields of management and leadership. How can this be accomplished?

Once I was part of a panel discussing the basic question, what can managers learn from sports coaches. One of panel members was at the time the most successful professional basketball coaches in the world, named Red Auerbach of the Boston Celtics. Red, who had a gruff demeanor and puffed on a cigar throughout the discussion was getting increasingly frustrated by the difficulty of putting into words the essence of what he did as a coach. Finally, in what could be called a moment of spontaneous exasperation, he slammed his hand down on the table and exclaimed to the international TV audience, 'Goddammit, I'll tell you what I do… I love the bastards!' Underneath all the complexities of coaching models, and different styles, and strategies, I this says it all.

W Timothy Gallwey
Author of The Inner Game of Tennis,
The Inner Game of Work *and* The Inner Game of Stress

Introduction

Dr Jonathan Passmore

This book is the fourth in the coaching series with Kogan Page and the Association for Coaching. In the first book in the series, *Excellence in Coaching: The industry guide*, we explored coaching models and core coaching concepts such as ethics, supervision and cross-cultural working. That book has become one of the best-respected introductions to coaching, which is a reflection of the high quality of the contributors who shared their work in it. The book has now been through a series of reprints since its first publication in 2006, and as a result we have worked to update the book, with a second edition containing both updated material in the existing chapters and several new chapters on new models, research and evaluation. In the second book in the series, *Psychometrics in Coaching*, we explored psychometrics and their use in coaching. The book aimed to encourage coaches to take a broader view of their role and extend their practice into a wider range of psychometrics. Such tools can be a useful guide that to help coachees reflect on their own behaviour, personality and abilities, as well as providing a language for a discussion about these attributes, and how the coachee can change and develop to become more effective in their role. The third book, *Diversity in Coaching*, applied a similar approach to diversity, reviewing gender, national and cultural differences, and how these differences may influence the coachee (and coach) in the coaching relationship.

In this book we are returning to a more popular issue: leadership. Once again I as editor have taken the approach of providing writers with a clear and explicit structure. In this case I asked them to write about a specific model, review the research that supports the model and then explore how the model can be of help in a coaching relationship, including offering the reader a detailed case study. However rather than just offer the 12 most well known, we have tried to combine well-known models, such as Porter's strategy model (1985) and Goleman's model of leadership styles (2000) and transformational leadership, with less well-known ones such as the leadership radar. We have also tried to draw work from both the Western view of leadership and other traditions such as Asia, using the ancient writings of Sun Tzu, and African myths.

In the first chapter, I have offered an overview of leadership coaching, signposting the reader to the research, as well as reflecting on how concepts and models in leadership can help some coaches to think more broadly about their role. A brief overview of one model has been offered, drawing on the concept of servant leadership.

In the second chapter Graham Lee and Ian Roberts explore the concept of authenticity. The chapter draws on their thinking about authentic leadership and how this can be used to achieve significant and enduring transitions for leadership performance through coaching. The writers make explicit reference to psychodynamic concepts drawn from the work of Winnicott (1971) and describe how attachment is a key influencer to future behaviour at work.

In the third chapter, on integrated leadership, Doug Strycharczyk, Dr Peter Clough and Dr Nollaig Heffernan have contributed their thoughts on a model developed for the Institute for Leadership and Management (ILM). They describe their integrated model as a 'macro' model. By this they mean it has been designed to enable the coach to take a high-level view of leadership and enables the coach to work within a 'big picture' view of leadership.

The fourth chapter is on emotional intelligence. The chapter, written by Jonathan Perks and Reuven Bar-On, draws on Reuven's work in developing a model of emotional intelligence. The chapter both offers insights into how the model works and indicates how the coach could use this framework in coaching conversations.

In the fifth chapter Stuart Duff and Ceri Roderick offer a new framework for leadership, drawing on their work at Pearn Kandola. The framework provides a structure that they suggest can raise self-awareness in coachees, enabling them to monitor their behaviour and actions on a daily basis and reflect on their role and responsibilities.

The sixth chapter steps back to ancient times and the work of Sun Tzu, a Chinese military advisor. In this chapter Dr Ho Law offers a modern day version of the model, and suggests ways that this text can be used in the executive coaching relationship to help managers plan and win.

In Chapter 7 Professor Adrian Furnham takes a critical look at leadership derailment, and how the coach can work to help leaders identify potentially derailing behaviours and manage this threat as their roles within the organization change.

In Chapter 8 Martin Egan draws on the work of Ken Wilber (1996) to offer a model of integral leadership. Egan seeks to draw together the diverse voices on leadership to build a meta-model of leadership, and in so doing help coaches and their coachees to explore the complexity and inter-relatedness of work and organizations.

In Chapter 9 Professor Jean Hartley and Kate Pinder offer a public-sector view of leadership. They have drawn on their work with central and local government to build a leadership model for political leaders. They note that such leaders, both in national government and in state and regional government, are turning to coaches to help them manage the large, complex organizations for which they are responsible.

In Chapter 10 one of the best-known coaching practitioners, Dr Marshall Goldsmith, offers his insight into leadership coaching with a model for feedback that he has titled 'feedforward'. The chapter offers readers a practical, step-by-step guide to why and how the approach can be used with managers.

In Chapter 11 Barry Oshry, a systems thinker, brings his ideas to a coaching audience. He suggests that managers can often find themselves in places that lead others to behave towards them in certain ways. Such behaviour is not personal, but systemic. He describes these positions as 'bottoms', 'middles' and 'tops'. Barry offers coaches a deeper understanding of these processes and how the coach may bring this understanding into play in the coaching relationship.

Chapter 12 explores transformational and transactional leadership approaches, which have been made popular by the work of Bass (1985) and Alimo-Metcalfe *et al* (2008). In this chapter Juliette Alban-Metcalfe and Glenn Mead explain the importance of transformational leadership and how coaches may help their coachees to move toward more transformational styles.

In Chapter 13 Gerard Fitzsimmons and Samantha Guise from Hay explore a contingency model of leadership, made popular by Daniel Goleman. The model suggests that leaders need to use a variety of leadership styles when working with different people and in different situations. The best leaders adopt all six styles, although they suggest that two of the six styles should be used sparingly.

In Chapter 14 Declan Woods reviews how coaches can help leaders on strategy development. He draws on the work of three of the main writers on business strategy: Gary Hamel, Henry Mintzberg and Michael Porter. He argues that to be effective coaches need to help senior managers recognize the range of different approaches to strategy and provide an independent voice in the strategy building process.

In Chapter 15 Katharine Tulpa and Georgina Woudstra review the arena of working with top teams. They suggest a variety of tools and techniques that the coach can draw on to help engagement and support the one-to-one and team coaching processes.

In Chapter 16 Judith Okonkwo draws on myths and stories in African traditions to inform our thinking about leadership in general and how these ideas in particular may be used in coaching to help leaders think about their leadership roles.

We hope that this book will add to your thinking about leadership development and how you can enhance and extend your coaching practice to draw on evidenced-based thinking and the experience of some of the world's top leadership writers and of coaching practitioners to build your own coaching practice.

References

Alimo-Metcalfe, B, Alban-Metcalfe, J, Bradley, M, Mariathasan, J and Samele, C (2008) The impact of engaging leadership on performance, attitudes to work and well-being at work: a longitudinal study, *The Journal of Health Organization and Management,* **22** (6), pp 586–98

Bass, B (1985) *Leadership and Performance: Beyond expectations*, Free Press, Oxford.

Goleman, D (2000) Leadership that gets results, *Harvard Business Review*, March–April, pp 78–90

Porter, ME (1985) *Generic Competitive Strategies, Competitive Advantage: Creating and sustaining superior performance*, Free Press, New York

Wilber, K (1996). *A Brief History of Everything*, Shambhala, Boston, MA

Winnicott, D (1971) *Playing and Reality*, Tavistock Publications, London

1

Leadership coaching

Dr Jonathan Passmore

INTRODUCTION

This chapter offers an overview of leadership coaching. In the first section I will explore the benefits that models and concepts offer the coach in working with managers in organizations. In doing this, it is recognized that models are shorthand ways to view the world and they can be helpful in exploring the diverse ways of leading others. In addition they can be useful heuristics for managers in guiding their decision making.

In the second section I will discuss the growing evidence base in leadership coaching. While many coaches work in this domain, the evidence of coaching's impact (at least in scientific terms) is still relatively weak when compared with other organizational interventions. However this is slowly changing with increasing numbers of coaching studies being published. This chapter includes a brief account of this growing evidence. In the final part of the chapter I will briefly discuss ways in which the coach can use models and frameworks in their work and review one model that I find useful in my own coaching practice.

THE OPPORTUNITIES OF CONCEPTS AND FRAMEWORKS

There is no shortage of leadership models. Walk into any bookshop or library and there will be plenty of choice in the section on leadership and management. Most offer the reader a unique model, sometimes developed from research but more often the product of the author's thoughts and experiences. Examples include John Kotter and Charles Handy, who have both offered multiple insights into leadership and how leaders can improve what they do. Many are personal accounts of well-known leaders such as Louis Gerstner, former Chief Executive of IBM, or Barbara Cassani from Go airlines, who offer their perspectives on what it takes to be a successful leader.

Sadly many readers, and some writers, interpret these models as universal truths: a model that can be applied in both sunshine and rain. However, it is misleading and unhelpful if leadership theories are ex-pressed in this way. The context is important, as many of the writers in this book and others have emphasized (Grint, 2005; Porter and McLaughlin, 2006). The best leaders select from a wide palette and make informed choices about their interventions and the approaches that suit the individuals, the culture and the context.

I would argue that models are useful heuristics for leaders, but they are not the answer. Conceptual models offer the leader (and the coach) a number of advantages when discussing leadership and leadership dilemmas. First, they offer a lens through which to view the situation. Such a lens provides positioning points that can frame the problem, like longitude and latitude. The model does not exist by itself but these points help to measure, assess and explore the issue. Second, models offer both the coach and the manager a common language with which they can talk about the issue. Models use different words and phrases to describe leadership behaviours. They can be helpful and provide a common way to engage with and discuss the issue. In some instances the issue itself may be outside the manager's awareness and the coaching conversation can help deepen their reflection and self-awareness. Third, models can help normalize events, enabling managers to recognize that they are not alone in experiencing these events, and also challenge their perspective when wider issues have been left unconsidered. Finally, in some cases the model has been developed into a questionnaire. The questionnaire offers feedback for managers on their personal situations or styles and, combined with the common language, can help in building a plan of action. We have explored this concept in more detail in an earlier book, *Psychometrics in Coaching*, but a few of the authors in this book have linked their models to accompanying questionnaires.

Coaches need to be able to draw on a range of useful models, which they should be able to describe and discuss with their coachees. However in doing this the coach needs to be confident the approach fits with the learning style of the coachee, and that the model's language or insight provides a shorthand aid that would help cut through a longer discussion of the problem.

EVIDENCE-BASED COACHING: THE IMPORTANCE OF RESEARCH

There has been a growing body of research in coaching over the past decade (Passmore and Gibbes, 2007) and much of this has focused on the benefits of coaching within organizations. However the area of coaching's contribution to leadership is still relatively under-researched when compared with other areas of leadership development. Organizations are asking more questions about their development decisions: What are the benefits of this approach? What is the return on investment? Does it really work?

I would argue that coaching can contribute in a number of ways to leadership development. The first is in helping leaders and managers to transfer learning from the classroom to the workplace, personalizing the material, and making links from theory to practice and from conceptual to previous knowledge. While this is limited in its scope, Olivero, Bane and Kopelman (1997) argued that such benefits could be achieved through combining training with coaching to enhance learning.

A second benefit of leadership coaching is to enhance skills. As noted above, learning is part of this process, but applying conceptual learning to a new behavioural skill is a specific aspect of it. In this part, leaders with their coaches can use coaching to develop the new skills identified from the learning engagement, through developing a personal plan about how they may apply the new learning, as well as considering the barriers and assessing who may support their new behaviour change. What we know is that forming new habits is difficult, and that support from our wider network is a critical part in successfully breaking habits or forming new ones.

A third area is the development of greater self-awareness. This may come from training; however the Socratic questions of coaching can also bring new insights and learning. This may be achieved through reflecting on feedback or through discussion about a model.

One model I frequently use in my own practice is the six leadership styles described by Fitzsimmons and Guise (2010, Chapter 20). Leaders can often relate well to the six styles, as these are simple to describe and are few enough to remember without reference to notes. From personal experience, many managers often observe that they use two or three styles frequently and ignore the others. Discussing the styles with managers offers two useful paths for conversation, depending on the coachee and the stage of the coaching contract and its goals. The first is to explore why these one or two styles have been ignored. Frequent examples are pace setting and commanding. These can be ignored by some managers as they want to be liked and hold the view that a more authoritative style would be conflictual and negative. This opens the arena of self-esteem, the nature of being a manager and what team members look for in a manager. The second area is to focus on the development of these absent aspects of behaviour, and explore in what situations and in what ways the manager could authentically use these styles.

A fourth potential benefit of leadership coaching is through enhancing the motivation of managers. The role of managing others can be difficult and challenging, and in senior positions can be an isolated one. It is not surprising that being able to talk in confidence to someone who does not have a personal interest in the outcomes is viewed by leaders as intrinsically motivating. This may result from goal setting, which in itself has strong motivational properties, as well as the use of interventions such as motivational interviewing that foster a desire to overcome ambivalence (Passmore, 2008; Passmore, 2007).

The fifth area where coaching can demonstrate a positive contribution in leaders is in helping them develop stronger personal confidence or self-regard (Evers, Brouwers and Tomic, 2006). This confidence may come through reflection on strengths and recognition that these strengths are adequate to achieve the tasks in hand. Alternatively, it may come from developing plans to address perceived weaknesses.

The final area where coaching can impact on leadership is through well-being. A host of studies have been undertaken in this area. These include the positive effects of coaching on stress reduction (Taylor, 1997; Palmer and Gyllensten, 2008) and in building resilience and hope (Green, Grant and Rynsaardt, 2007).

Others have argued that the impact of coaching on leaders is slightly different, preferring the headings: people management, relationships with managers, goal setting and prioritization, engagement and productivity, and dialogue and communication (Kombarakaran et al, 2008). But what can be concluded is that the evidence from coaching research demonstrates the value of coaching as a significant tool for leadership development.

I have drawn a selection of studies together in Table 1.1. They show a sample of the studies that have been undertaken by research in the area of leadership development coaching. There have been relatively few publications focusing on the topic but both *Consulting Psychology Journal* and the *International Coaching Psychology Review* have published special editions on leadership coaching. These contributions have drawn on the experiences of coaching practitioners and offer case studies of the application (Goldsmith, 2009) and value of leadership coaching (Linley,

Table 1.1 A brief sample of leadership coaching research

Study	Brief summary
Jones, G, & Spooner, K (2006)	An exploratory study involving 11 managers. The study found coaching increased self-reported managerial flexibility.
Evers, W J, Brouwers, A and Tomic, W (2006)	A study involving 60 federal government managers. The study found the coached group scored significantly higher than the control group on two variables: outcome expectancies to act in a balanced way and self-efficacy beliefs to set one's own goals.
Barrett, P T (2007)	A study involving 84 managers in group coaching and a control group. The study found that group coaching reduced burnout but did not increase productivity when compared with the control group.
Bowles, S *et al* (2007)	A study involving 59 middle and senior managers. The study found the coach group improved more than the uncoached group.
Feggetter, A J W (2007)	A study involving 10 high-potential UK military personnel. The study concluded that coaching had a positive ROI.
Czigan, T K (2008)	A PhD study examining the development of leadership competencies using multi-rater feedback. The study found coaching contributed towards the development of the competences.
Kombarakaran *et al* (2008)	A study of 114 USA managers. The study found coaching had positive effect on people management, relationships with managers, goal setting and prioritization, engagement and productivity, and dialogue and communication.

Woolston and Biswas-Diener, 2009), as well as offering models for leadership development within coaching (Kemp, 2009).

WORKING WITH SENIOR LEADERS: SERVANT LEADERSHIP

In this final section of this chapter I will explore one leadership model that may be returning to popularity, servant leadership, and how coaches can use this model and others in their coaching practice (Greenleaf, 1977) as an illustration of what is to follow in the remaining chapters of this book.

Greenleaf offered a different approach from many models of leadership, one that emphasizes service to others, a sense of community and the sharing of power and decision making.

While the 10 labels offered in Figure 1.1 do not directly accord with the model or language used by Greenleaf (1977), the approach and the themes are consistent with the overall approach of servant leadership. Its focus is on changing from traditional leadership of controlling to empowering, from the more traditional directing to coaching.

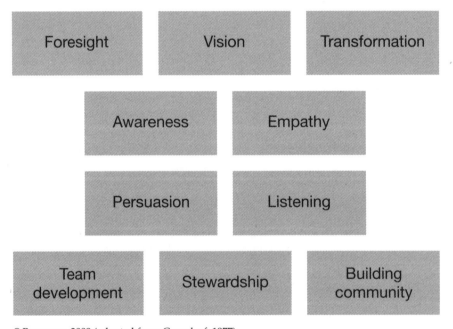

© Passmore, 2009 (adapted from Greenleaf, 1977)

Figure 1.1 The key components of servant leadership

The servant leadership model

The first three themes of team building, stewardship and community building reflect the outward-facing approach of the leader towards stakeholders and employees. The servant manager recognizes the value of developing others, not only for their future contribution to profits or in their current role, but in the wider belief that human development is a virtue that will bring both tangible and intangible benefits to the individual, the organization and the community.

The second theme in the three building blocks of the model is a focus towards building the community. In the past 50 years institutions have become increasingly removed from a single local community, from which they draw their employees and which they serve. As a result organizations can become disconnected from these communities. This is just as true for public sector bodies, local councils and health trusts as it is for multinationals. Most organizations now need to find ways to reconnect. This may be through charity giving to local projects, or positively encouraging senior staff to live locally and contribute to the community with time off for service on local bodies.

The last of these building blocks, stewardship, is the recognition that the chief executive and senior managers are not the organization, but simply hold the organization in trust for future generations.

The next set of four themes, persuasion, listening, awareness and empathy, are the core skills of effective interpersonal behaviour. Listening is often an underused skill. Leaders in Western culture, as contrasted with Japan for example, are more used to expressing their opinions in the hope of influencing the debate. Like many of us, leaders when listening can be just waiting for their turn to talk. Real listening involves not just hearing the words but paying attention to the body language, including changes in breathing, skin colouration and body animation. It also involves aiming to listen beyond the words into the context of what the speakers really mean, and checking this out with them through summaries and paraphrasing. Leaders also benefit from awareness both of others and of themselves. This may draw on awareness of their personality, their preferences, their changing emotions and a recognition that others are different. Managers are then conscious of days when they feel sad or happy, and this, along with other factors, can be managed as part of their interactions with others.

The two elements described above lead towards the third element in this set: empathy. This is the ability to understand the world of others 'as if it were our own'. Empathy can be easy for those we are close to or relate to, but can take effort when we do not know someone or when we recognize wide differences between them and us.

The last element is the skill of being able to persuade. Servant leaders need to be able to listen, empathize and maintain personal awareness, and these skills can be used to influence others. Empathy contrasts with a more directive or commanding style, which instructs and gives out orders. In this element the servant leader is seeking to gain the commitment of others, through reflecting back their values, concerns and views in the communication to produce a win–win outcome. This may come, for example, by consulting staff and including their views as factors in the decision, and when communicating the decision by linking this back to the feedback from staff.

The final set of three – foresight, vision and transformation – is about the longer-term relationships. Leaders need to be able to scan the environment, make sense of the mass of information and translate this into useful information for their teams. They need to hold to a clear vision about where they and the organization are going, and most importantly communicate this in a language that staff can understand. Finally they need to be able to bring about transformational change, responding to the environment and taking forward their vision. Such transformations should affect both the organization and the individuals in a positive way.

Using the model with coachees

The set of 10 elements is a useful set of themes that leaders can consider. In coaching where I have a coachee who is reflective and interested in ideas, and the focus is on leadership development, I would explore what makes a good leader. In most instances I find such coachees talk about their personal experiences or their views of a leader who they admire. One frequently quoted example is Richard Branson; another is Nelson Mandela. In these instances I would encourage the coachees to talk about their perceptions of these individuals and what they do that makes them great leaders. This leads us into building a set of competences, and at this point a leadership model can be useful.

Having gained agreement to talk about a model, I tend to briefly describe the model and if, like Greenleaf's ideas, it contains a number of elements or important relationships, I would write these down for the coachees to help them visualise the model. The 10 categories are easy to remember, so it's the type of model that as a coach you can keep in your head, and the use of modern language gives it resonance for today's manager.

One way to move forward would be to ask coachees to rate themselves from 1 to 10 for each of the elements, with 10 being an exceptional personal strength and one being 'I need to do significantly better in this area.' As self-perceptions give only one perspective, I would then invite the coachees to repeat the rating and imagine it was their boss who was rating them.

The rating provides a great starting point for discussion. One direction is to explore the differences between self and 'imagined boss' rating. It can be useful to get coachees to think about the evidence in each element, and having reflected on this make amendments to both their and their imagined boss rating so these reflect a stronger evidence-based view rather than an initial reaction.

With the ratings available, the coach can explore with coachees their views on what matters most in their roles. In general I would argue that, with a model such as this, all aspects are important but I recognize some are more important than others and this varies between roles. Having identified the important aspects and the areas of lower rating, I would invite the coachee to select areas to focus on for a discussion, selecting two or three for a coaching session.

The discussion would encourage the coachee to talk about what they do, and what an exceptional performer might do in this element. Take listening as an example. Coachees may reflect back that they do listen but that it takes time they don't have, so they often find they interrupt staff or talk over them. We might then explore techniques for them to encourage their staff to stay focused and use a 'lift speech' approach – delivering their message in a limited time. Alongside this we might explore the perceptions of staff when their managers talk over them, and also how the coachee might develop patience to be able to stay focused and fully attentive for the whole conversation. These two or three elements might in turn lead the coachee to develop an action plan of 6–10 objectives they will go away and try out. In closing I tend to encourage coachees to think about how they will stay on track towards these goals over the next three or four weeks. In particular I encourage them to think about who will hold them to account and who will support and encourage them when they are doing well. Ensuring support mechanisms are in place increases the likelihood of the manager returning, having found he or she has successfully maintained these new behaviours throughout the period.

A second way of exploring these elements would be to invite coachees to tell a story about their experience of each. This approach works better with coachees who are more extroverted and who enjoy the narrative as opposed to a more numerical rating approach. The end process however is similar in encouraging them to think about what they are doing well and what aspects from the model they could choose to strengthen.

The model also provides a useful aid in two further ways. First, I have found many managers enjoy reading about business and leadership, so being able to recommend a book or magazine article from *Harvard*

Business Review, *People Management* or the *Director* for example, is helpful. The recommendation often follows a conversation in shorthand about the model, and getting the manager to read the long version encourages them to re-engage with the material. To support this process, I tend to ask the manager to consider a series of questions that I suggest will be the basis for our conversation next time. These questions might relate to: What aspects of the model are critical for the organization/manager now? What would the manager add to the model to make it a more appropriate fit? What does the manager need to change about his or her style? How are they going to do this?

A model, lastly, can be used as an evaluation device. The coach might usefully return with the coachee to consider the leader's progress against the model, after six months. This can be particularly effective when managers are asked to rate themselves and the original scores are then compared with the self-rating. The contrast again provides data about what changes have taken place and why these have occurred. With the manager's agreement it would be possible to use the model in a self and boss-rating exercise in the tripartite closure meeting, when the coach, coachee and coachee's manager meet to review the progress made.

CONCLUSIONS

In this chapter I have offered a brief review of the emerging literature on coaching's contribution to leadership development. The conclusion is that coaching is a useful tool in this process, and the research evidence from studies is beginning to demonstrate this value in scientific research terms beyond case study and personal experience. The chapter then offered a model of leadership and set out how leadership models can be a useful aid in the coaching relationship to enhance leadership development.

As with psychometrics or coaching models, the application of a leadership model requires a judgement by the coach about what will be of most use and value for the coachee. Models can be a shorthand guide to helping leaders understand themselves, provide them with a language for developmental conversations and offer them a heuristic to take into the office for their future development and decision making.

References

Barrett, P T (2007) The effects of group coaching on executive health and team effectiveness: a quasi-experimental field study, *Dissertation Abstracts International Section A: Humanities and Social Sciences*, **67** (7-A), p 2640

Bowles, S, Cunningham, C J L, Rosa, G M, De La Picano, J (2007) Coaching leaders in middle and executive management: goals, performance buy-in, *Leadership and Organization Development Journal*, **28** (5), pp 388–408

Czigan, T K (2008) *Combining Coaching and Temperament: Implications for middle management leadership development*, PhD study, Capella University, USA

Evers, W J, Brouwers, A and Tomic, W (2006) A quasi-experimental study on management coaching effectiveness, *Consulting Psychology Journal: Practice and Research*, **58** (3), pp 174–82

Feggetter, A J W (2007) A preliminary evaluation of executive coaching: does executive coaching work for candidates on a high potential development scheme? *International Coaching Psychology Review*, **2** (2), pp 129–42

Fitzsimmons, G and Guise, S (2010) Coaching for leadership style, in *Leadership Coaching*, ed. J Passmore, Kogan Page, London

Goldsmith, M (2009) Executive coaching: real world perspective from a real life coaching practitioner, *International Coaching Psychology Review*, **4** (1), pp 22–24

Green, S A, Grant, A and Rynsaardt, J (2007) Evidence-based life coaching for senior high school students: building hardiness and hope, *International Coaching Psychology Review*, **2** (1), pp 24–32

Greenleaf, R (1977) *Servant Leadership*, Paulist Press, New York

Grint, K (2005) Problems, problems, problems: the social construction of 'leadership', *Human Relations*, **58**, pp 1467–94

Jones, G and Spooner, K (2006) Coaching high achievers, *Consulting Psychology Journal: Practice and Research*, **58** (1), pp 40–50

Kemp, T (2009) Is coaching an evolved form of leadership: building a trans-disciplinary framework for exploring the coaching alliance, *International Coaching Psychology Review*, **4** (1), pp 105–10

Kombarakaran, F, Yang, J, Baker, M N and Fernandes, P B (2008) Executive coaching: it works, *Consulting Psychology*, **60** (1), pp 78–90

Linley, A, Woolston, L and Biswas-Diener, R (2009) Strengths coaching with leaders, *International Coaching Psychology Review*, **4** (1), pp 37–48

Olivero, G K D, Bane, K D and Kopelman, R E (1997) Executive coaching as a transfer of training tool: effects on productivity in a public agency, *Public Personnel Management*, **26** (4), pp 461–69

Palmer, S and Gyllensten, K (2008) How cognitive behavioural, rational emotive behavioural or multimodal coaching could prevent mental health problems, enhance performance and reduce work related stress, *Journal of Rational-Emotive and Cognitive Behaviour Therapy*, **26** (1), pp 38–52

Passmore, J (2007) Addressing deficit performance through coaching: using motivational interviewing for performance improvement at work, *International Coaching Psychology Review*, **2** (3), pp 265–75

Passmore, J (2008) Character of workplace coaching, unpublished doctoral thesis, UEL

Passmore, J and Gibbes, C (2007) The state of executive coaching research: what does the current literature tell us and what's next for coaching research? *International Coaching Psychology Review*, **2** (2), pp 116–28

Porter L and McLaughlin G (2006) Leadership and the organizational context: like the weather? *Leadership Quarterly*, **17**, pp 559–76

Taylor, L M (1997) The relation between resilience, coaching, coping skills training, and perceived stress during a career threatening milestone, *DAI-B*, **58/05** (Nov), p 2738

2

Coaching for authentic leadership

Graham Lee and Ian Roberts

INTRODUCTION

The aim of this chapter is to show how the concept of authentic leadership can be used to achieve significant and enduring transitions in leadership performance through coaching. Its core premise is that authentic leadership is conscious leadership, and that conscious leadership is the most effective in tackling complex challenges. Drawing on psychological research, particularly in relation to early attachments, our aim is to provide coaches with two things: first, an accessible frame for understanding the current status of a leader's capacity for reflective awareness, and second, to show how this understanding provides the basis for recommending a number of tailored interventions to support shifts in awareness, judgement and ultimately leadership effectiveness.

THE AUTHENTIC LEADERSHIP MODEL

There is a tension at the heart of leadership. In one respect effective leadership requires managers to be able to draw on core character strengths and to remain true and grounded in these enduring qualities. We want leaders to know and to express their courage, their creativity, their persistence, their drive and enthusiasm. However, if these character strengths are expressed inflexibly, without awareness or subtlety of application, then the leader will not meet the rapidly changing demands of a complex environment. Thus, in another respect, effective leadership requires managers to tune in to others, to understand how to motivate, to be sensitive to their environment and to adapt an approach according to shifts in context. This capacity to match and express core character strengths in ways that are optimal to different contexts is what we mean by authentic leadership (Lee, 2003) (see Figure 2.1).

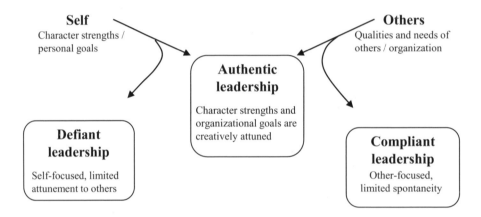

Figure 2.1 Three leadership positions

This picture of authenticity emphasizes the paradoxical nature of leadership; it contains not only the personal authenticity of leaders being true to themselves, accurately representing their intentions and commitments with emotional genuineness (Petersen and Seligman, 2004), but also the 'social authenticity' (Gergen, 1991; Wang, 1999) of being true to the needs of the situation, attuned to others and the context, and to the impact the leaders are likely to have on others. Leadership is what is co-created in the space between the leader and the led (Jones and Goffee, 2006), the self and the other.

Table 2.1 Reflective awareness in authentic leadership

▌ Standing back; paying attention to one's focus of attention.
▌ Acknowledging, labelling and tolerating (difficult) thoughts and feelings.
▌ Teasing out the mental states (cognitions and emotions) underlying the behaviour of self and others.
▌ Understanding personal triggers and their historical origins; autobiographical awareness.
▌ Being open to multiple perspectives; embracing paradox and ambiguity.
▌ Shifting attention to different levels of meaning-making (eg events, patterns, structure).
▌ Fostering the reflective stance in others/groups/teams.

THE REFLECTIVE STANCE IN AUTHENTIC LEADERSHIP

The defining characteristic of authentic leadership is the quality of reflective awareness that managers are able to bring to their leadership challenges. By taking a reflective stance (see Table 2.1), and attending to the mental states (thoughts and feelings) underlying the behaviour of self and others, the leadership repertoire is substantially expanded.

With self-awareness, managers can harness different facets of their character strengths and can also acknowledge what they struggle with, what the triggers are that disrupt their capacity to lead effectively. With curiosity about the mental states of self and others, managers can enter into insightful dialogue with colleagues and so collectively shape an understanding of how best to lead different individuals and groups. They can think and create with others without having to dominate, and yet can take charge and drive effort towards an urgent solution. They can play to their strengths and, acknowledging personal gaps, know when to seek out colleagues with complementary qualities. They can immerse themselves in necessary detail, and also recognize the need to empower others to take responsibility. They can model openness, humility and curiosity in the service of shared learning, but can also hold clear boundaries, show confidence and be willing to end a discussion in the service of delivering a result.

Authentic leadership therefore is not defined by a particular style, but by the quality of consciousness and the level of reflective and integrative awareness that informs, intuitively or more explicitly, a manager's choices, judgements and interpersonal behaviours. It is not that managers need perfect awareness and adaptability to be authentic, but they do need a 'good enough' awareness to get the best out of themselves in relation to their colleagues and organizations.

DEFIANT AND COMPLIANT LEADERSHIP

Without sufficient reflective awareness managers are less adaptable and tend to swing towards one of two more defensive leadership positions, of either defiance or compliance (see Table 2.2 for a comparison with authentic leadership). In the position of defiant leadership the manager is unconsciously focused on personal agendas at the expense of others, and is typically experienced as controlling and emotionally distant. In

Table 2.2 Characteristics of three leadership positions

Defiance	Authenticity	Compliance
Self-assertive stance, at the expense of the other awareness.	Conscious balancing of needs of self and others.	'Other'-focused bias, at expense of self-expression.
Controlling, critical, confrontational.	Potential for rumination or complacency.	Lacking spontaneity, timid, needy.
Decisive, individual, idiosyncratic.	Adaptable, self-disclosing, motivating.	Responsive, collaborative, steady.
Implicit fear of failure and longing for intimacy.	Implicit sense of perspective and concern for others.	Implicit fear of abandonment and longing for safe autonomy.
Regulates emotions through unconscious dissociation and ignoring others' needs.	Regulates emotions through reflection and dialogue.	Regulates emotions by unconscious matching to others and ignoring personal needs.
Interpersonally awkward, emotionally distant, and inflexible.	Interpersonally attuned, empathising with self and others.	Interpersonally eager to please or overly bound by rules and process.
Evokes competitiveness, resistance or obedience.	Evokes vitality, collaboration and creativity.	Evokes process compliance rather than inspiration.

this position the manager may be charismatic, but fails to draw out the best in others. In the position of compliant leadership the manager is unconsciously focused on matching the expectations of others at the expense of self-expression, and is typically experienced as responsive and supportive, but lacking in individuality and creativity.

Although some managers have a distinct bias towards the defiant or compliant positions, it is usual to find managers who tend to operate across all three of the leadership positions, shifting according to different contexts and relationships. The goal in coaching managers in relation to this model is, first, to raise their awareness about the positions they are adopting, and second, where necessary, to develop their capacity to shift their position in order to be more effective in their leadership function.

THEORETICAL AND RESEARCH UNDERPINNINGS

We highlight two primary areas of research and theorizing that underpin the authentic leadership model: attachment theory and developmental theory. We outline these, showing how they have informed the leadership model, and their implications for coaching.

Attachment theory: the origins of authentic leadership

Based on extensive research with children and adults, attachment theory has demonstrated the importance of early relationships (or attachments) with parents for psychological development (Bowlby, 1973). The attachment process in humans closely resembles the largely instinctual processes in animals whereby infants seek proximity to carers in the face of threat. Bowlby argues that in infancy the child develops an internal 'attachment model' – mental structures representing the degree to which others can be trusted – based upon early experiences. If children experience responsiveness from parents – parents who are available and ready to respond when called upon to encourage or assist, but who do not intrude – they develop a 'secure base'. They have an internal sense of confidence that allows them, as children and as adults, to venture into the world, to show curiosity and openness to new experiences, and to form trusting and rewarding relationships.

However, if the early parenting experience is less reliable, attachments and emotional development are less secure. In addition to the secure form of attachment, two primary forms of insecure attachment have been identified (Ainsworth et al, 1978). Avoidant attachment occurs where parenting is experienced as unresponsive or rejecting; in these circumstances a child tends to be emotionally cut off, and this quality of distance can persist into adulthood. Ambivalent attachment occurs where parenting is experienced as inconsistent, sometimes ignoring and sometimes intrusive, and in these circumstances a child learns to be constantly alert to the caregiver's state of mind, clinging to his or her carer and with a tendency to be overwhelmed by emotions. In adulthood, ambivalent attachment is seen in the desire to please others, to cling to relationships and to be 'needy' for recognition. Although attachment patterns established in childhood can change, there is accumulating evidence that patterns of emotional attachments learned in childhood often extend into adult relationships (Ainsworth, 1989; Main, Kaplan and Cassidy, 1985; Fonagy et al, 1993; Brennan, Clark and Shaver, 1998).

Relating these findings to the model of authentic leadership, we argue that managers' capacities to lead more authentically are directly related to their implicit learning from experiences of secure attachment at earlier phases in their life. Those with an insecure avoidant attachment pattern are more likely to adopt a position of defiance in relation to stressful leadership challenges, whilst those with an insecure ambivalent attachment pattern are more likely, under stress, to adopt a position of compliance.

Implications for development

In aligning authentic, defiant and compliant leadership positions with secure, avoidant and ambivalent attachment patterns, what clues might research into treating patients with insecure attachments give us about coaching managers? Psychotherapy research indicates that a therapist with a high capacity for reflective awareness can, through techniques and interactions that evoke reflective awareness of self and other, help patients to develop this same capacity (Allen, Fonagy and Bateman, 2008). We would suggest that in coaching it is through a similar process of increasing self-awareness and tuning into the minds of others that managers can make more conscious choices about the most effective leadership position to adopt in relation to specific tasks and contexts.

Spirals of development

As developmental theory suggests in arguing that development proceeds through a series of stages (Erikson, 1950; Piaget, 1954; Torbert, 1987; Cook-Greuter, 1990; Wilber, 2000), authenticity, compliance and defiance are not discrete categories, with authenticity as the 'best' place to be. Rather, these positions are necessary parts of the spiral journey through which we cycle on the path to increasing awareness, integration and

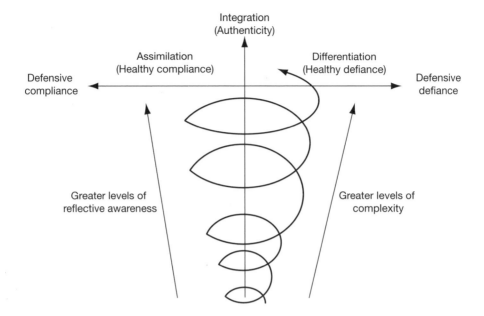

Figure 2.2 Spiral development of leadership

authenticity (see Figure 2.2). Vertical progression is achieved through the movement from assimilation (healthy compliance), giving oneself over to receiving new knowledge, to differentiation (healthy defiance), making the knowledge one's own. Through successive cycles, increasing integration and authenticity is achieved. Compliance and defiance represent defensive and somewhat 'stuck' forms of assimilation and differentiation that can occur at different levels of development. Thus the coaching challenge is to keep a dynamic relationship between the focus on self and others, moving back and forth between differentiation and assimilation in order to achieve greater integration and authenticity.

USING THE AUTHENTIC LEADERSHIP MODEL WITH COACHEES

In this section we outline a number of approaches that we have found particularly effective for helping coachees apply the insights and learnings from the model of authentic leadership.

Creating a safe space

The first step in using the model is the need to create a safe 'holding' environment (Winnicott, 1971): a safe and secure space in which established patterns of identity and the associated defences can be loosened. Safety and security within the coaching relationship is partly facilitated by setting clear boundaries through the contracting process, but above all it is the coach's capacity to stay curious and reflective that builds rapport and trust, and eventually the belief that this is a space where difficult thoughts and feelings can be held, examined and ultimately transformed. We can think of the coach containing the coachee's anxiety, modelling the possibility of thinking about feelings, holding and thinking about feelings.

The kind of responsiveness needed to create an experience of holding for the coachee will depend on the coachee's position in relation to the coach. For example a coachee in a 'defiant' position may be wary or critical of the coach or coaching process. By holding the likely vulnerability of the coachee in mind and by normalizing feelings of uncertainty, the coaching space is experienced as one in which all feelings and thoughts can be entertained. A coachee in a 'compliant' position may show a friendly and keen to please manner, or an overly transactional approach. The coachee needs to be supported to think more systematically and to find his or her own sense of worth in the coaching relationship. Those in a more authentic position may be more open to immediate challenge and exploration, and the coachee can work towards deepening self-awareness and identifying areas of greatest challenge.

It is also important to note that the working relationship between the coach and the coachee can be supported or undermined by the sponsor for the coaching, typically the coachee's manager. For example a sponsor who shows little interest or engagement in the coaching process, or who even disrupts the process – for example by causing sessions to be cancelled – will potentially make the coaching space unsafe and so block the potential for useful change.

Developing hypotheses

Throughout the coaching process the coach will be collecting information and developing tentative hypotheses about the coachee's development challenges. The authentic leadership model represents one possible lens for collecting and making sense of information about the coachee, and in this respect the coach looks for evidence of the coachee operating from a defiant, compliant or authentic position. In conversation coaches invite coachees to talk about themselves: their role, the challenges and dilemmas they face, their relationships, what motivates them or demotivates them, their lives when they are not working, and about formative experiences.

At the surface level, forming provisional hypotheses about defiant or compliant behaviours is relatively easy, because controlling or pleasing behaviours are not difficult to spot. However, drawing on research into attachment theory, a subtler indicator of the underlying attachment pattern, and therefore the leadership position that is likely to predominate, comes from work on narrative competence, and the adult attachment interview (George, Kaplan and Main, 1984).

Narrative competence relates to both the coachee's ability to tell his or her story and the story itself. The coach seeks information on the coachee's capacity to think and talk clearly and coherently about him/ herself and his or her life challenges. It is possible for the coach to identify characteristic narrative patterns that are indicative of specific attachment patterns. This understanding is held 'lightly' or provisionally by the coach to avoid overly deterministic or simplistic hypotheses.

Defiant, compliant and authentic leadership positions can be aligned with avoidant, ambivalent and secure attachment patterns. Authentic narratives tend to be coherent, clear, factual and relevant, whereas defiant narratives tend to be brief and disjointed, and may contain factual contradictions. There is a distancing of the emotional in defiant narratives, typified by often bland, unelaborated accounts of childhood and self. Some individuals may present idealized or dismissive thoughts about relationships. Compliant narratives tend to be rambling, indirect and incomplete, which can overwhelm the coach with unresolved and unsorted emotions from the past (Waters, 2004).

A further key area for picking up information about the coachee's leadership position is through counter-transference. Counter-transference, a concept developed in psychoanalysis (Racker, 1957), refers to the feelings, bodily sensations, thoughts and behaviours that can be unconsciously evoked in the coach by the coachee. By silently examining these internal experiences the coach can gain insight into the coachee's unexpressed feelings. If the coachee is operating from an authentic position, then the coach is likely to feel confident and attuned in the work. If the coachee is operating from a defiant position, the coach may perhaps notice an impulse to prove him/herself or to defensively compete with the coachee, suggesting the coach may be experiencing the coachee's unconscious fear of rejection. If the coachee is operating from a compliant position, the coach may perhaps notice an impulse to collude and engage in mutual admiration, suggesting the coach may be experiencing the coachee's unconscious denial of frustration. Learning to work with the counter-transference is a powerful dimension to the work of coaching, but needs to be approached with caution because it is all too easy for the coach to attribute feelings to the coachee that really belong with the coach. In our view, receiving supervision from a clinically qualified supervisor is the most effective way of learning how to use counter-transference effectively.

Teaching the model to coachees

When we first began to work with the authentic leadership model we were cautious about presenting it to our coachees..We preferred to use it as a 'behind the scenes' tool to help with sense making. However, over time we came to experiment with showing the model and the descriptions directly to our coachees and were impressed by how helpful they seemed to find them. The model is generally experienced as accessible and insightful, and most remarkably, it rapidly moves coaching conversations towards deep, hidden and potentially key factors that are blocking leadership effectiveness.

We present the model to our coachees, sometimes in the first or second session, sometimes further into the work – using tables and figures such as those in this chapter to do this – and ask clients to consider which positions they typically see themselves as occupying. This approach is particularly effective when presenting the defiant or compliant positions in terms of patterns of actions, cognitions and emotions, or ACE patterns (see Table 2.3). After glancing down the conscious aspects of the ACE patterns, coachees look with great curiosity at the unconscious column, and particularly the unconscious emotions. In our experience even quite resistant coachees readily identify themselves when the characterization is presented in this way, thus substantially supporting our efforts to raise awareness and to integrate unconscious and problematic emotional agendas.

WORKING WITH PARTICULAR TOOLS AND APPROACHES

Using ACE records

An ACE record – loosely based on 'thought records' used in cognitive behaviour therapy (Padesky, 1985) – is a method for capturing the patterns of actions, cognitions and emotions that are enabling or limiting coachees in achieving specific leadership challenges. The record, completed with the coachee in relation to key goals (intentions), provides the basis for planning alternative strategies based on a more authentic way of relating. An example of the use of the ACE record is given in the case study of William on page 32.

Table 2.3 Indicative 'defiant' and 'compliant' ACE patterns

	Example of a 'defiant' ACE pattern	
	Conscious	*Unconscious*
Actions (What you say or do)	▌ Controlling, directive, autocratic ▌ Critical or dismissive	▌ Looking for approval/ recognition ▌ Looking for support/ intimacy
Cognitions (What you think)	▌ 'I must take control to make sure things work' ▌ 'Others cannot be trusted'	▌ 'I am not competent' ▌ 'I am not likeable' ▌ 'I am not lovable'
Emotions (What you feel)	▌ Driven ▌ Irritability, anger	▌ Fear of failure ▌ Fear of rejection ▌ Longing for intimacy

	Example of a 'compliant' ACE pattern	
	Conscious	*Unconscious*
Actions (What you say or do)	▌ Collaborative, concerned, appeasing ▌ Working and searching for recognition	▌ Appears withdrawn and lost ▌ Occasional outburst of anger
Cognitions (What you think)	▌ 'I must keep the peace' ▌ 'I will succeed if I follow the rules'	▌ 'I am not significant or worthy of attention' ▌ 'I am furious' ▌ 'I am misunderstood'
Emotions (What you feel)	▌ Anxiety about getting it wrong ▌ Fear of upsetting others	▌ Fear of abandonment ▌ Frustration, anger ▌ Longing for safe autonomy

Shifting perceptual position

Perceptual position refers to the idea that we can look at relationships from a number of different perspectives, such as self, other and observer. The methodology enables coachees to gain perspective on their current ACE patterns and to increase their reflective awareness (for further information see McDermott and Jago, 2001).

The coach invites the coachee to relive a past leadership interaction or imagine a future one, and to occupy each of the three perceptual positions. Coachees can then explore:

▌ the impact of existing and potential ACE patterns, and their effectiveness;
▌ their hypothesis about the ACE patterns of others;
▌ how their own authenticity would be experienced by themselves and others.

Taking the lead from the Gestalt technique of the open chair (see Perls, 1973), coachees often access hidden or untenable ACE patterns by imagining a significant other in an empty chair placed in front of them and being helped by the coach to verbalize such patterns. The coachees are then asked to inhabit the mind and body of the significant other by sitting in the empty chair and observing themselves. The coach both facilitates inquiry from these two perspectives and reflects back what is going on from the position of observer.

Making the link to break the link

The coach can invite the coachee to cast his/her mind back over past relationships and situations to find where the learning for a particular leadership position may have formed – the coach may already have an intuition about this based on conversations about formative experiences. It is often useful to begin by normalizing the feelings that the coachee has experienced in the past, and the way in which they may still be shaping current behaviour. This lays the ground for accepting often difficult or shameful feelings, and opens the way for a fuller understanding of how they may be influencing thoughts and behaviours. The coach may encourage the coachee to notice what is brought from past learning into present work relationships and contexts. For example a coachee may have had experiences of unresponsive or rejecting relationships that were unconsciously managed by learning to dismiss feelings and to be self-sufficient, which in the working environment now is manifest as being emotionally remote and controlling – a defiant pattern of relating. Having made these links, the coach encourages the coachee to break the link by exploring the differences between the past and present, and so be more able to approach the present from a more conscious, resourceful and adaptable perspective.

Mindfulness training

Authentic leadership depends on the capacity for reflective awareness, and reflective awareness in turn depends on the coachee's state of mind. Mindfulness training is essentially a process of 'being here now', attending to the present moment with openness and curiosity (Kabat-Zinn, 1994; Lee, 2009). By bringing attention to the present moment coachees can gain a measure of control over their states of mind, calming them and evoking a more spacious awareness, a shift from 'doing' to 'being'. Common approaches involve focusing attention on the flow of the breath or on sensations in the body. Over time, and with regular practice, this kind of training can help coachees to manage their states of arousal and so more reliably sustain their reflective awareness in challenging leadership contexts.

Developmental swings

The spiral nature of development (see the section on Spirals of development, above) means that it is important that both the coach and coachee recognize the ebb and flow between authenticity, differentiation and assimilation. For example a 'high-potential' leader may need a period of assimilation (or healthy compliance) on moving to a more senior role or from a functional leadership role to a broader corporate one – this more receptive position is a necessary part of being open to new learning. Similarly an individual tending towards a compliant leadership position may need to swing towards a defiant stance in order to overcome the inertia of established compliant patterns. Integrating the earlier compliant bias with more recent defiant aspects, the coachee is able to move to a more balanced, authentic position.

Moreover, as mentioned above, authenticity should not be seen as a final fixed state: it is a continuous and dynamic pursuit that demands awareness of when one becomes defiant or compliant. The challenge is therefore one of a continuous cycle of awareness and learning rather than final enlightenment.

COACHES' SELF-AWARENESS

Above all the coach needs to be a role model of reflective awareness. Therefore it is essential that coaches explore through supervision their own biases towards compliance or defiance, and how these can trip them up in drawing out the best in others. It is important for coaches to recognize that individual coachees, as well as the coaching process, may activate their own attachment system and draw them towards particular interventions. Figure 2.3 shows the potential interactions between the attachment systems of the coach and coachee.

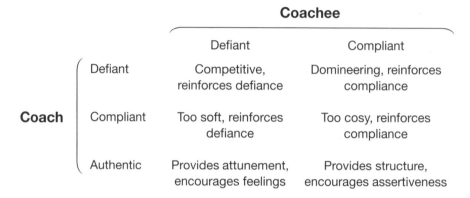

Figure 2.3 Coach–coachee interventions

CASE STUDY

William, a senior manager within the sales and client service function, had been recruited a few months before coaching began to address the poor reputation of the department. In the brief from William's manager, the coach was told that she thought he was 'too stressed out' and was 'clashing with key colleagues' in the product development area. This description suggested that a possible construction of the coaching challenge was to understand William as needing to shift from a defiant 'clashing' position in relation to certain key colleagues, and to find more productive ways of relating. This initial construction was partly confirmed in William's own account of what he wanted from coaching. However, interestingly, in relation to his coach he seemed more tentative and eager to please, suggesting that, at least in this first meeting, he was operating from a more compliant position. The coach construed that, although clearly in touch with his frustration with key colleagues, William was able to adapt his style to different contexts and was demonstrating that he was open to learning through coaching.

In the second session the coach shared the authentic leadership model with William, describing the distinctions between authenticity, defiance and compliance (see Table 2.2) and the actions, cognitions and emotions that drive these positions (see Lee, 2003). When William was asked to describe which leadership positions he more typically adopted in different contexts, he noted that he was often able to be authentic within his own team. However in relation to key product development colleagues, and in particular Charlie, he found himself firmly stuck in defiance, undermining trust and cooperation through his challenging and bullying approach.

Over the next few sessions the coach worked with William to develop a much richer picture of the factors that were triggering William into defiance. Table 2.4 shows the ACE record that William and his coach completed together to capture both those defiant aspects that were limiting William's relational effectiveness, and those more authentic aspects that would enable him to make a positive shift.

The coach used a number of techniques to increase William's reflective awareness about his relationship with Charlie. William was invited to imagine a conversation with Charlie, physically moving to different positions in the room to represent the self, other and observer perceptual positions, or the defiant, compliant and authentic positions, thus helping him to see situations from others' perspectives. The coach also helped William to link his experience of not being respected by Charlie and other product development colleagues with childhood memories. Specifically, William felt that his father appreciated him less than his brothers, and he had learned to adopt a defiant, 'I'll show them' attitude. This was also linked to the relatively buried emotion of 'longing to be valued' (see Table 2.4). By 'making the link to break the link', William recognized that his frustrations with Charlie in part belonged with his father, and so was able to attend more inquiringly to what Charlie was really like.

William's increase in reflective awareness was strongly reinforced by the coach introducing him to techniques for developing mindfulness. This approach enabled him to become more curious about his feelings, and he learned to focus on his body sensations as a source of internal knowledge about himself in relation to others. He began to practise mindfulness on a daily basis, which supported his growing capacity to observe his own thoughts and feelings, and to have space to wonder about the thoughts and feelings of others. In fact William became quite fascinated and liberated by the discovery that he did not need to react to others, and felt increasingly able to adopt a more enabling ACE pattern of authenticity. He reported that his relationship with others was being transformed, at home as well as at work. He had connected with a capacity to stand back from situations that would have been triggering for him, to tune in to thoughts and feelings in himself and others, and so work to find common ground with colleagues and to solve problems collaboratively. Over time William substantially raised the credibility both of his own potential and of his department, and he is now viewed as an important figure in collectively shaping and driving the success of the organization.

Table 2.4 ACE record for William

Intention: *What do you wish to achieve?*		**Result:** *What is the current outcome?*
To develop a more productive working relationship with Charles		Confrontations and then distance

	Limiting	*Enabling*
Actions: *What behaviours do you use in relation to this intention?*	▌ Cool, steady, logical. ▌ Dismissive statements. ▌ Point scoring. ▌ Rapid, cursory, 'rifle-fire' speech.	▌ Choosing when to talk to others. ▌ Finding common ground. ▌ Inquiring rather than solving. ▌ Lighter, more spacious and nuanced speech.
Cognitions: *What thoughts, attitudes and beliefs about yourself or others do you have in relation to this intention?*	▌ 'They don't respect me' (anticipating rejection). ▌ 'I'll show them'. ▌ Black-and-white thinking.	▌ 'They value my knowledge'. ▌ 'I'm good at finding solutions'. ▌ 'It's interesting to notice my impulses and reactions and to wonder about those of others'.
Emotions: *What feelings about yourself or others do you have in relation to this intention?*	▌ Anger and resentment. ▌ Longing to be valued.	▌ Desire to have an impact. ▌ Enjoying a sense of perspective.

Effectiveness: *To what extent is this ACE pattern successful? (What is the gap between intentions and results?)*
The 'Limiting' ACE approach is causing a rift with Charles, and undermining the interdepartmental relationship

Changes: *What changes do you need to make to achieve your intended results more effectively? Consider changes in actions, cognitions, and emotions.*
▌ Make time for mindfulness practice to get more perspective on cognitions and emotions in self and others.
▌ Enact the 'Enabling' actions.

CONCLUSIONS

The model of authentic leadership emphasizes the reflective awareness that underpins the capacity of managers to be effective in relation to their shifting challenges and contexts. The model provides coaches with a tool for making sense of the possible unconscious dynamics that limit a coachee's ability to change, and with an explicit frame for understanding the coachee's tendency to adopt particular positions relative to different contexts. Through the use of this model and a range of techniques that foster more expansive and integrative forms of reflective awareness, coachees become more able to make conscious choices about the leadership position that will be most effective in a particular context.

References

Ainsworth, M D S (1989) Attachments beyond infancy, *American Psychologist*, **44**, pp 709–16

Ainsworth, M D S, Blehar, R M C, Waters, E and Wall, S (1978) *Patterns of Attachment: A psychological study of the strange situation*, Erlbaum, Hillside, NJ

Allen, J G, Fonagy, P and Bateman, A W (2008) *Mentalizing in Clinical Practice*, American Psychiatric Publishing, Washington, DC

Bowlby, J (1973) *Attachment and Loss, Vol 2: Separation, anxiety and anger*, Hogarth Press, London

Brennan, K A, Clark, C L, and Shaver, P R (1998) Self-report measurement of adult romantic attachment: an integrative overview, in *Attachment Theory and Close Relationships*, ed J A Simpson and W S Rholes, pp 46–76, Guilford Press, New York

Cook-Greuter, S (1990) Maps for living: ego-development stages from symbiosis to conscious universal embeddedness, in *Adult Development, Vol 2: Models and methods in the study of adolescent and adult thought*, ed M L Commons, C Armon, L Kohlberg, F A Richards, T A Grotzer and J D Sinnott, pp 79–103, Prager, New York

Erikson, E H (1950) *Childhood and Society*, Norton, New York

Fonagy, P, Steele, M, Moran, G S and Higgit, A C (1993) Measuring the ghost in the nursery: an empirical study of the relations between parents' mental representations of childhood experiences and their infants' security attachment, *Journal of the American Psychoanalytic Association*, **41**, pp 957–89

George, C, Kaplan, N and Main, M (1984) *The Adult Attachment Interview*, unpublished manuscript, University of California at Berkeley, CA

Gergen, K (1991) *The Saturated Self: Dilemmas of identity in contemporary life*, Basic Books, New York

Jones, G and Goffee, R (2006) *Why Should Anyone Be Led By You?* Harvard Business School Press, Boston, MA

Kabat-Zinn, J (1994) *Wherever You Go, There You Are: Mindfulness meditation in everyday life*, Hyperion, New York

Lee, G (2003) *Leadership Coaching: From personal insight to organizational perform-ance*, CIPD, London

Lee, G (2009) *Developing the Mindful Leader: Coaching at work*, forthcoming

Main, K, Kaplan, N, and Cassidy, J (1985) Security in infancy, childhood, and adulthood: a move to the level of representation, in *Monographs of the Society of Research and Child Development*, Serial No 209 50: Nos 1–2, ed I Bretherton and E Waters, University of Chicago Press, Chicago, IL

McDermott, I and Jago, W (2001) *The NLP Coach*, Judy Piatkus Publishers, London

Padesky, C (1985) *Clinician's Guide to Mind Over Mood*, Guilford Press, New York

Perls, F S (1973) *The Gestalt Approach and Eye Witness to Therapy*, Science and Behavior Books, Ben Lomond, CA

Petersen, C and Seligman, M E P (2004) *Character Strengths and Virtues: A handbook and classification*, Oxford University Press, Oxford

Piaget (1954) *The Construction of Reality in the Child*, Basic Books, New York

Racker, H (1957) The meanings and uses of countertransference, *Psychoanalytic Quarterly*, **26**, pp 303–57

Torbert, W (1987) *Managing the Corporate Dream: Restructuring for long term success*, Dow Jones Irwin, Homewood, IL

Wang, N (1999) Rethinking authenticity in tourism experience, *Annals of Tourism Research*, **26** (2), pp 349–70

Waters, T (2004) Learning to love: from your mother's arms to your lover's arms, *The Medium (Voice of University of Toronto)*, **30** (19), 9 February

Wilber, K (2000) *A Brief History of Everything*, 2nd edn, Shambhala Publications, Boston, MA

Winnicott, D (1971) *Playing and Reality*, Tavistock, London

3

The integrated leadership model

Doug Strycharczyk, Dr Peter Clough and Dr Nollaig Heffernan

INTRODUCTION

This chapter introduces the coach to the integrated leadership model (2007), its structure and content and its value as a framework for assessing leadership style and leadership effectiveness.

It is a 'macro' model in that it enables the coach to take a high-level view of leadership and to work within a 'big picture' view. It is integrated because it integrates well with virtually every leadership model in popular use around the world – and provides context for the application of many of these models.

This is particularly valuable and important for the leadership coach. There is no shortage of leadership models and many do work reasonably well. Indeed many are described elsewhere in this book. The challenge for the effective coach is to identify how to select and to use the most appropriate model or framework for each situation.

This chapter provides an overview of six elements in which all leadership models seem to be rooted. These describe different aspects of leadership style and enable the coach to define and assess it.

It also provides an overview of three higher-order factors that are derived from these aspects of style. These describe factors that are relevant to assessing and developing leadership effectiveness.

THE INTEGRATED LEADERSHIP MODEL

An examination of most accepted definitions of leadership confirms that it is a quality that is concerned with performance and with engagement with others. More specifically it is about developing exceptional performance through some process of engagement with others such that they, individually or collectively, give their discretionary effort – often without seeing this as additional effort.

The integrated leadership model has two main components: a) the global factors and b) the specific leadership bi-polar elements.

Global factors

Our research showed that there are three high-order (global) factors that seem to be key requirements for highly effective leadership.

▌ A determination to deliver (high) performance
  The extent to which there is a single-minded determination to achieve – in the short and long term.
▌ Engagement with individuals
  The extent to which a leader attends to the capability, confidence and commitment of individuals.
▌ Engagement with teams – engaging the organization
  The extent to which the leader understands the variety of teams and relationships in the organization, harnesses their collective strengths and enables their effectiveness.

These are described in greater detail in the section below on 'Using the integrated leadership model with coaches'.

These three factors are each enablers and each contributes independently to effective leadership. A key message here is that the first of these, determination to deliver, is a vitally important enabler. Many models that focus on the engagement with people elements can underplay this.

The global factors also resonate strongly with an overview of many popular and effective models – particularly the action-centred leadership model developed by Professor John Adair (1973) almost 50 years ago, with which there are strong similarities.

There are subtle differences however. First, in the integrated leadership model the three global factors emerge as reasonably independent factors. Moreover one of the factors, determination to deliver, appears more significant than the other two.

There is also some indication that these factors are related to leadership effectiveness. The more you do in each area, the more likely you are to be assessed as a highly effective leader and the more likely it is that followers will respond to the leader.

This has implications. First, focus on performance is a core requirement for effective leadership. It may even be possible for leaders to demonstrate only this to create some level of followership, although this may only be effective in the short term.

Either engaging with individuals or with teams/organization will enable more effective leadership. Doing both will enable highly effective leadership.

The integrated leadership model has two major components. The global factors described above emerged from six specific leadership elements.

The specific elements

The research that led to its development showed that all leadership models have their roots in six specific bi-polar scales. These emerge as six different aspects of leadership style and give us the ability to describe leadership style (Browne, 2008).

The global factors described above emerged from these scales, which are shown in Figure 3.1.

The evidence shows that there is no particular combination of style that correlates uniquely with high performance in all situations. The clear

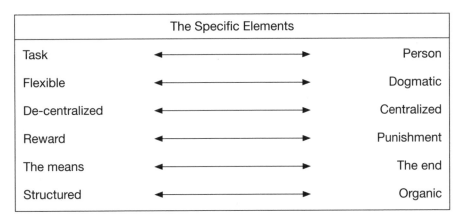

Figure 3.1 Integrated leadership model: the specific elements

implication is that leadership style is situational. Different profiles might work better in different situations.

This framework also works at the organizational level. The specific scale framework is useful as a map for defining key aspects of the organization's culture. This is important for a coach engaged in development activity. It is rarely possible to develop individuals without taking into account the context within which they will act and behave.

Examining each element in more detail:

▌ Task versus person
  This reflects and measures the extent to which the individual is oriented towards meeting the needs of the task or is concerned with the needs of individuals. A central theme in most models, this reflects how a leader believes people are motivated to perform more effectively.
▌ Flexible versus dogmatic
  Describes the extent to which the leader prefers to involve others in analysis and decision making in the organization. It may also reflect the extent to which making a decision is important in the sense that making a decision quickly is more important than making the best possible decision, which might take time to achieve.
▌ De-centralized versus centralized
  Describes the extent to which leaders feel they are central to the operation and to what extent they will empower others to exercise authority.
▌ Reward versus punishment
  Describes the extent to which the leader believes that people respond to reward or to punishment.
▌ The means versus the end
  Describes how important hitting goals and targets is to the leaders – and what they are prepared to sacrifice to get there.
▌ Structured versus organic
  Describes the extent to which structure, planning and personal organization are important to the people who lead, and to what extent they will rely upon their presence, intuition and instinct to achieve them. The implication here is that leadership is learned one way or the other.

These too are described in greater detail in the section on 'Using the integrated leadership model with coaches'.

THE RESEARCH

The research was carried out over four years between 2005 and 2008 by AQR Ltd and Dr Peter Clough, Head of Psychology at Hull University, and Dr Nollaig Heffernan.

The original project was triggered by a discussion with a director of the Institute of Leadership and Management who observed that there was a plethora of models being used in leadership development but there was little that showed whether and how they were connected. It became apparent that an integrated model of leadership would offer a way forward within the complex and often contradictory field of leadership.

A small number of writers have attempted to produce a fully integrated model of leadership. For example, Chelladurai and Saleh's (1980) multidimensional model of leadership and Bass's multifactor leadership theory (1985, cited in Tejeda, Scandura and Pillai, 2001: 32). The former was derived specifically from path–goal theory (1971) and adaptive–reactive theory (Osbourne, Hunt and Jaunch, 2002) and investigated aspects of situational leadership theory, whilst the latter emerged when Bass (1985) combined Burns' (1978) observations on transformational and transactional leadership and added the third dimension of laissez-faire leadership. Both these models had a number of omissions and other methodological shortcomings that call into question their usefulness, and the lack of a simple and robust measure directly related to them also raised some questions about their utility.

The starting point of our attempt was to utilize Dansereau's framework of leadership models (Dansereau, Yammarino and Markham, 1995). This over-arching framework included 13 separate leadership models, which were divided into four categories: classical, contemporary, alternative and new wave. Whilst this framework went some of the way towards a fully integrated approach, a number of theories/models were still not included. These included a small number of occupational models. There were a number of omissions, especially those models that might be labelled 'commercial'.

After an extensive literature review a consensus was reached that the research team had identified all the then existing models and theories of leadership. These included 'academic models' such as contingency theory, behavioural theory, cognitive and social psychology, the multi-level approach and neo-charismatic approaches amongst others. Leading models included the work of Fiedler (1967), Bass (1985), House (1971) and Fleishman (1957) and 'commercial' models such as the work of John Adair (1973), Covey (1989), Hersey and Blanchard (1977) and the situational models, McGregor (1960), Bennis (1998) and Berne (1964).

The next task was to identify the commonalities between these models. This process resulted in the identification of six commonalities or themes, the root concepts underlying the models. Items were then written to measure these root concepts. After an extensive iterative process, 124 items were produced that were deemed to be appropriate.

These items were then trialled on 1,339 managers/leaders/supervisors from over 50 different private and public sector organizations. There was a roughly even split between the public and private sectors.

The initial analyses showed that the six specific scales appeared to be robust. After the exclusion of items that were confusing or unclear, six distinct scales were produced with reliability scores ranging from 0.66 to 0.80.

A further factor analysis showed the existence of the three higher-order 'global' factors described earlier in this chapter. These scales had reliability scores ranging between 0.82 and 0.90.

An important by-product of the research has been the development of a reliable psychometric questionnaire called the ILM72, which assesses individuals on each of the specific and global scales. This supports diagnostic work as well as enabling the impact of interventions to be assessed. ILM72 measures adopted behaviours as opposed to preferred behaviours (see: www.aqr.co.uk).

USING THE INTEGRATED LEADERSHIP MODEL WITH COACHES

The integrated leadership model offers the coach a number of features that are potentially valuable:

▮ It is applicable at all levels in an organization or in society. All of us have the opportunity and need to perform at different times, and our performance is often dependent on our engagement with others. This is particularly important where distributed or dispersed leadership is a consideration.

▮ The model provides a high-level context within which the coach can work. By using it, the coach can do two things. First, all popular leadership models can be applied within this context, often in combination. Second, it enables coaches to take factors like organizational culture into account in their work.

▮ Two frameworks. Both are interrelated and both are described in very accessible language.
    The first describes three areas of competence that are directly related to leadership effectiveness. These are the global factors.

The second describes how leaders behave. These are the six specific scales that measure the key aspects of leadership style. These emerge as situational.

Working with the global factors

Briefly introduced earlier, the global factors are discussed below.

A determination to deliver (high) performance

Effective leaders appear to see delivering what has been identified and what has been promised as an overriding requirement that leads to success and the feeling of success. Having this determination and demonstrating it emerges as a key enabler for a leader.

The evidence suggests that most followers will respond to someone who appears to know what he/she is doing, is determined to achieve results and wastes no time in doing so. It is therefore a core requirement. Whatever else leaders do, they are unlikely to be effective unless they demonstrate this quality.

Similarly it may be possible in some circumstances for a leader to demonstrate only this. However, this may only be effective in the short term, for example to deal with a crisis.

A checklist of characteristics associated with this factor would include some of these behaviours and traits:

- commitment to deliver on target;
- a willingness to discomfort people when necessary in order to achieve goals and objectives;
- a sense of one's own importance in the scheme of things – you can make that difference;
- recognition that work and business exist in a competitive world with winners and losers;
- a preparedness to adopt 'telling and selling' to get things going quickly and to have an emphasis on action;
- a belief in strong leadership – that you are strong so everyone else needs to be strong too;
- an interest in McGregor's theory X – that people may need to be cajoled into action;
- awareness of how far you can push people;
- not worried about popularity – and not offended by a lack of popularity;
- a concern with the long term as well as the short term – particularly in terms of succession planning.

The coach can use this kind of checklist to work with coachees to reflect on their level of determination to deliver and their commitment to achieve high performance. The response will guide the coach in proposing interventions and development actions

Engagement with individuals

Effective leaders focus on enhancing the capability, confidence and commitment of individuals to enable them to contribute to the organization and to fulfil themselves. The emphasis here is on ensuring that people have the skills, knowledge and behaviours to carry out their roles in the organization, and on providing the means and the environment to enable staff to fulfil their potential.

If a leader is to persuade the follower to give that additional discretionary effort and do it contentedly, then the leader should provide the follower with the best opportunity to respond as comfortably as possible.

Attending to the organization's needs will normally be more of a priority than attending to the personal needs of the individual – although an effective leader will be aware of both.

A checklist of characteristics associated with this factor would include some of these behaviours and traits:

▌ awareness that the welfare of employees is important;
▌ concern with capability of employees to respond to challenge and pressure;
▌ awareness that a contented worker is a productive worker;
▌ concern with formation of meaningful relationships with individuals;
▌ an interest in McGregor's Theory Y – aware that giving the followers attention releases the feeling that they will more readily work for the organization and buy into its goals and values, etc;
▌ An interest in the feelings of others – these are important – the leader wants contented and satisfied employees;
▌ viewing a key aspect of the role as creating harmony and team spirit;
▌ probably emotionally intelligent but won't be driven by it – will be aware of the significance of feelings but will probably be logical and calculating about dealing with that.

Again this can form the basis of a checklist with which a coach can work with coachees to reflect on the extent to which they will engage with individuals and what they can do to enhance it where appropriate.

Engagement with teams: engaging the organization

Effective leaders focus on and give attention to harnessing all the potential in an organization so that problem solving and decision making can occur more efficiently and more effectively. One emphasis here is on enabling groups of people to gather their knowledge, experience and skills and apply these to managing the day-to-day operation within the organization.

This factor also recognizes that in most organizations individuals do not perform a role in isolation. In order to do their job efficiently and effectively they will participate in often a large number of business processes. Where there are several participants in a process, they are in fact members of a team whose goal is to deliver the same output from that process.

This is not always recognized and understood but is where a great deal of organizational inefficiency is created. It is easy to recognize the highly visible functional or departmental team – they often sit together and identify themselves as a team.

So another major emphasis is the capability to identify all the myriad teams in the organization – the cross-functional and process-based as well as the departmental or functional teams. This is often where the highly effective leader makes a significant impact.

A checklist of characteristics associated with this factor would include some of these behaviours and traits:

- respecting the abilities of others;
- encouraging others to use own initiative – adopting a decentralized approach;
- accepting there is value in sharing ideas and getting others' points of view;
- being consultative;
- avoiding being dogmatic – prepared to be flexible and to delegate;
- maximizing the use of the skills and capabilities within the work force;
- being aware of the main business processes within the organization – how work actually gets done and where people have to work together to deliver tasks;
- understanding how to make people aware of business processes and the need to work more effectively with others;
- not feeling that you are the centre of everything – knowing you are not irreplaceable;
- understanding that this is not about being soft – nor is it necessarily concern for feelings; realizing that you don't have to like each other, but you do have to listen to one another and work together.

Again this can form the basis of a checklist with which a coach can work with coachees to reflect on the extent to which they will engage with teams and what they can do to enhance it where appropriate.

A useful generic approach for a coach to work with the coachee would be to:

1. Assess to what extent the coachee demonstrates strengths in the three global factors. This can be achieved though careful discussion, using the above checklists as a guide. Another option is to use a 360° process or the ILM72 questionnaire.
2. Assess to what extent this explains the response the coachee gets from 'followers'.
3. Assess how far this explains performance for which the coachee is responsible or to which the coachee makes a significant contribution.
4. From this, identify where differences or improvements need to be achieved and what would be the benefit of so doing.
5. Identify priorities for attention and appropriate activities.
6. Plan for their implementation – and review.

The global factors can also help the coach to work with the coachee to understand how and why leadership effectiveness can be developed even where there is already some evidence of effective leadership.

There may be different levels of 'good' leadership. The term 'good' here means only that the leader is effective. It does not imply an ethical or moral position.

A GOOD or EFFECTIVE leader would, as a minimum, demonstrate a keen determination to deliver.

A BETTER or MORE EFFECTIVE leader would demonstrate a determination to deliver and some form of engagement with the follower – either as an individual or as a team member.

The BEST or the HIGHLY EFFECTIVE leader would demonstrate competence in all three areas – a determination to deliver as well as engaging with the follower at the individual and the team levels.

This suggests that there is a spectrum of effective leadership. This is shown in Figure 3.2.

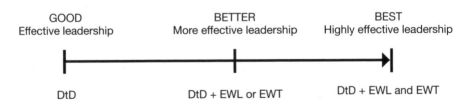

Figure 3.2 Spectrum of effective leadership

This is a very useful notion for a coach working with coachees who already enjoy success. Even if they are good leaders it helps to point the way to becoming better and more effective in their roles.

Although the specific scales are situational, there is evidence that the global scales are less so. It suggests that whatever your situation, the leader's determination to perform matters.

WORKING WITH THE SPECIFIC SCALES

Introduced earlier, the specific scales describe the different aspects of leadership style. The research showed that these scales were situational – there appeared to be no particular set of styles that were consistently shown to be more effective than any other. The research also showed that people adopt styles, which weren't always necessarily their preferred ones.

In many instances leaders will find that the circumstances and the situation in which they operate changes and there may be a need to adjust the adopted style. However if they are not aware of the former and do not realize the implications for the latter, then they might find that they are becoming less effective.

The specific scales provide a robust framework for coaches to assist them in working with coachees to reflect upon and develop their leadership style and behaviours.

The specific scales are bi-polar. They have two ends that represent 'opposites'. They are not necessarily right or wrong, they simply describe the characteristics of the individual. Typically 20–30 per cent of people will adopt a position that is firmly rooted to some extent at one end or the other. Most, 40–60 per cent, will be capable of adopting a position that enables them to adopt a certain degree of flexibility in that they can deploy tactics that are appropriate across the spectrum.

The first concern for the coach will be to establish with the coachee where the coachee is positioned on each scale. From this, the discussion can move to identifying a preferred position and then appropriate actions to get there.

The scales are outlined below.

Task versus person

The task-oriented leader believes that success breeds success and that people will work more enthusiastically for a successful organization.

Focusing on the task can ensure that the coachee and the organization achieve a great deal and can create a sense of success. Attending to the needs of people can often become secondary in importance in achieving that success. This can either be a conscious and deliberate approach or can be a by-product of an intensely focused approach.

However, ignoring the needs of people can also lead to problems and can lead to underdevelopment of the individual and ultimately a decline in performance.

The person-oriented leader believes that one must focus on individuals' needs in order to motivate them to greater performance. A balanced leader deploys both approaches as appropriate.

Focusing on people and relationships can create a good atmosphere that is a basis for success. However ignoring the need to complete key tasks can lead to problems. People may develop the notion that the task is not important and fail to grasp its significance. In turn, processes for task completion are unlikely to be supported and compliance will suffer. Both of these can have an impact on task completion – which can be critical to creating focus and a sense of achievement.

Flexible versus dogmatic

Dogmatic leaders will have a strong belief that 'they know how things should be done around here.' They may believe being decisive is important and valuable. They can also believe that if you dither or are unsure you may send the wrong message to others. Sticking to a firm view can project an aura of confidence that can be infectious.

Whilst many people do respond well to firm leadership of this type and it can be very effective as a means of doing things quickly (particularly in a high-pressure situation where action must be taken quickly), it can be flawed in some situations.

Where the culture is that one person's view holds sway all the time, it can create a form of 'learned helplessness'. People begin to feel that they have no role in problem solving or decision making, and fail to recognize the opportunity to take such a role when it arises.

A dogmatic approach can result in reducing challenge and discussion from subordinates and staff. It can be easy for sycophancy to develop, and this can affect the quality of decisions made. Similarly the responsibility for coming up with ideas falls to one person – the dogmatic leader. No one is perfect and over time some poor decisions may be – and probably will be – made. These can be evident to everyone else and can undermine the leader's credibility in the eyes of colleagues and clients.

Flexible managers are open to ideas and suggestions, understand that they don't have a monopoly on ideas and may be prepared to accept that decisions can be changed.

Whereas many people respond well to consultation, and involvement can be empowering and motivating, this can carry potential downsides.

Where the culture is flexible it can appear that the leadership is indecisive. Keeping decisions open to harness a wide range of views is useful but sometimes there is a need to strike a greater sense of urgency and importance.

Encouraging debate and discussion can allow people to continue to dwell on an issue even when a decision has been made – potentially undermining commitment. Similarly a consultative process can be slow at times, and consumes time and resources.

Both of these can have a negative impact on the organization, reducing its capability to perform when needed. There can be benefits in adopting a firmer more dogmatic style.

De-centralized versus centralized

Centralized leaders are those who prefer that everything goes through them. They may have a strong need to control or they may have a less mature group to work with where there is need for strong guidance.

This style can be very effective where the organization is comparatively small and/or where others are not as mature as the leader. However it has disadvantages too, which can grow over time if not checked.

Speed of decision making can be slow and comparatively trivial decisions are made at too high a level in the organization. Development of the team members is inhibited and their capacity to solve problems at the level at which they occur diminishes – which can encourage inefficiency.

The development of the leader may slow too. The leader's time is taken up with issues and tasks that should be handled elsewhere.

De-centralized leaders are happy to delegate to others and to work through others. Their ethos is one of empowerment.

A de-centralized style can be effective in creating an organization that has a strong internal capability to solve problems and perform. However this approach can develop problems over time.

Not everyone will be comfortable about making decisions without some guidance from above. Furthermore most people appreciate some degree of visibility from the leadership of the organization – and will accept a reasonable degree of control for all the signals it sends – indicating direction, pace and so on.

Reward versus punishment

The reward-oriented leader is prepared to reward and recognize acceptable and high performance. This can take the form of a tangible benefit or it could be 'warm strokes'.

The 'carrot' can be effective in making people aware of the need to do things right and to set standards, but persistent use and over-use of this style can create complacency. People may begin to expect reward – even when their achievement is minor. Poor performers are not dealt with, except in the sense that they do not receive a reward. Being over-generous or lavish with praise diminishes its worth. People need to earn it for their efforts and their achievements.

There may be benefits to adopting a more punishment-oriented style. The punishment-oriented leader accepts good or high performance as the norm ('that's what I pay the person for already') and thus finds it acceptable to punish a shortcoming in performance in some way.

The 'stick' can be effective in making people aware of the need to do things right and can help to establish standards, but again there will be situations where persistent use of this style can wear people down and create problems. People learn to adopt a minimalist approach – they do as little as possible because there is less risk of punishment for getting it wrong. They learn to hide mistakes and errors; these don't get solved and are repeated. Many may take their cue from the leader and punishment becomes a cultural feature of the organization, leading to bullying and/or a blame culture.

The means versus the end

The leader focused on the end is someone for whom the result matters more than anything. Much can be sacrificed for that goal. This does not necessarily mean that such leaders are immoral or amoral – they are simply very focused.

Focusing on the end rather than the means can be valuable in some circumstances. For example threatened liquidation, critical delivery, restructuring, merger, takeover or business failure may create situations where survival and/or performance is the paramount concern. However there is a risk that 'out and out' focus on the end can lead people to ignore environmental, social, interpersonal and legal factors, all of which can have equally severe implications. It also touches upon people's (customers', suppliers', employees' and stakeholders') concepts of values and morality – making some unwilling to contribute to the cause. This can have an adverse impact on capability and performance.

Leaders who are focused on the means are concerned about how the goal is achieved and will adopt standards and values to ensure that it is done properly. They will also take into account the implications of what they do – and will typically tend to be concerned about environment and capability in people and process.

Focusing on the means rather than the end can be valuable. It can ensure that what you do is in line with values, ethical standpoint and standards that are important in the conduct of any organization. However, if insufficient attention is given to the end, then in some circumstances there will be a risk of underperformance where achievement is critical.

There can be benefits to maintaining a better balance between the means and the end.

Structured versus organic

Organic leaders appear to operate naturally. They learn about leadership in a more casual manner by observing others' behaviours and selecting what they feel works. This can be very effective because it is such a natural style (and often has a charismatic appeal). Followers tend to see this as an expression of commitment and find it appealing.

However an organic approach can also present problems. Followers can find the style of leadership appealing but may not be able to see the substance. They will not always see clearly what the leader stands for and what the core strategies are. And the highly reactive approach makes it difficult to see commitment to process and structure, which is what guides many people – particularly those within the organization.

There are often benefits to adopting a more structured style. The structured leader operates more formally, using an approach drawn from education, models or training, and following detailed plans and processes to achieve things through others. Such leaders will often articulate a clear vision about what they wish to achieve.

The structured style can be very effective because it often relies on use of well-researched models, logic and structure that provide a good deal of clarity and transparency. It can be based on application of good practice and role modelling on the experience of others.

However a highly structured approach can also present problems. Outputs can appear dull, lifeless and semi-academic; as a result, personal presentation can also appear to be short of enthusiasm, suggesting that the sell is from the head and not the heart.

Note that one implication here is that leadership is learned, one way or the other.

A useful generic approach for a coach to work with the specific scales would be to:

1. Assess the coachees' position on each of the six scales. To what extent do they favour one position or another, or are they balanced in some

way? This can be achieved though discussion, a 360° process or the ILM72 measure.

2. An important and useful aspect of the discussion is to identify whether these are the coachees adopted or preferred positions. If adopted rather than preferred, why do the coachees think they have adopted this style?
3. Given that leadership style is situational, assess what might be a more effective leadership style and how benefits would arise.
4. Identify how any gap would be closed.
5. Assign priorities for attention.
6. Plan for implementation – and review.

CASE STUDY

In late 2007 a major UK local authority had set out to improve its organizational performance. It had succeeded in previous years in transforming itself from an average authority to a high-performing one, as measured by independent national government inspectors. This had been achieved through a highly centralized approach where the organization's development had been closely controlled by a small group at its top.

The commonly held view was that engaging with staff at all levels through empowering them and developing better teamworking would lead to better organizational performance.

A plan was developed and implemented, but disappointingly this didn't produce any significant impact.

The organization had participated in the research behind the development of the integrated leadership model, and we were able to establish profiles for the (97) senior managers of the organization for the three global factors though a combination of the ILM72 measure and one-to-one discussions. The analysis was revealing and informative. This case study shows only the patterns for the global scales. The analysis found:

❚ In assessing *determination to deliver*, there was a comparatively low level of such committment (see Figure 3.3 below). We would expect that senior management team would have a high determination to deliver (Stens 7–10). Individual discussions confirmed this pattern. Many managers were not confident about their role in delivering the proposed plan.

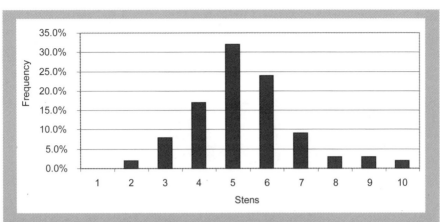

Figure 3.3 Determination to deliver

▮ In assessing *engagement with individuals*, the analysis found again that there was a relatively low level of engagement on the part of the senior managers (see Figure 3.4).The expectation is that senior managers should have a higher than average interest in this factor – half appeared not to have this level of interest.

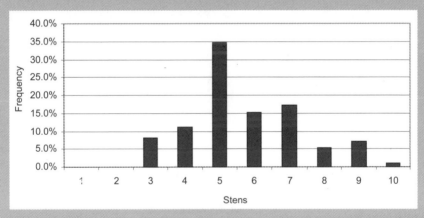

Figure 3.4 Engagement with individuals

▮ The most significant of the findings was examining the extent to which senior managers were engaged with *teams and with teamworking*. The organization had set teamworking as a key aspect of the development strategy. Only a tiny proportion of the senior management team were focused on developing and using teamworking (see Figure 3.5).

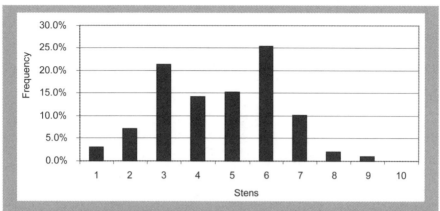

Figure 3.5 Engagement with teams

The conclusion reached was that the organization had achieved its previous successes though a very centralized and directive approach. Teamworking had not featured at all highly in the 'dash for success'.

The organization had correctly identified that a different style and a new set of strategies were needed 'to get to the next level'. However, the managers were simply so rooted in the prevailing style that they had been unable, individually and organizationally, to make that shift. Consequently the followers, the staff, didn't recognize any new behaviours and took the view that the senior managers were simply saying one thing but doing something else entirely. They were carrying on as before.

This has led to a review of the OD strategy that is being implemented as we write and that includes provision for coaching interventions.

The case study illustrates the importance of taking a global view as well as a specific view.

CONCLUSIONS

In this chapter the development of an integrated model of leadership and the construction of an instrument to measure leadership style have been briefly described. There is a clear need for an integrated model.

The use of specific models has been helpful, but they can sometimes produce an almost evangelical fervour. No single approach can provide all the answers.

Leadership models appear to come into, and drop out of, fashion at an alarming rate. This leads to both confusion and suspicion by the end users. Additionally, there has been a strong tendency to 're-invent the wheel'. This has been made worse by the fact that different disciplines have their own language and there is very little cross-over between them.

It is hoped that the integrated leadership model offers a practical and non-partisan approach to leadership coaching.

References

Adair, J (1973) *Action Centred Leadership*, McGraw-Hill, London

Bass, B M (1985) *Leadership and Performance Beyond Expectation*, Free Press, New York

Bennis, W (1998) *On Becoming a Leader*, Arrow, London

Berne, E (1964) *Games People Play*, Grove Press, New York

Browne, M N M (2008) *An Integrated Model of Leadership*, PhD Thesis, University of Hull, UK

Burns, J M (1978) *Leadership*, Harper, New York

Chelladurai, P (1978) *A Contingency Model of Leadership in Athletics*, unpublished doctoral dissertation, Department of Management Sciences, University of Waterloo, Canada

Chelladurai, P (1990) Leadership in sports: a review, *International Journal of Sport Psychology*, **21**, pp 328–54

Chelladurai, P and Saleh, S D (1980) Dimensions of leader behaviour in sports: development of a leadership scale, *Journal of Sport Psychology*, **2**, pp 34–45

Covey, S R (1989) *The Seven Habits of Highly Effective People*, Simon and Schuster, London

Dansereau, F, Yammarino, F J and Markham, S E (1995) Leadership: the multiple-level approaches, *The Leadership Quarterly*, **6**, pp 97–109

Fiedler, F E (1967) *A Theory of Leadership Effectiveness*, McGraw-Hill/Harper and Row, New York

Fleishman, E A (1957) A leader behaviour description for industry, in *Leader Behaviour: Its description and measurement*, ed R M Stogdill and A E Coons, pp 103–34, Bureau of Business Research, Ohio State University, Columbus, Ohio

Fleishman, E A, Zaccaro, S J and Mumford, M D (1991) Individual differences and leadership: an overview, *The Leadership Quarterly*, **2**, pp 237–43

Hersey, P and Blanchard, K H (1977) *The Management of Organizational Behaviour*, 3rd edn, Prentice Hall, Upper Saddle River, NJ

House, Robert J (1971) A path-goal theory of leader effectiveness, *Administrative Science Quarterly*, **16**, pp 321–39

McGregor, D (1960) *The Human Side of Enterprise*, McGraw-Hill, New York

Osborne, R N, Hunt, J G and Jaunch, L R (2002) Toward a contextual theory of leadership, *The Leadership Quarterly*, **13**, pp 797–837

Tejeda, M J, Scandura, T A and Pillai, R (2001) The MLQ revisited: psychometric properties and recommendations, *The Leadership Quarterly*, **12**, pp 31–52

4

Coaching for emotionally intelligent leadership

Jonathan Perks and Professor Reuven Bar-On

INTRODUCTION

This chapter provides the theory, research and practical guidance needed to help individuals become more emotionally intelligent leaders. Our aim is to give a pragmatic guide to leadership coaches and leaders, who in turn are responsible for developing leadership in others. It explains how to use emotional intelligence (EI) to develop more successful leadership.

We start by providing the reader with a brief background on EI and then describe our personally preferred model of leadership coaching, which is based on EI. We will also briefly discuss key research findings that support the value EI adds to leadership and business results. After a more detailed explanation of the Bar-On model of emotional intelligence and how to apply it in coaching, we will describe an authentic case study demonstrating the ability to produce a successful outcome through more effective emotionally intelligent leadership.

THE EMOTIONALLY INTELLIGENT LEADERSHIP MODEL

In order to explain what the emotionally intelligent leadership model is and how to apply it in coaching, we must first describe what an emotionally intelligent leader looks like and then describe the Bar-On model of emotional intelligence (Bar-On, 1997b), which is the basis of our approach to coaching described in this chapter.

Characteristics of emotionally intelligent leaders

Emotionally intelligent leaders often display the following characteristics:

- They cope proactively with life's demands and pressures without caving in.
- They build and leverage cooperative, effective and rewarding relationships with others.
- They are able to set and achieve personal and professional goals in a manner that is compatible with what is best for them and others.
- They seek first to understand, and then to be understood.
- They are sufficiently assertive to act with authority in making difficult and courageous decisions when the need arises.
- They are typically positive and lead by example.
- They are realistically optimistic about maximizing their potential and able to get the most out of others.

Emotional intelligence (EI)

Emotional intelligence has become a major topic of interest, since the publication of a bestseller by the same name authored by Daniel Goleman (Goleman, 1995). In this and his follow-up book, *Working with Emotional Intelligence* (Goleman, 1998), Goleman created a tremendous amount of publicity for the topic. This set in motion a surge of energy that was directed to the study, understanding and application of the concept worldwide. Despite the heightened level of interest in this 'new idea', scholars have been studying this concept for the greater part of the 20th century; its historical roots can be traced to Charles Darwin's 1872 publication on the use of EI in survival and adaptation (Darwin, 1872/1965).

Over the past century, a number of different approaches to EI have appeared, creating some degree of confusion about the way it should be defined, measured and applied. To help clarify this situation, the *Encyclopedia of Applied Psychology* (Spielberger, 2004) suggests that there are three major EI models: a) the Mayer–Salovey model (Mayer and Salovey, 1997), which defines this concept as the ability to perceive, understand, manage and use emotions to facilitate thinking, measured by an ability-based tool (Mayer, Salovey and Caruso, 2002); b) the Goleman model (Goleman, 1998), which views it as an assortment of competencies and skills that contribute to managerial performance, measured by a 360° multi-rater assessment (Boyatzis, Goleman and Hay Group, 2001); and c) the Bar-On model (Bar-On, 1997b), which describes it as an array of interrelated emotional and social competencies and skills that impact on intelligent behaviour, measured by self-report (Bar-On, 1997a) and multi-rater assessment (Bar-On and Handley, 2003a, 2003b).

The basic strategic differences between these three EI models have influenced the way they are measured and, possibly, their ability to predict leadership performance. The Mayer–Salovey model focuses on the potential for emotionally intelligent behaviour, which requires an ability-based assessment to determine someone's ability to behave in an emotionally intelligent manner. On the other hand, the Bar-On model and the Goleman model focus on overt behaviour that requires self-report and multi-rater assessment respectively; the former asks the individual, while the latter asks others about his or her behaviour to determine how emotionally intelligent it is. It is much easier to work in coaching with one's overt behaviour, including perceived strengths and weaknesses, than with one's potential for behaviour; and this might also explain the fact that the Goleman and, especially, the Bar-On model are better predictors of effective and successful performance in the workplace than the Mayer–Salovey model (Geher, 2004).

Most descriptions, definitions, models and measures of emotional in-telligence have included one or more of the following key components: a) the ability to recognize and understand emotions and to express feelings; b) the ability to understand how others feel and to relate with them; c) the ability to manage and control emotions; d) the ability to manage change, adapt and solve problems of a personal and interpersonal nature; and e) the ability to generate positive mood and be self-motivated.

THE BAR-ON MODEL OF EI

This section describes the Bar-On model of emotional intelligence; its comprehensive and multi-factorial nature makes it very applicable and meaningful in coaching. Moreover, this model has proven to be a significantly valid predictor of leadership performance (Bar-On, 2006b), proving it to be a valuable tool in leadership coaching.

According to the Bar-On model: 'Emotional–social intelligence is an array of interrelated emotional and social competencies and skills that determine how effectively we understand and express ourselves, understand others and relate with them, and cope with daily demands and challenges' (Bar-On, 1997b, 2006b). The emotional and social competencies and skills referred to in this general definition are grouped into five meta-components that are divided into 15 sub-components (or factors). All of these EI factors are measured by the Emotional Quotient Inventory (EQ-i; Bar-On, 1997a) and described briefly in Table 4.1, which is also used as a worksheet to help understand, discuss and work on the coachee's EI strengths and weaknesses in the initial stage of coaching.

The EQ-i is briefly described here, because it is not only the measure of the Bar-On model of emotional intelligence, but was used to develop that model scientifically. It also determined the most powerful EI predictors of leadership and its use can unquestionably strengthen emotionally intelligent leadership coaching. The EQ-i is a self-report measure of emotionally and socially intelligent behaviour that provides an estimate of one's overall emotional–social intelligence. A detailed description of the psychometric properties of this measure and how it was developed, validated and standardized for use is found in a number of publications such as *The Bar-On EQ-i: Technical manual* (Bar-On, 1997b), Buros *Mental Measurement Yearbook* (Plake and Impara, 1999), *Handbook of Emotional Intelligence* (Bar-On and Parker, 2000) and *Measuring Emotional Intelligence* (Geher, 2004). This instrument contains 133 brief items and uses a five-point response scale. There is also a 125-item inventory that is used extensively in the corporate world as well as a 360° multi-rater version of the EQ-i and a 51-item short version (www.mhs.com). The EQ-i is suitable for individuals 17 years of age and older and takes approximately 20 minutes to complete online. The individual's responses to the EQ-i produces a total EQ score and scores on five composite scales and 15 sub-scales, which are described in Table 4.1.

THE RESEARCH

The executive leaders with whom we work are pragmatic people who are interested in practical solutions to problems, rather than the theory and research behind emotional intelligence. They are primarily interested in knowing if 'it', be it EI or anything else, can help them and their colleagues be more effective, productive and successful.

When the reader is confronted by sceptical executive leaders and HR directors who need evidence that will demonstrate the value of applying EI in their organization, there are some good sources to refer them to, such as the chapter in Goleman's 1998 book on the hard case for soft skills, where he summarizes one of the most important findings from an extensive data analysis conducted by Hay/McBer (Goleman, 1998):

> Emotional (and social) competencies were found to be twice as important in contributing to excellence as pure intellect and expertise; [and] emotional competence is particularly central to leadership, a role whose essence is to get others to do their jobs more effectively.

For those who need additional evidence that EI can help their business be more profitable and get staff to be more motivated, productive and willing to work for their leaders, you might suggest that they review the Gallup findings (Buckingham and Coffman, 1999). The researchers who conducted this study conclude by suggesting that 'people join great organizations and leave poor managers!'

For the hardcore sceptics, who are not yet convinced that the application of EI in organizations is beneficial, we can help them 'connect the dots' (Bar-On, 2003) between EI, occupational performance and organizational productivity by showing that:

- With the Bar-On model, we have a clear, comprehensive and meaningful working definition of EI that can easily be used in group training and individual coaching.
- With the EQ-i, we have a valid EI measure that can accurately pinpoint what needs to be worked on and then assess how successful coaching was from an emotional intelligence perspective.
- Based on numerous studies to date, EI significantly impacts on various aspects of occupational performance, including leadership.
- Based on past and current projects, we know we can hire and promote emotionally intelligent individuals.
- Based on empirical findings, emotionally intelligent leaders increase organizational productivity and the bottom line.
- We can train, coach and develop leaders to be more emotionally intelligent, and thus more effective, productive and successful.

The following sources, which appear in the reference section, convincingly provide the empirical evidence needed to connect the above dots and make the case for applying emotional intelligence in the workplace to improve performance, effectiveness and productivity leading to measurable profit growth:

- Bar-On, R (2006b) The Bar-On model of emotional–social intelligence (ESI), *Psicothema*, 18, supplement, pp 13–25.

Table 4.1 The emotional intelligence (EI) worksheet based on the Bar-On model

EI factors	Definition of EI factors	Areas to be strengthened	Effective functioning	Enhanced functioning
Intrapersonal	*Self-awareness and self-expression*			
Self-regard	To accurately perceive, understand and accept oneself			
Emotional self-awareness	To be aware of and understand one's emotions and feelings			
Assertiveness	To constructively express one's feelings and oneself			
Independence	To be self-reliant and free from emotional dependency on others			
Self-actualization	To strive to achieve personal goals and actualize one's potential			
Interpersonal	*Social awareness and interaction*			
Empathy	To be aware of and understand how others feel			
Social responsibility	To identify with one's social group and cooperate with others			
Interpersonal relationship	To establish mutually satisfying relationships and relate well with others			

EI factors	Definition of EI factors	Areas to be strengthened	Effective functioning	Enhanced functioning
Stress management	*Emotional management and control*			
Stress tolerance	To effectively manage emotions			
Impulse control	To effectively control emotions			
Adaptability	*Change management*			
Reality testing	To objectively validate one's feelings and thinking with external reality			
Flexibility	To adapt and adjust one's feelings and thinking to new situations			
Problem solving	To effectively solve problems of a personal and interpersonal nature			
General mood	*Self-motivation*			
Optimism	To be positive and look on the brighter side of life			
Happiness	To feel content with oneself, others and life in general			

▌ Bar-On, R (2006a) *The Bar-On EQ-i Leadership User's Guide*, Multi-Health Systems Inc, Toronto, Canada.

▌ Bar-On, R, Maree, J G and Elias, M J (eds) (2007) *Educating People to be Emotionally Intelligent*, Praeger, Westport, Connecticut.

▌ Bharwaney, G, Bar-On, R and MacKinlay, A (2007) *EQ and the Bottom Line: Emotional intelligence increases individual occupational performance, leadership and organisational productivity*, Ei World Ltd, Bedfordshire, UK.

▌ Druskat, V, Sala, F and Mount, G (eds) (2006) *Linking Emotional Intelligence and Performance at Work: Current research evidence with individuals and groups*, Lawrence Erlbaum, Mahwah, New Jersey.

▌ Langhorn, S (2004) How emotional intelligence can improve management performance, *International Journal of Contemporary Hospitality Management*, 16, pp 220–30.

THE SIX MOST IMPORTANT EI FACTORS THAT PREDICT SUCCESSFUL LEADERSHIP

To identify the most powerful EI predictors of successful leadership, the second co-author of this chapter re-examined the findings that emerged from a study conducted with Marian Ruderman at the Center for Creative Leadership (CCL) in 2003 (Bar-On, 2006a). In this study, a large sample of 300 executive leaders from a wide variety of industries completed the EQ-i. Their performance was then rated by seven to eight co-workers on CCL's Benchmarks, which is a 360° multi-rater assessment tool, designed to evaluate 16 competencies related to 'successful leadership' and five factors related to 'derailment' (unsuccessful leadership).

The overall impact of EI on leadership was examined by using three different types of multivariate statistics. The specific impact of EI was then examined on seven different leadership orientations (people, process and organization) and leadership styles (centred and grounded, action-taking, participative and tough-minded). Findings from 26 additional validity studies comprising a total sample of more than 26,600 individuals confirmed and clarified these results (Bar-On, 2006b). The six EI competencies and skills that consistently emerge as the most powerful predictors of leadership performance across the above-mentioned studies are:

▌ accurate self-awareness ('Self-regard' in Table 4.1);
▌ the ability to manage emotions ('Stress tolerance' in Table 4.1);
▌ the ability to control emotions ('Impulse control' in Table 4.1);

▌ responsible social interaction ('Social responsibility' in Table 4.1);
▌ optimism and positive thinking ('Optimism' in Table 4.1);
▌ happiness and self-motivation ('Happiness' in Table 4.1).

Individuals who match the above model, by demonstrating significant strengths in these six areas, are expected to be successful leaders capable of being people oriented, process oriented and organization oriented, as well as well grounded, action taking, participative and even tough minded when they need to be. From a purely EI perspective, they would also be expected to understand their strengths and limitations, to manage and control their emotions, to work well under pressure, relate responsibly and cooperatively with people, and be optimistic, positive, happy and self-motivated. This is what an effective, productive and successful leader looks like, based on the large number of studies that were reviewed.

USING THE EMOTIONALLY INTELLIGENT LEADERSHIP MODEL WITH COACHEES

There is a wide variety of approaches to leadership development that coaches can choose from. In the present chapter, we recommend using the emotionally intelligent leadership model, as a valuable adjunct to leadership coaching. This approach can easily be woven into any other approach that is normally used by the coach. The following 14 recommendations were developed by the second co-author of this chapter; they were based on his personal approach to interpreting EQ-i results and have appeared in numerous publications (see, for example, Bar-On, 1997b) and presentations (see, for example, Bar-On, 2008).

Before meeting with the coachee for the first time:

1. *Collect all available collateral information on the coachee before the initial coaching session.*
   Before the initial coaching session, the coach needs to collect as much information as possible on the coachee. This often includes letters of reference, correspondence with former bosses, previous interviews and, at times, psychometric results. In order to receive a rich source of information, we recommend that the coachee complete an EI measure such as the EQ-i (www.mhs.com) prior to the initial coaching session; this provides a reliable and valid indication of the individual's current level of emotional intelligence and how it might be affecting his or her leadership performance. Within the context

of the emotionally intelligent leadership model, the coach should begin to note indications of EI strengths or weaknesses based on the information available. The coach should begin to record indications of possible strengths and weaknesses on the EI worksheet provided in Table 4.1. At the beginning, these are 'indications' at best, especially if there is little collateral information to work with and in the absence of test results. The coach needs to confirm or refute these assumptions during the initial coaching session and to collect additional information regarding the coachee's emotional intelligence at that time.

2. *Focus on the 15 EI factors described in Table 4.1, especially those that have the greatest impact on leadership.*

   As the coach is reviewing available collateral information before the initial coaching session, he or she should focus primarily on the 15 EI factors in Table 4.1. Among the 15 factors, it is most important to concentrate on those EI factors that significantly impact on leadership (stress tolerance, impulse control, self-regard, social responsibility, optimism and happiness in Table 4.1).

3. *Begin to identify what appear to be the individual's strongest and weakest EI competencies and skills.*

   As more collateral information is collected, attempt to see what appear to be the coachee's strongest and weakest EI competencies and skills. Then, note which of these strengths and weaknesses are associated with those EI factors that are the best predictors of leadership (those listed in Recommendation No 2 above). Where do most of the EI strengths appear to cluster, and where are all the EI weaknesses and limitations clustering? Begin to think what the apparent weaknesses may have in common and what they may mean from an emotionally intelligent leadership perspective, and what needs to be addressed in coaching to enhance leadership. Identify what are thought to be the most serious weaknesses. Begin to think what needs to be addressed first and what may need to be addressed later in coaching. Weaknesses in one or more of the six EI factors that have a significant impact on leadership should be the coach's top priority.

4. *Attempt to understand the coachee's 'story' on the basis of what is beginning to emerge from the EI worksheet prior to the initial coaching session.*

   The coach should look at what is beginning to appear on the worksheet in Table 4.1 as 'bits and pieces of valuable information' that begin to tell something important about the individual. It may suggest what his or her strengths and weaknesses are, how well he or she is presently functioning, and where there are problems that might be limiting performance. Build the story carefully by developing a picture that slowly emerges from the EI worksheet and not on the basis of what you 'assume' or 'feel' should be the story. Follow a well-grounded, focused and flexible problem-solving process to determine what the story might be. Avoid forming rigid opinions by widening the various possibilities that might explain the individual's current performance.

5. *Prepare for the initial session carefully.*
   The initial session is designed to discuss what appears to be emerging, what this might mean on a personal and leadership level, and to think about what needs to be addressed in coaching. Plan what you are going to say, why, how and when. Use your cognitive intelligence in organizing the content that has been collected, and your emotional intelligence in planning how best to convey what you want to discuss. This initial session represents a very important meeting, because it is typically the beginning of the coaching process.

6. *The initial meeting with the coachee.*
   Promise confidentiality; and if you cannot, clarify why that is so.
   It is not only ethically correct to promise confidentiality at the outset of the coaching process, but is a valuable way to build trust so as to facilitate the successful continuation of this process. If you cannot promise confidentiality, you are obliged to convey this information from the outset. Tell the individual if the contents of the coaching sessions will be shared with others within the organization. If decisions related to employment, recruitment, advancement or redundancy are to be made on the basis of these discussions, the individual should be informed of this possibility during the first session. Being honest and straightforward facilitates trust, openness and co-operation in the coaching process.

7. *Use the initial session to collect additional information that fine tunes and adds to what has been emerging from the EI worksheet.*
   The individual's reaction to the initial session, what is said and how it is said will provide an additional source of information that helps clarify the emerging story.

8. *Explain that the EI worksheet is a self-awareness tool.*
   Tell the coachee that the EI worksheet is a valuable tool that is applied in coaching to help better understand and develop leadership performance. Explain something about emotional intelligence and the idea behind emotionally intelligent leadership coaching. Discuss how EI is connected with leadership performance. Begin to discuss how the EI worksheet will be used during the initial session. Then begin to discuss the 15 EI factors and explore how the individual sees his or her strengths and weaknesses in these areas.

9. *Compare the individual with himself or herself and not with others.*
    From the beginning of the coaching process it should be explained that individuals who have completed the EQ-i should be compared with themselves, not with others or the national average. Insight and performance enhancement come from first understanding their weakest EI areas in comparison with their strongest ones.

10. *Summarize what has emerged from the discussion regarding the EI strengths, and work down to those areas that need to be improved.*
    In order to ease the individual into the initial coaching session and strengthen cooperation, begin by discussing the strongest EI factors and what they mean with respect to leadership. Explain that these factors drive various aspects of successful leadership. Stress that 'effective functioning' does not mean mediocre performance, but rather functioning as most other people function in those particular EI areas. It should be conveyed that relative weaknesses suggest 'opportunities for improvement'. Coachees should be made to feel that this is an excellent way for them to learn more about themselves and improve leadership performance.

11. *Ask how it felt to discuss the 15 EI areas and whether the coachee learned something new about himself or herself.*
    Asking how easy or difficult it was to discuss these EI areas often generates additional information about what the person has learned about himself/herself and leadership performance from an EI perspective. This typically provides the coach with valuable input that can be used in coaching.

12. *Ask what the coachee wants to change, why, how and when.*
    To make the transition to the actual coaching process and to effect-ively advance this process, it is important to ask what the coachee would like to change based on the discussion. To enhance personal commitment, it is important that this comes from the coachee and not from the coach. The coach should facilitate clarification as to a) what exactly the individual wants to change and b) why; c) how he or she wants to achieve these goals; and d) when to begin in order to become a better leader. The responses to these important questions provide the content for the coachee's action plan.

13. *Mobilize as much commitment for change as possible, and ask why that would be important for the coachee and his or her organization.*
    It is important to get as much commitment as possible from the coachee in order to set the stage for a successful leadership coaching experience. To facilitate this, it is imperative for the coachee to verbalize why that change is important for the organization and for him or her personally. Then begin to work out a detailed action plan for change in the following coaching sessions.

14. *Do not promise that the coachee will be transformed into a new person, or a legendary leader, but do explain it may improve leadership.*

    It is counter-productive to create grandiose expectations, which should not be encouraged by the coach in any way whatsoever. Do say, however, that the coachee's leadership performance is expected to improve should emotional intelligence improve as a result of the coaching process. Once again, stress the importance of creating and working with a well-defined action plan, which is one of the most important components of the coaching process.

CASE STUDY

In this real case study, which exemplifies coaching for emotionally intelligent leadership, the coachee's actual name and the identity of his organization are not revealed in order to protect his anonymity and privacy. His name appears as 'Gary' and his organization is referred to as 'a global bank'.

Last year, Gary took on a challenge that might have overwhelmed even the most talented of managers; newly appointed to the role of managing director in a famous global bank, he was charged with the task of bringing together two underperforming businesses, with a combined total worth of £8bn in assets and turning them into a single, profitable division. Shortly after starting his new appointment, Gary requested executive coaching, in order to enhance his leadership skills. He was assigned a coach trained in the emotionally intelligent leadership model.

To effectively build his team and lead 200 colleagues through rapid change, Gary needed to rely on high levels of resilience. Without that, inevitable conflicts could have resulted in a depletion of group energy, decline in morale and a failure to inspire colleagues with his vision for change. He wished to make himself and his new team 'fit for purpose' and ready for the storms ahead. Despite the pressure to deliver huge change in a new culture and a new market, Gary knew that he needed clarity of thought to generate an effective strategy and well-thought-out solutions. To achieve this, he wanted to create 'thinking time' in a role that threatened to impose a 24-hour-a-day, seven-days-a-week lifestyle!

Gary was under considerable time pressure, since his organization wanted to see results quickly. He needed support that could be delivered promptly and effectively, and emotionally intelligent leadership coaching was his preferred approach, after discussions with his coach. The coach's approach at the very start was to co-design with Gary a 'coaching contract' – a document that clearly defined the desired outcomes of coaching for his organization and for Gary himself. The contract was then reviewed with his two managers, who were both interviewed, to understand what Gary did well and what he could do even better as a leader.

In order to fully understand the organization's culture, the coach attended a two-day off-site team event with Gary and his team. This gave the coach a clearer understanding of how Gary's team operated, the levels of trust, how Gary responded to individuals and how they related to him. This was a pivotal moment in the team's development and opened up a culture of honesty, which helped Gary in his leadership style.

Changing a pattern of ineffective behaviour is a challenging process, and Gary was fully open to the resulting growth and learning. To do this, he needed to first understand the benefits and his motivation for change; and the coach helped by offering objective evidence of his current behaviour, based on observations that were made during the earlier team event. As part of several two-hour coaching sessions, Gary completed the EQ-i as well as other psychometric tools; these provided greater awareness of his leadership motivations in addition to his EI strengths and limitations. By using the self-scoring EI worksheet shown in Table 4.1, he reviewed his results together with his coach. They used this approach to identify those areas that he could most usefully leverage as well as those areas that needed to be improved in order to enhance his overall leadership performance.

Gary exhibited both determination and a very strong motivational drive to understand, learn and take action directed at strengthening the EI competencies that were holding him back from being a better leader. The previously described recommendations for applying the emotionally intelligent leadership model have proven to be an ideal approach for coaching leaders in Gary's challenging situation, as is illustrated here.

Gary's results are all the more significant, since by January 2009 the global recession had fully bitten; whilst other banks were losing millions, Gary swam against the tide and led his team through adversity to significant profit. Figure 4.1 compares Gary's EQ-i results at the beginning of coaching with results produced seven months later. Based on the pre-intervention assessment in Figure 4.1, which was completed in August 2007, Gary and his coach identified four EI competencies and skills in particular that they decided to work on in coaching: The ability to manage emotions (stress tolerance in Figure 4.1); the ability to control emotions (impulse control in Figure 4.1); accurate self-awareness (self-regard in Figure 4.1); and optimistic thinking (optimism in Figure 4.1). These represent four of the six EI factors that are the strongest predictors of leadership performance, nearly all of which proved to be Gary's significantly weakest competencies and skills at the beginning of coaching.

In brief, the approach adopted to enhance Gary's EI was to first make him more aware that the above four factors represented the primary

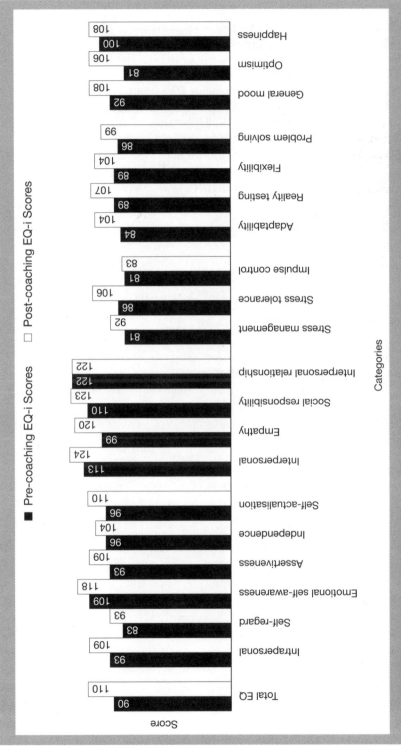

Figure 4.1 The before and after EQ-i scores for a recipient of emotionally intelligent leadership coaching

Legend:
- ■ Pre-coaching EQ-i Scores
- □ Post-coaching EQ-i Scores

Axis labels: Score (y-axis), Categories (x-axis)

Category	Pre-coaching	Post-coaching
Total EQ	90	110
Intrapersonal	93	109
Self-regard	83	93
Emotional self-awareness	109	118
Assertiveness	93	109
Independence	96	104
Self-actualisation	96	110
Interpersonal	113	124
Empathy	99	120
Social responsibility	110	123
Interpersonal relationship	122	122
Stress management	81	92
Stress tolerance	86	106
Impulse control	81	83
Adaptability	84	104
Reality testing	89	107
Flexibility	89	104
Problem solving	86	99
General mood	92	108
Optimism	81	106
Happiness	100	108

weaknesses that were holding him back, discuss their importance for leadership and then to explore ways to alter his behaviour that were designed to strengthen these factors. For example, optimistic thinking was enhanced by first having Gary recognize his natural tendency toward pessimism in terms of his ability to achieve his goals at work, and to think about the negative impact this was having on him, his colleagues and his organization. He learnt to purposefully turn pessimistic thinking, when it surfaced, into optimistic thinking; this eventually became a semi-automatic response for him.

Drawing out solutions and results

In addition to working on various ways of strengthening the previously mentioned EI competencies and skills, Gary raised live issues during his coaching sessions that were having an immediate impact on his performance at work, while his organization was experiencing ongoing change. Through a process of structured questioning, the coach was able to draw out Gary's own experience and abilities, enabling him to find solutions that best suited his own leadership style and strengths. Having begun with two failing businesses, the new division became the outstanding success of Gary's organization, producing a £200m profit just nine months after he began his new role. The impressive results of his division and so of his global bank helped significantly lift their share price.

Gary's general level of emotional intelligence began to show impressive changes in 13 of the 15 EI areas measured by the EQ-i, as can be seen in Figure 4.1 (above), with an average 20 per cent increase after seven months. Figure 4.2 (below) highlights this increase between the pre- and post-intervention assessments, revealing a definite increase in EI as a result of the intervention (emotionally intelligent leadership coaching). By examining the pre- and post-intervention changes shown in Figures 4.1 and 4.2, it can be seen that fairly strong increases occurred in three of the four EI factors that were addressed in coaching. The results presented here clearly indicate that coaching was successful, based on the increase of EI and especially in those areas that have the strongest impact on leadership performance.

Gary believes that the coaching process has already created a 'fundamental difference' in his self-regard and self-belief, as well as his ability to focus on issues that add the most value. This, in turn, provides him with both the clarity of thought he needs to build effective strategies and an improved work–life balance.

In reviewing the coaching relationship, Gary had a strong view about what worked and what did not work:

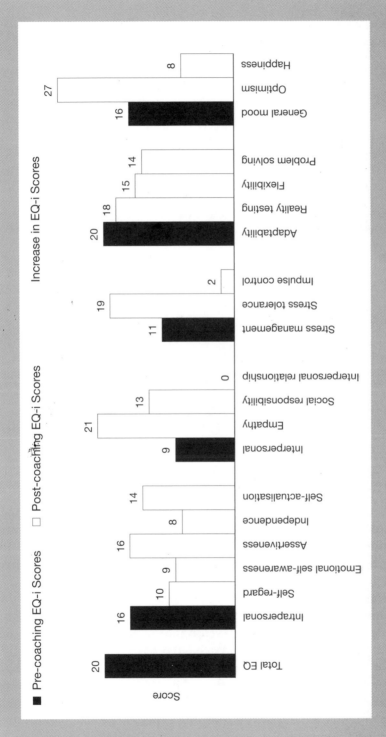

Figure 4.2 The increase in EQ-i scores (EI) for a recipient of emotionally intelligent leadership coaching

When I moved to the bank, I was initially tasked with leading a business that was underperforming significantly. Within two months, I was asked to take on an additional business, which was also undergoing substantial change.

Initially, I approached the role in my usual highly driven, impatient, solution-giving mode. I applied all my previous experience to drive out some quick wins and was marginally successful. I presented our strategy to our CEO, and he liked the approach; and we delivered one or two quick wins. However, I didn't feel as though I was getting the wholehearted support of my colleagues, or was delivering a sustainable improvement in performance. This became a very lonely job, and my usual charm tactics didn't seem to be working this time.

Then I met my coach, and we started working together to understand how to alleviate this stressful situation and find a way of gaining more support across my network. Using my coach's wise counsel, I began to think about the challenges differently, seeking first to understand, then to be understood. This approach began to pay dividends very quickly; and having adapted my style, I began to gain more support for my plans.

We delivered one of the most successful campaigns in the bank's history, and suddenly everyone wanted to be part of our success. I relaxed and realized that I was 'good enough already.' Our sales and profitability results got better and better. I recruited some great talent, who wanted to be part of our transformational story, and suddenly my division was no longer seen as the two problem children, but was the rising star of the bank.

My coach has played a pivotal role in helping me transform this business and myself over the past 12 months. The business is succeeding, and I am enjoying life so much more because of my coach's insightful and skilful coaching.

CONCLUSIONS

It is both a great honour and a daunting responsibility to work with some of the most able leaders of global brands and public sector departments. Through emotionally intelligent leadership coaching, coaches can be catalysts to help executives cope with adversity and become a positive force for good in their organizations.

This chapter has described the theory and research that support the development of the emotionally intelligent leadership model and its application in coaching: to help develop more effective, productive and successful leaders with less effort. We have provided a practical step-by-step guide to using this model, as well as a method to accurately pinpoint the EI factors that need to be strengthened in order to improve leadership performance and to evaluate progress achieved in this type of coaching. The case study describing Gary's coaching experience demonstrates that there are hard numbers and significant benefits behind the soft skills of emotionally intelligent leadership and this new and unique approach to coaching.

Ultimately, we are leaders who aspire to inspire and develop leaders, who in turn grow other leaders. Through enhancing their own EI, leaders can truly help ordinary people achieve extraordinary performance with high levels of energy, passion and motivation.

References

Bar-On, R (1997a) *The Bar-On Emotional Quotient Inventory (EQ-i): A test of emotional intelligence*, Multi-Health Systems Inc, Toronto, Canada

Bar-On, R (1997b) *The Bar-On Emotional Quotient Inventory (EQ-i): Technical manual*, Multi-Health Systems Inc, Toronto, Canada

Bar-On, R (2003) The impact of EI on leadership and organizational productivity: how to make the case in 45 minutes, a presentation delivered at The Consortium for Research on Emotional Intelligence in Organizations, in Boston, 30 October 2003

Bar-On, R (2006a) *The Bar-On EQ-i Leadership User's Guide*, Multi-Health Systems Inc, Toronto, Canada

Bar-On, R (2006b) The Bar-On model of emotional–social intelligence (ESI), *Psicothema*, **18**, supplement, pp 13–25

Bar-On, R (2008) An advanced Bar-On EQ-i practitioners workshop, a workshop delivered at The British Psychological Society, in London, 7 November 2008

Bar-On, R and Handley, R (2003a) *The Bar-On EQ-360*, Multi-Health Systems Inc, Toronto, Canada

Bar-On, R and Handley, R (2003b) *The Bar-On EQ-360: Technical manual*, Multi-Health Systems Inc, Toronto, Canada

Bar-On, R, Maree, J G and Elias, M J (Eds) (2007) *Educating People to be Emotionally Intelligent*, Praeger, Westport, Connecticut

Bar-On, R and Parker, J D A (2000) *Handbook of Emotional Intelligence: Theory, development, assessment and application at home, school and in the workplace*, Jossey-Bass, San Francisco

Bharwaney, G, Bar-On, R and MacKinlay, A (2007) *EQ and the Bottom Line: Emotional intelligence increases individual occupational performance, leadership and organisational productivity*, Ei World Ltd, Bedfordshire, UK

Boyatzis, R E, Goleman, D and Hay Group (2001) *The Emotional Competence Inventory (ECI)*, Hay Group, Boston

Buckingham, M and Coffman, C W (1999) *First Break All The Rules: Gallup study into managers*, Simon and Schuster, London

Darwin, C (1872/1965) *The Expression of the Emotions in Man and Animals*, University of Chicago Press, Chicago

Druskat, V, Sala, F and Mount, G (eds) (2006) *Linking Emotional Intelligence and Performance at Work: Current research evidence with individuals and groups*, Lawrence Erlbaum, Mahwah, NJ

Geher, G (ed) (2004) *Measuring Emotional Intelligence: Common ground and controversy*, Nova Science Publishers, Hauppauge, New York

Goleman, D (1995) *Emotional Intelligence*, Bantam Books, New York

Goleman, D (1998) *Working with Emotional Intelligence*, Bantam Books, New York

Langhorn, S (2004) How emotional intelligence can improve management performance, *International Journal of Contemporary Hospitality Management*, **16**, pp 220–30

Mayer, J D and Salovey, P (1997) What is emotional intelligence, in *Emotional Development and Emotional Intelligence: Implications for educators*, ed P Salovey, and D Sluyter, pp 3–31, Basic Books, New York

Mayer, J D, Salovey, P and Caruso, D R (2002) Mayer–Salovey–Caruso Emotional Intelligence Test (MSCEIT), Multi-Health Systems Inc, Toronto, Canada

Plake, B S and Impara, J C (eds) (1999) *Supplement to The Thirteenth Mental Measurement Yearbook*, Buros Institute for Mental Measurement, Lincoln, Nebraska

Ruderman, M and Bar-On, R (2003) The impact of emotional intelligence on leadership, unpublished data

Spielberger, C (ed) (2004) *Encyclopedia of Applied Psychology*, Academic Press, San Diego, California

5

The Leadership Radar

Stuart Duff and Ceri Roderick

INTRODUCTION

This chapter presents a framework for leadership that has, over many years, proved to be a valuable tool in coaching leaders from all walks of life. The framework derives from several major sources, including our own research into the paths that leaders choose at critical moments in their careers (Kandola, 2008), a number of established models of leadership, such as Adair's (1998) three circle model and Blake and Mouton's (1978) *Managerial Grid*, the transitions that leaders experience when moving across and upwards in their organizations, and our own experience of designing and implementing many leadership competency models for organizations across different industry sectors.

The model that we have developed over the years has been most widely used to raise awareness of the breadth of leadership challenges and, in many senses, to shed light on the often ambiguous challenges that leaders encounter on a daily basis. This approach to coaching leaders attempts to simplify and clarify the answers to the most important question – what is it that helps any individual to demonstrate the qualities of leadership at critical moments when leadership is required?

The model, known as the Leadership Radar™, provides a structure that can raise self-awareness in coachees. It can, for instance, enable them to monitor their behaviour and actions on a daily basis, and to maintain

...icopter view of their role and responsibilities, and ultimately of their
...ontribution as leaders.

THE LEADERSHIP MODEL

Over the past 25 years we have worked with organizations of all kinds
and sizes, helping their leaders to acquire new skills and improve their
performance. Our work with these many different, committed and talented individuals and teams, who are tackling challenges in very different environments, exposes similarities that they all share by virtue of
their leadership experiences. These common facets led us to develop our
own unique model: the Leadership Radar.

The model is based on three overlapping screens or 'arenas' of activity (Figure 5.1). The task leadership, thought leadership and people
leadership screens represent each of the core facets of leadership. These
are expressed differently for different leaders in different environments.
The three-dimensional shape of any one leader is influenced by factors
such as personality and temperament, business objectives, organizational
culture and personal experience.

Given that these three screens, in our view, represent the totality of
the leader's role, it follows that effective leaders will want – on balance
– to pay equal attention to all three screens. And that's why we use the

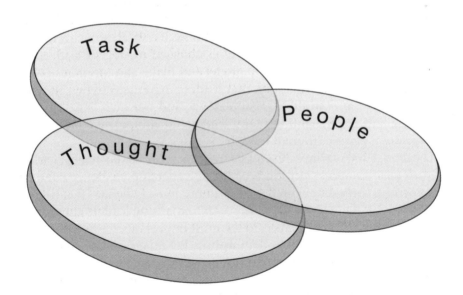

Figure 5.1 The leadership radars

metaphor of the radar for the model. The three screens direct a leader's attention to the areas that matter, and provide a way of ensuring that he or she acknowledges and responds to all the facets of the role – at some time or another.

Each of the three screens of the radar is relevant to leadership at every level. But different leadership roles place different pressures on leaders. Situations can cause individuals' use of their mental radar to change, leading them to ignore one or other of the screens. This behaviour quickly shows itself in the way leaders are spending their time. Periods of transition from one leadership role to another, or from one level of leadership to another, are particularly prone to this kind of narrowing or exclusivity.

It is important for leaders – and those around them – to recognize the changing pressures affecting them at these times, and the likely effects on their performance. If leaders aren't aware of their changing attention to the three screens, and the pressures prompting their behaviour, then they may lapse into a restricted comfort zone, rather than recognizing and tackling the challenges of their new situation.

The radar model helps leaders in transition to realize that a new role isn't just quantitatively different, but qualitatively different too. Each new role requires us to dissolve and reconstitute our approach to leadership, while holding on to and trusting the personal qualities that have served us well in the past. Change is about giving up what we've done before as much as it is about taking on new functions.

But it is also about applying what's best about ourselves to a situation that demands our distinctive contribution. Even when we move to fill another person's shoes, we still must walk our own path. Using the radar gives leaders a tool to reflect on and reorganize – if they wish to – their leadership approach in any environment.

People describe the key points in their careers in different ways, but there is a set of milestones that most would recognize as marking the main stages in leadership careers (eg Charan, Drotter and Noel, 2001). These career milestones form a series of 'firsts', including:

▌ first role requiring significant people leadership;
▌ first role requiring large-team leadership and the leadership of other managers;
▌ first role with functional leadership and responsibility for direction setting;
▌ first role requiring a contribution to leadership of the business as a whole;
▌ first role requiring personal leadership of a significant business unit or the business as a whole.

These transitions are of course generic, and the specific context will mould each leader's experience of any one milestone. For example, moving to a new leadership role in a steady-state environment, where the area to be led is well established, insulated from external change pressures and optimally resourced, is a very different proposition from the turnaround opportunity, where a leader is tasked with retrieving a failing situation, or even reinventing an entire business.

Progressing from one leadership role to another usually demands a re-evaluation of the relative priorities of each radar screen. At the same time, the nature of activity within each area changes qualitatively. For example, as responsibility increases, leaders have a greater requirement for managing multiple stakeholders and perceptions, which affects the quality of their people leadership screen. This screen is also implicated in an increased emphasis on role modelling and living corporate values, communicating strategy clearly, and developing the skills of other leaders.

Increasing responsibility affects the task leadership screen through a greater requirement for initiating tasks, defining processes and systems, and challenging the status quo. The quality movement is a clear expression of an evolution in task leadership. Thought leadership is also affected by increasing responsibility. In fact, thought leadership is traditionally regarded as the exclusive preserve of top leaders, rather than a legitimate concern of leaders at all levels. However, increasing responsibility brings in its train a new focus on enterprise issues and strategic direction. Increasing responsibility also places a greater demand on the leader to ask 'why' questions rather than 'what' and 'how' questions.

THE RESEARCH

Our work has brought us into contact with the best – and worst – of leadership competency frameworks over the past decade, alongside reviewing and developing frameworks for organizations in diverse industries through primary research in them. These experiences led us to develop the Leadership Radar.

The area in which we find greatest commonality is the matter of how leaders spend their time. We've observed that leaders occupy their time in three activities: delivering results, managing people and providing future direction. Drop in on any competent leader and he or she will be engaged in at least one of these activities. Many leaders manage to combine all three types of activity in a single situation. For example, a leader may bring together a task group to generate and assess possible solutions to a problem facing the business (West, Tjosvold and Smith, 2005).

None of us has any more time than anyone else, so how we choose to allocate this resource is often a key indicator of what we hold to be important. Leaders invest their time, looking for healthy returns that contribute to their goals (Kouzes and Pozner, 2008). In our experience, time is a proxy measure for attention. We can think of time spent as attention directed. And we can think of leaders as people who direct their attention to the concerns of delivering results, managing people and providing future direction (Blake and Mouton, 1978).

We also know, both from our own research (Kandola, 2008) and our experience of working with a huge number of organizations that almost all organizational competency frameworks, despite their apparent complexity, can be broken down into the same three core categories of activity; thought leadership, task leadership and people leadership. These reflect the areas where leaders invest their attention. Thought leadership relates to developing a vision and setting direction, task leadership relates to results delivery, and people leadership relates to the motivation and coordination of people.

These observations fit strongly with what we know of human nature and social psychology. They also provide a valuable framework for organizing, explaining and – most importantly – developing leadership that can apply to all leaders in all situations. Organizational research going back over two decades also makes it clear that the world of work, especially as it relates to leading, clusters into three key areas of skill or competence. And our analysis of the competency frameworks used by a wide variety of organizations confirms this pattern. We capture and illustrate these three areas in the Leadership Radar. It is important to stress that the three screens of the radar do not simply represent skill sets. They indicate leaders' personal preferences for where they habitually focus their attention. And as well as representing underlying personal preferences, the three radar screens often represent the hot spots where organizations focus the rewards they offer to their people.

USING THE MODEL WITH COACHEES

The Leadership Radar gives equal weight to each of the three overlapping arenas in which leaders operate: task leadership, people leadership and thought leadership. As a model, it enables coachees to make sense of their experiences, to balance their attention and to stay alert to problems. The idea is that they recognize the existence of the three screens and the screens' abilities to capture and represent every facet of their role. As leaders take on the everyday challenges in their role, they become increasingly mindful of the three screens. All that each screen needs is a brief glance, while the daily challenges that need to be dealt with can be likened to 'blips' on any of the radar screens.

The radar is a model that has strong face validity, as it closely matches the way the most successful leaders instinctively behave. So, for example, in a meeting a leader will be continually checking that the team is on task, doing what it is meant to be doing. The leader will also be paying attention to people issues: for example, making sure that everyone has their say on each item, and that each contribution is valued. The leader will also check that the group is working creatively and challenging its own assumptions, which is thought leadership. Good leaders may not consciously think of themselves as radar users. But importantly, coachees who consciously use the radar can become better leaders.

It's a simple yet essential model of leadership activity. But how can it be used in coaching to go beyond understanding and start to improve leadership performance? This section sets out seven different examples of applications of the radar that coach and coachee can apply immediately.

Application 1: Setting a leadership baseline

In this application, the coach can introduce the radar as a way of enabling coachees to establish a baseline that reflects their current leadership practice. This isn't intended to match the coachees against any ideal shape. It's simply meant to give honest feedback on what they actually do as leaders. The key question to explore in coaching is: 'What proportion of time does the coachee spend in each arena?'

One way to do this is for coachees to keep a simple diary recording activities (Figure 5.2). They might want to record segments to the nearest

09:00 – 09:15   Answering overnight e-mails: **Task**
09:15 – 10:15   Weekly progress meeting: **Task, People**
10:15 – 10:45   Coffee with John: **People**
10:45 – 12:30   Writing executive summary: **Task, Thought**
12:30 – 13:00   Lunch at desk – surfing the net: **Thought**
13:00 – 15:00   Facilitating product development workshop: **Task, People**
15:00 – 16:30   Sat in on sales presentation: **???**
16:30 – 18:00   Catching up on e-mails: **Task**

Figure 5.2 The leader's record diary

quarter-hour – or even less if they find themselves constantly switching arenas. They don't need to write a long description of activity, and they don't need to make it understandable to anyone else.

Encourage coachees to keep the diary for several consecutive days, so that they don't inadvertently set a baseline according to an unusual day's experience. They shouldn't be concerned if they can't allocate an activity to some of the screens. Sometimes – as in our example – we're all afflicted by downtime or periods when we feel we're neither leading nor contributing. However, awareness of the Leadership Radar can help coachees to reappraise their activities and their value.

Note that the leader in the example log can't say what leadership arena she was using during her attendance at a sales presentation. This may mean she shouldn't have been there, or it may mean she was unsure what kind of leadership she needed to provide. Was she there to give feedback to the presenter? In that case, people and task leadership will have been uppermost in her mind. If she was there to learn about the product being sold or assess the impact of the sales process on customers, then people and thought leadership may have been more important.

So what? Most interestingly, it is very common that the coachees' records will show a lower proportion of actual leadership behaviour than they might like – or expect – to see. This is often because the way that we think we spend our time often bears little relationship to the way we actually spend it. We're all experts at finding ways of doing what we want to do rather than what we think we should do – and rationalizing our actions in order to hide our deceptions from ourselves. A very important message in using the Leadership Radar is that there is no 'right' way of apportioning leadership attention: the model simply insists that all leadership activity can be found on the radar's screens. With a clearer view of where the coachee's main areas of focus lie, the process of identifying desired outcomes can begin.

As part of setting a baseline, the coachee may also seek the views of colleagues and team members: to share their observations on the way that the coachee apportions time according to the three arenas. This can produce surprising results. Managers who thinks of themselves as predominantly task leaders but who force themselves to pay attention to people issues may be thought of by their team members as strong people leaders. Team members may even differentiate such leaders from other leaders by saying that they don't sacrifice people leadership to task leadership. In such cases, coachees can be reassured that their consciously forced attention is having the intended effect.

Application 2: Identifying organizational distortions

This application uses the Leadership Radar as a means of measuring the pressure points generated by the organization around the coachee. It's a way of characterizing the climate within the organization, in terms of the impact it has on the coachee's leadership style. The important question here for the coach and coachee is: 'Do organizational pressures drive the coachee into one arena at the expense of others?'

Both coach and coachee can interpret 'organizational pressures' quite widely when considering this question. The organization's pressure points can be composed of many smaller triggers acting on different levels. For example, high-profile corporate situations, such as takeovers, can strongly influence leadership style in a certain direction.

It may be that coachees are closely involved with such situations as part of their responsibilities, and that a sense of strategic mission amongst colleagues tends to encourage thought leadership behaviours. On the other hand, coachees could be detached from the front line of such a situation, but affected by the climate of uncertainty it creates within their team, and across the organization as a whole. Hence, they may find then that they are spending more time on people leadership as they seek to reassure people in a time of stress.

In our experience, organizations develop cultural preferences that reward, or at least appear to reward, one arena of leadership above the others. Sometimes a preference for one style of leadership is promoted by key individuals who have learnt it through their predecessors and mentors, and see it as the determining factor in the organization's success. These cultural preferences don't just stem from the biases of individuals. They tend to grow more subtly, whereby the organization evolves a distorted sense of what's important to success through its accumulated experience.

In particular, organizations learn from their successes that they should repeat whatever actions they took prior to their success. This is a perfectly reasonable way of interpreting outcomes, but it leaves organizations vulnerable to changes in their operating environment and market. It also causes organizations to lose their ability to act in other ways. As with muscles, if an organization doesn't regularly exercise each leadership arena, then it will become weak in neglected areas, with subsequent deficits becoming a significant risk to the coachee and the organization.

Of course we're not suggesting that there's any one 'right' organizational culture, or that there is a need to change the organization's culture before coachees can improve their leadership performance. The key use of the radar here is to enable the coachees to better understand how their immediate environment is influencing their behaviour (eg Lee, 2003).

And the effect of environment is not necessarily malign – it may also be helping coachees to be better leaders. For example, a bias towards task leadership may be forcing coachees to spend too much time in this arena. On the other hand, they might respond to this pressure by compensating in the other arenas. Such coachees may have been hired for their task orientation, but they are serving the organization more fully by stretching to correct its myopia.

Organizational pressure is difficult to characterize succinctly, and coachees may feel that it's too big an issue to track adequately in relation to their own leadership situations. If so, they will benefit by limiting their exploration to their immediate environment. Local pressures are likely to be the main determining factors in their day-to-day performance, and in our experience are always the easiest for coachees to grasp. The main consideration when exploring the local environment can often be the composition of the coachees' teams and the priority given to their goals. Is their team full of verbal jousters tasked with formulating policy? Or ex-firefighters kicked upstairs to the control room? Has this team been thrown together by a corporate restructuring, and do its members spend time competing for resources and visibility? Are the people around the coachee happy to be there, or running for the lifeboats?

The key to this application of the radar is to use it as a way of objectifying the coachee's current leadership style. The process of questioning the organization's effect on the coachee's preferences may look like a diagnostic attack on the organization, but it's really intended to illuminate four related truths about leadership:

▌ The behaviour of coachees is modulated by their environments.
▌ How the coachees behave is not who they are.
▌ Changing the coachees' environments might change their performance.
▌ Changing the way coachees react to their environments might change their performance.

Application 3: Personal preferences

The organization is a powerful influencer on the way we behave at work, but it doesn't account for our entire experience of leadership. We don't necessarily respond equally to all the organizational pressures that we encounter. And we often fight back against them. How we see the world as individuals is a major factor in how we decide to act (Downey, 2003). This use of the radar allows coachees to explore the contribution that their own preferences make to their leadership habits. The key question to ask in coaching is: 'Does the coachee's personal proclivity push him or her into one arena more than the others?'

This doesn't mean that coachees should necessarily label themselves as task leaders, people leaders or thought leaders. Instead, it means that they might find themselves consistently spending more time in one arena than the others because they enjoy acting in that arena more than the others.

As we've seen, it's entirely normal for individuals to have different preferences for how they direct their attention. We all have different talents, and we're usually rewarded for using our talents rather than suppressing them. That means we'll take opportunities to exercise those talents. But when our talents are not explicitly rewarded in the organization, or are downplayed, then we may find more subtle ways of following our preferences. For example, people who have a preference for thought leadership may find themselves drafted on to industry bodies, supposedly because no one else wants to do the job. Similarly, we know salespeople whose strong people leadership interests drive them to construct complex offers that necessitate many customer workshops, with multidisciplinary teams drawn from both supplier and customer.

Most commonly, we find leaders in all walks of life who prioritize task achievement above all else. This may be because of the formal rewards offered for task achievement, but it's also because many of us simply enjoy getting things done.

Ask anyone why they go to work and they'll give one of three answers – after they've mentioned their need to feed themselves or their family:

▌ I like working with people.
▌ I like getting things done.
▌ I want to make a difference.

These statements closely match the three arenas, and therefore often give a clue to a coachee's leadership preference. But the Leadership Radar can give a better idea of how people's personal preferences play out in the organization. For example, self-proclaimed 'people people' may be expressing a desire, rather than a truth, about themselves. The radar can help coachees to reflect on what they actually do, rather than what they might wish to do – or what they think other people value in them as leaders.

Application 4: Setting standards

This application of the model challenges coachees to question what leadership demands of them. It allows them to question their assumptions about the kind(s) of leadership they need to provide, and their mix. The key question to explore here is: 'Does the coachee need to be equally competent across all three arenas?'

Most of us assume that we have to be equally competent in all areas of leadership. Once we have measured the organizational pressures acting upon us, and our personal preferences, we may be convinced that there's a structural mismatch between what we're doing and what we need to do in order to be successful. It's natural to think in terms of gaps – and the actions we can take to close those gaps.

However, this application of the radar isn't intended to put a value on the coachee's 'fit' to an ideal. The question is an innocent one. Does the coachee have to be an all-rounder? If they do, that's worth knowing. If they don't – that's worth knowing too. But the question at the heart of this application does have a hidden payload. While coachees think about this question in relation to their working experience, they'll have to confront a fundamental issue. And that is: Whose expectations is the coachee attempting to meet? In other words, for whom do they have to be competent?

The source of the demand for competence is an important motivator for our behaviour. If we believe that the organization corporately sets objective standards of competence, then we'll tend to have a bureaucratic approach to leadership. This means we'll be interested in ticking boxes: in demonstrating competence. In turn, this may mean that we believe that all areas of competence are equally important – but that they are all addressable through clear, unambiguous and organizationally approved actions. People who believe in this kind of corporate demand can be found 'going through the motions' in organizations of all types and sizes. Cohn, Katzenbach and Vlak (2008) observed that: 'Companies usually develop leaders who replicate rather than innovate.' At the heart of this was a desire to ensure that those leaders tick the box of the incumbent competency framework.

The liberation that this application offers is this. No leader has to be equally competent in every arena of leadership. But there's a responsibility that goes along with this liberation. And that is the need for everyone who leads to respect, and address, each arena when it's appropriate to do so.

Application 5: Risks and consequences

The applications so far have been ways of analysing what leadership means to coachees and how they may begin to question their fundamental assumptions about leadership. This application raises the question of consequences. Specifically: 'What are the personal risks for the coachee in taking his or her eyes off any of the radar screens?'

By 'personal risks' we mean any kind of outcome that could affect the coachee's performance, status or sense of well-being. So, for example, paying too little attention to task leadership could result in the coachee's team's failure to deliver its goals, which in turn will disappoint those with greater power in the organization, leading to uncomfortable discussions, loss of prestige – or even loss of the role. This may sound like an extreme example, but failing to monitor and react to any of the screens is, we would maintain, an extreme action.

What about intermittent attention? Are we better leaders if we pay some attention to all the screens? We believe so. Our experience with leaders strongly suggests that there's no single recipe for attention that works for all leaders. But our experience also suggests that some attention is better than none. And some attention, applied on a regular basis, creates a leader who can keep tabs on all the variables in his or her domain without having to master each one at all times.

If each screen of the radar is not addressed regularly, there will undoubtedly be consequences. Some may be immediate; others will be delayed. Some will be large, others small. And small consequences may well aggregate to become large ones. This is the most insidious danger of radar inattention.

To see what we mean, consider a leader who pays scant attention to people leadership. This leader has recognized – through the Leadership Radar – a need to do more in this arena, and therefore schedules a regular Friday afternoon meeting at which anyone in the team can say anything they like. Attendance is mandatory. Because they have to be there, team members suspect that there must be a hidden agenda to the meeting. And because there's no agenda, they imagine all kinds of dire reasons for the meeting. From the leader's point of view, this is an opportunity to tick the people leadership box, and leave for the weekend with a clear conscience.

Yet in fact, all this has done is create a fertile plot for disaffection. The regular meeting is launched as an open forum, yet rapidly becomes flooded with dissent, competition and mistrust. The 'people meeting' becomes a generator of people issues. And the leader, having tuned out the people leadership radar screen until the next Friday meeting, fails to see how these issues propagate. Until they begin to impinge upon the areas that are really important: when, for example, milestones start to be missed, staff fall ill and senior managers begin questioning the team's productivity.

Constant, albeit brief, attention to every radar screen is at the heart of the model's value to individuals. This is equally true for all the screens. Most people have little difficulty in seeing task leadership as an activity that demands constant attention. But we tend to see people leadership as something that happens at intervals: weekly meetings, annual appraisals. Yet we work with people every day; surely they deserve more of our brain cycles? Would we be happy to think that others only thought about us twice a year?

Thought leadership is often regarded as an even rarer matter for our attention. More often than not, any serious thinking tends to be scheduled for the occasional off-site conference. However, thought leadership is just as 'live' an arena as the others. Organizations often fail to respond adequately to customers, competitors, opportunities and threats, not because they lack the basic resources but because they do not register the relevant needs or take action to evaluate and analyse incoming information. More regular monitoring of the thought leadership screen means that – at the very least – the organization is alive to its environment.

Application 6: Exploring team demands

With this application, the emphasis of possible improvements shifts from the organization as a whole, to the part of the organization that coachees can affect most directly – their own teams. Rather than looking at the global requirements of the organization, we turn to what the coachees' people need of them. The key question for coach and coachee to explore is: 'Does the coachee's team need him or her to spend more time on one of the radar screens?'

It may be possible for coachees to answer this question by looking at the baseline radar and concluding that they're not visiting every screen often enough. However, this would be a fairly abstract response to what the radar is telling them. It might also suggest that they want to idealize their radar profile: to become more like the 'rounded' individual of legend. Also, it's fair to say that all leaders, once they have created a baseline, will see room for changes that they want to make. The purpose of this application is not to perfect the coachees as leaders, but to see how the needs of their teams might draw out the coachees' leadership skills.

One way to ask the question posed by this application is to ask the coachee's team members for their input. Encourage the coachee to share the Leadership Radar with the team. Ask the team how the coachee matches to the model. Some coachees may have already done this when they created their baseline. But now they can also ask team members how they rate the importance of each area to the team's goals, quality of experience and team cohesion.

Another way to answer this question of how much time to spend on the radar screens is for the coachee to compare his or her team's performance with other teams within the organization. In this way, the coachee may be able to work out how another team's situation benefits from a different mix of radar priorities and behaviours.

For most leaders, the answer to this question is instinctive and iterative. By this, we mean that leaders will quickly know the areas in which their team needs them to spend more time. But leaders will often be mistaken in their assumptions, and need to adjust their thinking as their team reacts to the changes they make. So, for example, in many situations leaders may note that their focus is over-devoted to task leadership and conclude that their team needs them to spend more time in thought leadership or people leadership. They rearrange their approach so as to apportion more time to these screens. Or they attempt to give equal weight to each screen as they multi-task. They may interpret the team's discomfort with the changed style as a reaction to change, and believe that the team members will become more comfortable as they get used to 'the new me'.

But it's also possible that the team needs its leader to address, say, some urgent task issues in a different way. The leader may spend lots of time on task leadership, but not on the boundary area where task leadership merges with thought leadership to produce strategic direction. Another possibility is that the team appreciates the leader's strong task leadership qualities, and looks to informal leaders within the group – or other formal leaders, if the organization has a matrix structure or loose reporting lines – to satisfy its people leadership and thought leadership needs. These, and the infinite variety of other potential team responses, are all perfectly valid.

Application 7: Setting personal goals

In coaching, this is at once the simplest and the most difficult of the radar applications presented here. The key question for the coach and coachee to explore is: 'Does the coachee need to improve performance in any of these arenas?'

The work that coachees have done already will have given some idea of how they use their radar. They should also have an appreciation of how their radar habits are influenced by their environment and their personal preferences. Exploring the radar so thoroughly almost always raises questions of potential change in the leader's mind.

Often the best way to break this question down is to look at which arenas coachees might consider candidates for changed behaviour. Do they feel that they could do more in task leadership, perhaps to ensure that their teams deliver their goal more predictably? Or perhaps it's thought leadership where they feel there's more work to be done: many leaders feel they are neglecting this vital aspect of leadership. They may decide that they haven't given equal weight to people leadership, perhaps treating the development of their team members as a discretionary activity that comes at the bottom of their to-do list. If they have any of these thoughts, they're by no means alone.

Most leaders perceive some kind of imbalance in their radar activity. But before rushing to make a plan of action, it's worth considering whether change is necessary. The coachee doesn't need to make changes just because a diagnostic tool seems to suggest change is in order. Though the radar will tell coachees much about themselves as leaders, and the way their leadership fits in with the people around them, it doesn't judge them. Whatever their work with the radar may suggest, it doesn't make them 'wrong'.

But if coachees identify areas where they need to change, they should take time to reflect on what the radar is telling them. They can observe their own behaviour to see if the messages continue to ring true. As they start to notice missed opportunities for better leadership, their 'wants' will start aligning with their needs. They will start to see the possibility of change in very tangible forms. In essence, they'll know what they're not doing.

Once coachees have decided which areas of the radar they want to address in terms of improvement, they may want an action plan. Happily, the action plan for leadership improvement using the radar is simple – and universal. It's this: pay more attention to the areas that deserve more attention. Using the Leadership Radar to improve performance isn't about juggling with theories. It's about redistributing energy and focus. The coachee decides in which arenas he or she wants to operate. Above all, changing leadership performance isn't about being somebody else. It's just about doing something different. That 'something' may be one big thing, or a collection of smaller things. The 'something' may change according to circumstances. But only the coachees themselves can decide what's important in the world they inhabit. The Leadership Radar will help them to stay on course – but the course is always theirs.

CASE STUDY: RAJ

Raj is a world-class synthetic chemist whose career has taken him from individual successes through team breakthroughs and on to management of laboratories and entire areas of global research. Raj is now at the very senior level of his organization – where the leadership approach he has used is considered too narrow for the business challenges he and his peers are facing.

Specialist field knowledge has always been crucial to his progression in the industry, and it's still a cornerstone of his capabilities. He managed the shift from being a solitary thinker, pursuing his own ideas and seeking guidance from others, to being a manager of other researchers. But at the lab and research theme level, he still had a hands-on role. If needs be, he could join the people he led as a team member, working with them to solve their problems.

On reaching the top, however, he quickly realized that he no longer had the time to be hands-on. In fact, if he was to perform at this level, he needed to be a hands-free leader. The personal challenge to his leadership style, therefore, was the need to people-lead other thought leaders. That meant using his technical skills and experience to empathize with people rather than synthesize molecules.

This highlighted, early in the coaching discussions, a need to risk-assess using the radar. He needed to use his conceptual understanding of what his people do – technically, systemically and socially – to make sure that the organization performed to its best potential. His concerns clustered around several questions:

▐ Are we hitting our business objectives?
▐ Are our processes cost-effective?
▐ Are we serving our professional interests above the interests of the business?

Raj did not need any help with his focus on thought leadership. Nor did he need to become a different person. But he did need to find a way of changing his daily activities so that he was covering the areas that had become a risk to his future success.

To bring the strategy into reality, it was helpful for our leader to think about his new role in terms of how much time he needed to spend in each radar arena. He could see his new leadership role as a practice rooted in proportionate attention. Just as he might design a research programme to investigate a particular area of promise, so he could design his leadership behaviour according to the needs suggested by his business goals.

If that sounds difficult to do – to translate the mystery of high-level leadership into a set of percentages marked on the three radar screens – consider this: in his technical field, the goal is always discovery. Researchers pursue the superficially paradoxical goal of discovering novelty via a highly controlled, manageable and accountable process. They may produce surprises, but not by stumbling around in the dark. In the same way, truly effective and even inspirational leadership can be generated from a fairly simple algorithm that states how much time a leader needs to spend paying attention to each radar screen.

Such a formula might be simple to state, but putting it into practice is harder. A new way of behaving will always feel unusual at first, even if it is made easier to adopt by being expressed in radar terms. How did Raj cope with his discomfort in applying the new formula? We didn't try to sell the change in behaviour to him, nor try to convince him that practice would make perfect. For one thing, he's one of the smartest people we've ever met, and he would have been suspicious of any attempt to do so. But, more importantly, we know that strong thought leaders need more than a solid practice they can follow; they also need a rationale that buttresses that practice, and that subjects it to repeated challenge as it is exercised.

We therefore used the coaching discussions as a vehicle to analyse the implications through his use of the radar. What personal choices would he have to make in order to use the radar in this way? In other words, if he was really to re-orientate his attention to include new areas of the task leadership and people leadership screens, what would he have to give up? We then worked with him to decide what activities he could give up, and which he was unwilling to let go.

It's hard for people to give up doing something that has brought them success in the past, even if there are plenty of clear signals in the environment telling them to change. Everyone can point to organizations that seem unable to update their behaviour to meet changing needs. But recognizing and correcting such errors in ourselves, or those close to us, is much harder.

Our leader is performing well in his new role, adapting to the changed expectations that his colleagues have of him, and using the radar as an instinctive means of staying on track. He is also beginning to find that his enlarged activities in the other two arenas are more than compensating for the activities that he has downgraded in the thought leadership arena. Curiously, it turns out that there's a great need for thought leadership within people leadership and task leadership.

The arenas of leadership aren't restricted to different types of people, though each may attract a different kind of person. Those who see themselves as 'people people' naturally gravitate towards people leadership, for example. This is one reason why people businesses often experience acute difficulty in growing or hiring high-level leaders: none of their existing people believe themselves capable of operating effectively in the other arenas. Or, more tragically, strong people leaders attempt to compensate for their lack of thought leadership and task leadership skills by doing more people leadership activity. And yet, just because someone was attracted to one arena, and has gained considerable experience and expertise in that area, that doesn't mean they can only operate in that area. We may need to exercise the muscles that we've neglected – but those muscles are still there.

CONCLUSIONS

The Leadership Radar provides an extremely practical, memorable framework within which any individual can evaluate, monitor and manage their leader behaviour on a regular basis.

There is no standard profile of the successful or desirable leader, though there are some commonly accepted aberrant behaviours that distinguish ineffective and derailed leaders. In a coaching context, reversing negative traits will not result in a profile of perfection. In fact, attempting to isolate any one strand of leadership and prioritize it above the others can be detrimental; there is no one absolute skill to leading. We have to treat all aspects of leadership in the round, because they are all interdependent and they all vary in their effect depending on circumstances.

In reality, leaders are more various and flexible than any ideal model, and the situations in which they act are often ambiguous, protracted and iterative. Through coaching with the Leadership Radar, individuals with outstanding strengths on one screen can quickly and effectively learn to manage their own coverage across the other screens. They can, as it were, adapt their interface to the organization. Most importantly, they don't need to change who they are, only some of the issues to which they pay attention.

References

Adair, J (1998) *Effective Leadership: How to develop leadership skills*, Pan Books, London

Alexander, G (2006) Behavioural coaching: the GROW model, in *Excellence in Coaching: The industry guide*, ed J Passmore, Chapter 5, Kogan Page, London

Blake, R R and Mouton, J S (1978) *New Managerial Grid*, Gulf Publishing, Houston

Charan, R, Drotter, S and Noel, J (2001) *The Leadership Pipeline: How to build the leadership powered company*, Jossey Bass, San Francisco

Cohn, J, Katzenbach, J and Vlak, G (2008) Finding and grooming breakthrough innovators, *Harvard Business Review*, December, pp 62–69

Downey, M (2003) *Effective Coaching: Lessons from the coaches' coach*, 3rd edn, Texere Publishing, New York

Kandola, R (2008) The Leadership Journey, *Asian Enterprise*, **1** (3), pp 21–22

Kouzes, J M and Posner, B Z (2008) *The Leadership Challenge*, 4th edn, Jossey Bass, San Francisco

Lee, G (2003) *Leadership Coaching: From personal insight to organizational excellence*, Chartered Institute of Personnel and Development, London

West, M A, Tjosvold, D and Smith, K G (2005) *The Essentials of Teamworking: International perspectives*, John Wiley, Chichester

6

An Asian perspective on leadership coaching
Sun Tzu and *The Art of War*

Dr Ho Law

INTRODUCTION

The chapter offers an Eastern perspective on leadership using Sun Tzu's *The Art of War* (a famous piece of Chinese classical literature). The historical and cultural context of Sun Tzu's work will be first described, with a brief overview of a leadership model constructed from the translation. The author will then show how the model can be used with coachees to help deepen their understanding in leadership operations. This is followed with a case study, which will demonstrate how some of the concepts derived from Sun Tzu's approach could be used to give insight in leadership coaching. From these illustrations, the essence of leadership is then distilled and summarized in the final section.

THE ART OF WAR MODEL OF LEADERSHIP

The Art of War was thought to have been written by Sun Wu in 500 BC. (In Chinese Sun is the surname and Wu is the personal name; Tzu is not a name but a title that means Educated Master, equivalent to Mister in the modern English expression.) The period in which Sun Tzu lived is known as the Classical period (Chou dynasty) and is linked to Confucius, who was born in 551 BC (and died in 479 BC). However, research by historians has suggested that the actual text of *The Art of War* was probably composed in the 4th century BC.

One could understand the rationale of the work by considering the historical backdrop in what is known as the Warring States Period (480–221 BC). During that time warfare evolved in such a way that it involved several hundred thousand soldiers with iron weapons and crossbows in campaigns lasting months or even years. Thus working out a military strategy was necessary.

According to historical records, Sun Wu was born in Chi State. He presented *The Art of War* to Ho Lu (King of Wu) toward the end of the 6th century BC. The book was made famous by the 'test' that King Ho Lu set for Sun Tzu. The test involved 180 beautiful women who were sent from the palace to be trained into a military force. Sun Tzu divided them into two companies and selected two women leaders to direct them. Although he trained them, the two leaders failed to direct the companies. Sun Tzu coached them again and both said they understood the approaches. They failed again. Sun Tzu said 'if the leaders understood the "know how" and failed, they are responsible for the failure' and ordered them to be beheaded, in spite of King Ho Lu asking him not to. After that, another two leaders were selected from the companies. This time all the women successfully followed the orders of their leaders. This story gave rise to a famous Chinese proverb for leadership: 'Kill one to warn 100.'

This approach (in a different form) is still practised in Asian management today, when managers are sacked for misconduct as an example to warn the other employees. *The Art of War* thus represents the essence of timeless wisdom in leadership.

Sun Tzu's essays were introduced to the West by Father J J M Amiot, a French missionary, shortly before the French Revolution. The first translated version was published in 1772. Russian, German and English translations also appeared around the early 20th century, including the early English translation by Lionel Giles (1910). The model translated in this chapter is based on the author's personal proficiency in both Chinese and English cultures and languages, written within the modern context of leadership coaching.

The Art of War consists of 13 essays:

1. Planning 計
2. Operation/implementation (Waging War) 作戰
3. Offensive strategy 謀攻

4. Tactical (military) disposition 形
5. Power 勢
6. Weaknesses and strengths 虛實
7. Operational leadership (military operations) 軍爭
8. Nine changes 九變
9. Manoeuvring the army 行軍
10. Topology (terrain) 地形
11. Nine terrains 九地
12. Incendiary attacks 火攻
13. Employing spies 用間

The 13 essays were written with such an amazing degree of consistency and inter-connectedness that historians have little doubt that they were written by the same person. Although the essays aimed to help army generals to achieve a victorious strategy, its philosophy can be adopted for leadership development and for coaching conversations.

Sun Tzu regarded the art of operational research as the most difficult aspect of leadership. It involves making complexity simple, the maximization of strengths, resources, revenues and other advantages, and the minimization of weaknesses, costs and losses. Thus if one compares Sun Tzu's strategic planning with Western approaches, it shares very little common ground with Western strategic thinkers such as Gary Hamel's (1996) view on strategy as revolution, Henry Mintzberg's (1994) evolutionary approach or Michael Porter (1996), who emphasizes the unique selling point, or with some of the other Western models offered in this leadership coaching book. On the contrary, Sun Tzu can be perceived as a forerunner of operational research and systems thinking that predates the Western practice. The operational aspects of strategic thinking in the West were developed from systems dynamics by Jay Wright Forrester (1918–), who has been regarded as the father of operational research (Forrester, 1961, 1968, 1973, 1987). Readers who are interested in applying systems dynamics may like to follow up references at the end of the chapter (for example, see Forrester, 1980, for economy, and Forrester, 1988, for management). The application of systems approaches to human systems in the modern era, known as soft systems methodology, has been developed by Professor Peter Checkland at Lancaster Business School in the UK (Checkland, 1999).

Using a general systems approach to capitalize on the interconnectivity of the 13 essays, the author has translated the useful principles and constructed a leadership model for coaching as shown in Figure 6.1.

In contrast to the stereotyped view that many people have of Eastern culture (eg the concept of time, see Rosinski, 2003), when waging war (or competing for business, as described in Essay 2), Sun Tzu focused

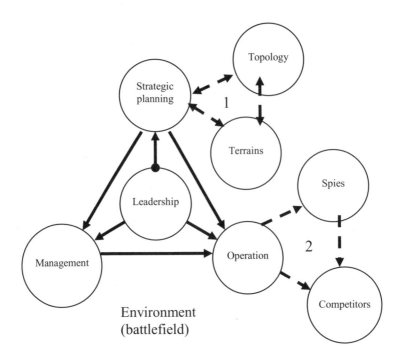

Figure 6.1 Sun Tzu's leadership model

on quantitative assessments: for example consideration of the topology and terrains (Essays 10 and 9), calculation of the resources required, and measurement of time and distance travelled by employees (army). The assessment is comparable to the modern operational research in the Western world (eg time is measured in a linear fashion).

This is because Sun Tzu believed that war is a business of life and death and thus one should treat it with extreme seriousness, total commitment, and plan it carefully. As Sun Tzu said (孫子曰), 'War is (兵者) a matter of vital importance to the nation (國之大事). It is a place of life or death (死生之地), a road to survival or to ruin (存亡之道). It is impossible [for one] not to study it thoroughly (不可不察也).'

The above opening statement in the first essay of Sun Tzu's *The Art of War* indicates the priority of strategic planning as a prerequisite for engagement in competition (battles, see Zone 1 in Figure 6.1).

By strategic planning, Sun Tzu implies that the plan should be made with such calculated detail and extent that the outcome of its implementation could be predicted. The more you plan and calculate, the more likely you are to succeed. When planning a strategy Sun Tzu said that every leader (commander) must consider the following five fundamental factors:

1. Tao (ethical/moral principle) 道
2. Heaven (meteorology) 天
3. Earth (geography) 地
4. The commander (leader) 將
5. Method 法

The word 'Tao' has a broad meaning in Chinese civilization, and includes philosophy, belief, value, reasons, a way of life, a rite of passage, ethics and moral principle. This is particularly important in transformational leadership in today's economic conditions. If a leader is to move people, he or she must move them with their hearts and minds so as to instil the team with a sense of great purpose, a mission that they are compelled to achieve. They and their leader share the same goal. To do that, the shared vision has to be grounded in an ethical principle. As Sun Tzu pointed out, when the war is a just cause, soldiers are willing to sacrifice their lives in battle. In an unjust war, they fight because they are told to. The leader's role is to create the circumstances for just wars.

Heaven (meteorology) – The word heaven in Chinese may mean the sky, weather or nature. Sun Tzu suggested that to win a battle, one needs to study the forces of nature (including weather forecasts and the geography of the land) to ensure that one can take advantage of the opportunities nature may offer.

According to Sun Tzu's model, the quality of leadership is at the heart of winning battles, or success in the competitive business market in our modern context. Sun Tzu said that the quality of a leader (commander 將) should consist of the following virtues: wisdom (智), trustworthiness (信), humanity (仁), courage (勇) and strict authority (嚴).

The Chinese word 'Fa' (法) could also have many meanings: approaches, disciplines, methods, methodology, solutions or techniques. According to Sun Tzu, in the context of leading an army into battle, the 'method' of leadership relates to its governance/control (曲制), organization (官道) and its major utility (主用).

The dos and don'ts in leadership – According Sun Tzu, there are three don'ts and five dos in leadership. The three don'ts that would weaken the company are:

▌ Moving the team to and fro without a sense of direction. Sun Tzu called this 'hobbling' the team. The team would become confused.
▌ Governing the team with bureaucracy like those in top-heavy administrations. The team would become inefficient.
▌ Selecting team leaders who have no knowledge of leading a team. Teams would lose their confidence in their leaders.

When employees in a company are confused, inefficient and lacking confidence, the company can easily be taken over by others. Five dos are offered to help the company succeed:

▌ Know when to compete (and when not).
▌ Know how to manage both strong and weak teams (or the strengths and weaknesses of employees).
▌ Ensure that all team members/employees share the same organizational mission ('spirit').
▌ Prepare oneself and wait to take the opponents/competitors by surprise.
▌ Avoid bureaucratic rules and regulations if these interfere with leadership.

The above five dos capture the essence of the ancient Chinese proverb: 'Know yourself and your opponents and you will win every time.'

Having developed a strategic plan, the second emphasis in *The Art of War* is placed on implementation (operational leadership, see Zone 2 in Figure 6.1). This may involve gathering commercial intelligence using informants (spies, Essay 13) and other tactics. Sun Tzu described five classes of spies:

▌ Native: these are local people who have local knowledge.
▌ Insiders: these people work inside the competitor's organization.
▌ Double agents (the converted): former competitors who have changed side.
▌ Sacrifice (expendable) spies: these agents are commissioned to deliberately provide competitors with false knowledge (in war, these agents would usually be captured and killed by the enemy, hence the term 'sacrifice').
▌ Surviving spies: these are employed as above, but it is hoped they will return to the base.

The rationale for using spies in competition is that what enables the wise leader to achieve things beyond the reach of ordinary people is 'foreknowledge'. When this foreknowledge cannot be elicited from 'spirits' (intuition), nor inductively from experience, nor by any deductive calculation (strategic planning), then this knowledge can only be obtained from other people who know about the competitor's dispositions. Sun Tzu concluded that: 'those who know how to use intelligent agents (智為間者) would achieve great results (必成大功).' Operations need intelligence, as forces depend on this information to make a move (decision). The use of spies (informants) is discussed further in the case study within the context of the operational leadership.

USING THE MODEL WITH COACHEES

This section shows how Sun Tzu's approach can be used with coachees in leadership development within the business competition or management context. For instance, the leadership triangle in Figure 6.1 can be extracted and further expanded (see Figure 6.2). This effectively describes three types of leadership:

▌ operational (Essays 2, 3, 4, 7 and 9);
▌ power (Essay 5);
▌ change (Essay 8).

Each of these styles of leadership can be drawn upon at different times and in different circumstances. However the most effective leaders are those who are able to make use of the full range of styles and select the right one for the challenge facing their business.

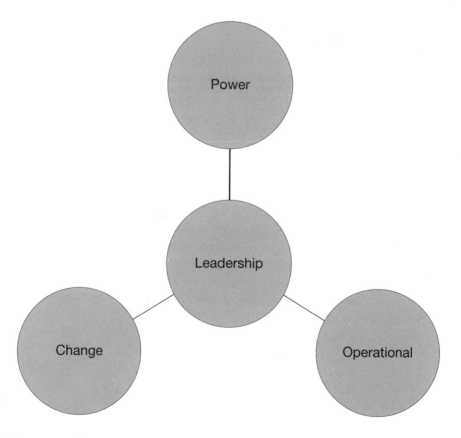

Figure 6.2 Sun Tzu's types of leadership

Power (勢) of leadership (Essay 5)

Sun Tzu said: 'The management of a large force is the same principle as managing a few: it is a matter of organization (divisions of the numbers).'

In other words, leading a large complex organization is the same as leading a small team. There are only two approaches that coachees can adopt in leadership: direct and indirect (Ying and Yang). Its possible combinations are infinite, like 'Heaven and Earth, the sun and moon, and four seasons'. One ends while the other begins. The direct and the indirect approaches lead on to each other in turn like a moving cycle.

The quality of leadership is in the decision making, which in turn depends on the timing. Sun Tzu used the metaphor of a falcon's strike, which can break the body of its prey. Coaches should develop their emotional intelligence as leaders who might appear to be disorganized when they are in fact highly disciplined underneath. They show fear to cover up their courage; and they are humble to hide their strengths.

The emotional intelligence in Chinese culture is different from that of the West; coachees operating in a Chinese business environment should appreciate that Chinese leaders are clever in utilizing their human resources and combining the strengths of their teams. Thus the combined power of the team/organization seems to achieve its mission effortlessly, like 'rolling logs or stones', as Sun Tzu puts it. That is the power of leadership. To realize this power, we would need to see its operation as described next.

Operational leadership

Sun Tzu said, 'In war, although the generals receive their order from the sovereign, once they have assembled the army and mobilized the masses, organized the teams and prepared for action, the generals become the leaders (kings) in the field of operation' (Essay 8).

As indicated in the previous section, Sun Tzu placed tremendous emphasis on the importance of operational leadership, as is shown by the fact that most of the essays are about operational aspects. This emphasis is echoed by the presence of many political leaders in China who were trained engineers (as observed by *The Economist*, 2009).

According to Sun Tzu's Essay 4 (Tactical dispositions), there are five steps in the operational process:

1. Measurement of space (度).
2. Estimation of quantity (量).
3. Calculation (數).
4. Comparison of chances (稱).
5. Opportunity for success (勝).

The above process could be utilized as a coaching model to help coachees who are operational directors/managers to consider the steps required to implement strategic plans and ensure success. This requires the coachees to first consider the physical space and resources required for the operation (Steps 1 and 2). They then need to perform a gap analysis by comparing the competing opportunities out there in the environment. Finally a probability for successful implementation can be computed (a classic resource allocation in operational research).

On implementation, Sun Tzu recommended that one should take action with all one's forces as if it were 'a pound's weight placed on the scale against a single grain' or 'the bursting of pent-up waters plunging into an abyss of a thousand fathoms deep'. 'That is the "form" of the peak performer,' said Sun Tzu. This wisdom resonates with the definition of coaching; for maximizing performance is at the heart of coaching (Whitmore, 1992, 2002). Underpinning this force is the coachee's commitment, as in coaching the coach usually asks the coachee:

▌ How committed are you in taking action for change?
▌ On a scale of 1 to 10, rate your commitment?

When the coachee replies, say, 7 or 8, the coach will ask, 'What can be done to raise your commitment to a higher number?' The next key coaching questions are: 'How do you achieve peak performance? Under what conditions will it be achieved?'

PEAK PERFORMANCE: FORM AND CONDITION (ESSAY 4)

Sun Tzu said:

> Good competitors first prepare, build up their strength an invincible level and wait and expose their opponent's vulnerable position [opportunities]. Thus it is up to oneself to prepare to achieve an invincible position. However, winning a competition depends on the others' weaknesses. So good competitors can ensure they are constantly at their peak performance, but still they cannot guarantee victory as that depends on the *opportunities* provided by their opponents [italics added].

Hence the Chinese proverb: 'Knowing how to succeed does not guarantee actual success.' The knowledge and outcome are two separate things. One could apply this knowledge to the coaching process. For instance, during the Option stage in Whitmore's (1992, 2002) GROW model, the coachees can be asked first to search for a list of all the possible opportunities 'out there' before they start thinking about the alternative courses of action. Thus the coachees should have two lists: A) the opportunities and B) action. List B should be the appropriate course of action that links to each item on list A.

Furthermore, Sun Tzu's principle implies that the first step toward seizing that opportunity is 'preparation'. The coach may ask:

- Are you ready to ...?
- How do you know if you are ready?
- What kind of resources would you need to prepare if Opportunity 1 happened?
- How much do you need (in terms of cost)?
- Whom do you need to inform as part of the preparation?
- What kind of information do you need to gather?

From the above, the coachee may generate a table as shown in Table 6.1.

Table 6.1 Option: Opportunities, action, preparation

Opportunities	Action	Preparation
Opportunity 1	Action 1.1 Action 1.2 etc	To do Action 1.1, I need: 1 2 3 etc
Opportunity 2	Action 2.1 Action 2.2 etc	
Opportunity n		

According to Sun Tzu, when one is facing an invincible competitor (for instance when a proprietor of a small company is in competition with a large multinational blue-chip corporation), the proprietor should be coached to prepare (defend) the market by continuous research and development (R&D) in order to build up to an 'invincible' position. It should be noted that this is a counter-intuitive strategy and is in contrast to the common assumption that R&D is the preserve of large corporate organizations (such as IBM and BP).

Thus coachees need to understand that strong companies take an aggressive strategy (attack/takeover) because they have spare resources. Company directors need to be aware of the weaknesses of their strategic position and protect themselves from the risk of being taken over. This requires companies to continuously evolve and develop their R&D capacity in preparation for opportunities.

In competition ('war') size does not matter. A smaller organization can compete against larger ones. All it means is that no direct competition should occur. The smaller companies should keep a close watch on the larger organizations, assess the situation, know when the opportunities arise and concentrate all their resources, and they can take over the larger competitor. The point (Sun Tzu's wisdom) here is that those comp-anies that have no strategic plan (their leaders have no foresight) and underestimate their competitors would eventually be taken over.

On an individual level, in terms of personal development, coachees need to be good at both 'defence' (learning) and 'attack' (doing). Thus one should continuously develop oneself professionally and apply one's knowledge in practice.

Traditionally those who are 'good performers' are those who achieve all the easy tasks. However from Sun Tzu's point of view, people who achieve excellence that is expected by everyone are not 'top performers', even though they may be regarded by everyone (or the general public) as such. Sun Tzu used the following metaphors to make the point: 'to lift a light hare does not demonstrate a great physical strength; the ability to see the sun and moon does not mean that one has sharp vision; to hear the sound of thunder does not mean one is good at hearing.' Thus it is because the achievement is so obvious that it has become public knowledge.

The true top performers are usually unknown by the public. Excellent performance is achieved by making no mistakes, and shown when competitors surrender without any conflict. No one would be aware of what actually happened, as it would be beyond their comprehension. Peak performers are those who always develop themselves to perfection (invincible position) and do not miss any opportunity for action.

In an open competition, the winners are those who have already planned for their success and selected those competitors whom they could defeat. The losers are those who engage in competition first and subsequently hope that they will win.

The peak performers continuously develop their ethical values ('Tao') and foster the social governance of justice and humanity. They thus could formulate an organizational policy/governance that is also invincible. Peak performers and top leaders have the same kind of quality. They have the power to decide the outcome of the operation. Thus in Sun Tzu leadership coaching, before the coach even asks the coachee, 'What will you do ... and when ...?' as in the 'Will' stage in the GROW model, the coach would ask:

▌ What will the outcome be?
▌ And when will this happen?

Thus Table 6.1 should have an extra outcome column, a 'when it happens' column as shown in Table 6.2.

Table 6.2 Will: Outcome plus when

Opportunities	Action	Preparation	Outcome	When
Opportunity 1	Action 1.1 Action 1.2 etc	To do Action 1.1, I need: 1 2 3 etc	Outcome 1	Eg 6 months
Opportunity 2	Action 2.1 Action 2.2 etc		Outcome 2	2 years
Opportunity n				

Ideally, one would expect that the outcome would match the final goal set by the coachee at the early stage of the coaching process. However, this is not necessarily the case. As Sir John Whitmore (1992, 2002: 58) points out in the goal-setting stage of his GROW model: the final goal 'is seldom absolutely within your own control. You cannot know what or control what your competitors will do.' This effectively captures the essence of Sun Tzu's observation that commanders 'could not guarantee victory [the final goal] as it depends on the opportunities provided by their opponents', mentioned earlier.

While Whitmore (1992, 2002) suggests coachees should set the performance goal (or objective), in contrast Sun Tzu recommended one should prepare, continue learning and wait for opportunities to come. The 'outcome' is more closely related to prediction (forecasting) in operational research (see Armstrong, 2001, for principles of forecasting). With the advance of e-technology, awareness about forecasting the outcome is increasingly relevant to today's leadership coaching in the global market.

For instance, IBM has adopted global connectivity technologies to run an e-business so that it can forecast and respond to changes, competition, customer preferences, market opportunity, supply and demand almost instantly (see http://www.ibm.com/ondemand).

Forecasting and planning have important implications for decisions that coachees would make for their organizations at a strategic level as well as at an operational level (for example, in inventory management, see Syntetos, Boylan and Disney, 2009). From the coaching perspective; the questions on outcome and on preparation are closely linked. For example:

▌ What does the outcome look like?
▌ When will this happen?
▌ How do you know you are getting there?
▌ How confident are you that you can predict the outcome?

Within the organizational context, the last question may be expressed quantitatively (confidence level) in terms of probability (for example, in terms of analysing minimum mean square error, see Lee, So and Tang, 2000). This of course depends on the technical competence of both the coach and coachee and on the operational context. For instance, in coaching a technical director for companies like IBM or Rolls-Royce (Aero), the coaching questions listed above may become:

▌ How confident are you? What is the value of the mean square error in your prediction (instead of rating on a simple 1–10 scale)?
▌ Is your confidence/decision based on statistical or judgemental forecasting?
▌ Is there any evidence to support your claim (if it is based on personal judgement)?
▌ Can you improve the outcome using your own judgement (if the decision is based on statistical forecasting)?
▌ What does the outcome look like? Is it a linear function, exponential or complex?
▌ If the performance could not be optimized because you said that it is a complex function, what would be the impact upon the inventory cost?
▌ When will this happen? Could you predict the pace of change? Is it going to be fast or slow (in statistical forecasting)?

As indicated above, Sun Tzu's principles for leadership coaching could take the coach and coachees to a level that is surprisingly technical and scientific in nature.

NINE MODES OF OPERATION (九變)

Depending on the operational conditions (referred to by Sun Tzu as 'grounds' on which armies operate), there are nine modes of operation. The first five are:

1. 圮地 Low-lying ground (difficult condition) – Do not encamp.
2. 衢地 Ground with many diversions (diverse and confused condition) – Seek unity (allies).
3. 絕地 Desolate ground (isolated and dangerous condition) – Do not linger.
4. 圍地 Enclosed ground (when surrounded by enemies) – Develop a strategy.
5. 死地 Death ground (in life and death situation or desperate condition) – Fight (struggle).

Coaches can make an analogy of the above ancient principles with modern location analysis (Smith, Laporte and Harper, 2009). In the first five grounds, which govern different modes of operation, there are four more operational rules where, under certain circumstances:

▌ Operational leaders (military generals) need not follow certain rules and procedures.
▌ They need not obey commands from the sovereign (head of organization).
▌ In addition, there are certain competitors ('armies' in the Sun Tzu context) that should not be competed against.
▌ Certain companies ('cities') should not be taken over. A good example is the RBS takeover in 2008 that led RBS into huge financial debt at a time when the market was already turning.

As operational leaders, coachees must know how to use these nine possible modes of operations appropriately in order to gain advantage and prevent loss. This wisdom is still applicable today, as found by Boffey and Karkazis (1993) in modelling for location and routing decision; they learnt that in practice (operation), multiple objectives (goals) frequently exist that require multiple solutions (modes of operation). This is achieved by weighing the pros and cons (cost–benefit analysis) of the given situation. The leader then makes a decision on applying appropriate modes of operation. One may not take action, but bring oneself or the team into a constant state of readiness so that one can always seize any opportunities that arise. In doing so leaders can ensure their company makes a sustainable profit and will survive even under harsh economic conditions. For example, when a coachee of a transport company was asked by a potential customer to solve the problem of where to store/process hazardous materials, a number of locations were assessed in terms of their cost and risk to the environment or human life (see Table 6.3).

Table 6.3 Location analysis

Opportunities	Cost	Risk
Location A:	Low	High
Location B:	Medium	Medium
Location C:	High	Low

Having been told by the company director to select Location A, the coachee might seek coaching advice due to the difficult nature of the decision. As a coach, what would you do?

The coach could map the location using the nine modes of operation and classify the location as shown in Table 6.4.

Table 6.4 Location and operational mapping

Opportunities	Cost	Risk	Ground	Mode
Location A:	Low	High	Low-lying ground (difficult condition)	Do not encamp
Location B:	Medium	Medium	N/A	N/A
Location C:	High	Low	Diverse and confused condition	Seek unity (allies)

Using Table 6.4 as a decision table, the coach could explain to the coachee that selecting Location A would place them in a difficult position that would not be acceptable in the light of the ethical principles that they hold. Selecting Location B might require the coachee to coordinate a campaign to unify the diverse opinions that exist in the company as well as persuading the potential customer to buy in to a decision that would cost them more money but would be a safer solution. The coachee could also be advised to combine the power of his/her teams with other regional divisions of the company to create a momentum.

According to Sun Tzu's strategy, the coachee could be advised that when competing (attack) with opponents, one may use the following tactics:

▌ Inflict damage by placing them in a disadvantageous position. (What if the media published the story? Consider the damage that it would cost the company in terms of its reputation?)
▌ Tire them out by keeping them busy and constantly occupied (provide them with a lot of information).
▌ Hurry them by offering them additional benefits. (Might more contracts be coming soon if Location C were selected?)

Despite all of the above effort, the coachee might ask: 'What if the director still decides on the unethical option?' Of course there is a bottom line; the coach may refer to the additional operational rule that under certain circumstances, operational leaders 'need not obey commands from the head of the organization', even though this might mean resigning and finding a different job.

When managing team leaders, as directors coachees need to look out for five dangerous weaknesses that their team leaders might have:

1. Recklessness: such operational leaders may make fatal mistakes and get killed.
2. Lack of courage: they would limit themselves and get stuck in the same position.
3. Hasty temper: they may act without thought and regret their action afterwards.
4. Over-delicate sense of honour: they may fear being humiliated.
5. Overly compassionate: they tend to be harassed and troubled by their team members.

Any failure must be due to one or more of the above weaknesses that team leaders are prone to. Thus one must observe these five dangerous weaknesses carefully. The points outlined above can be used to guide coachees in selecting team leaders and managing operational teams. According to Sun Tzu, the team leader should have a high intellect and all the team members should have high morale.

OPERATIONAL MANAGEMENT (MANOEUVRING THE ARMY) 行軍 (ESSAY 9)

Implementation is about encamping at a strategic advantageous position, observing the movement of competitors and making the correct interpretation. Applying Sun Tzu's principles to a modern business context, for instance a business start-up, when selecting a location or deciding on a venue for a marketing campaign such as workshops or conferences, you should select a location that gives you a strategic advantage. As the saying goes, 'location, location and location' – it matters. Again this relates to locations analysis as described above. For a competitive model within location theory, see Hakimi (1983).

COMMUNICATION (ESSAY 7)

On the battle field, because verbal communication cannot be heard at a distance, Sun Tzu suggested using banners and flags to communicate with large groups of soldiers during the daytime, and fire-signals and drums at night. Translate this into coaching for modern business expansion. Coaches could explore with coachees (who may be business owners or marketing executives) how they may use signs and symbols (logos) to enable their company to develop and be identifiable by a brand rather than relying on word-of-mouth for marketing. Companies may also use other media such as music to form associations; a good example of this is the Intel signature music.

CHANGE LEADERSHIP: WEAKNESSES AND STRENGTHS 虛實 (ESSAY 6)

Sun Tzu said, 'Of the five elements (water, fire, wood, metal, earth), none is always predominant (五行無常勝); of the four seasons, none always stand still (四時無常位); of the days, some are long and some short (日有短長); and the moon wanes and waxes (月有死生).

Finally coachees need to be reminded that the only constant is change. Leaders always ensure that they take up an advantageous position and that they will not be disadvantaged by their opponents. They take control and make decisions. They act when their competitors least expect them to. They can achieve a lot because their action does not encounter resistance/barriers. They hold the safest position where they cannot be attacked.

They seem to be 'invisible' and 'inaudible', yet they can determine the outcome. The winners run faster than their competitors. They know how to divide and conquer. However, the strategy has to be kept secret from opponents (the strategic commercial plan must be kept confidential). Do not repeat the tactics that helped you succeed. Change them according to the circumstances.

Operational tactics are like water. Water changes its shape according to the nature of the ground over which it flows; leaders work out their strategy in relation to the challenges that they are facing. Just as water has no constant shape, so in operation there are no fixed steps. Sun Tzu believed that those who could modify their tactics to take account of their opponents and succeed are natural born leaders (the champions in change leadership).

The wisdom of change leadership is that the coachees should understand that everyone has weaknesses and strengths (Ying and Yang). The art of winning is to align your strength against your competitors' weaknesses. In competition, avoid the strengths of competitors and compete with the weak.

In leadership, Sun Tzu coached the paradox of change (Ying and Yang). If you spend resources to strengthen one aspect, you will be weakened in others. If you attempt to be strong everywhere, you will be weak everywhere. Success may be produced by your competitors' own tactics. That is the reason why the winning strategy seems to have such a multiple nature that it cannot be comprehended by other people. Anyone can see the operation in action, but no one can see the strategy that leads to success. We shall demonstrate this with a case study in the next section.

CASE STUDY

In this section, the author will show how some of the concepts from Sun Tzu's leadership model could be used to give insight in coaching, using a single case study. This example is based on the ongoing experience of the author in coaching a Chinese highflier who was educated in the West and returned to lead an international company in China. For reasons of confidentiality, the coachee's identity is kept anonymous by using a fictitious name: Susan.

Susan, in her early 40s at the time of coaching, was from Northern China. She graduated from a top university in China and after further studies in the West obtained an international MBA, before returning to China and working as a business executive at a top global professional service firm. She was promoted quite a few years ago to be a regional director leading a particular business practice for the firm, with 15 consultants reporting to her.

As part of a restructuring her department was merged with the neighbouring region. The neighbourhood regional director became the deputy director, with his team working under Susan's control. While the change seemed to offer Susan a higher profile, with control over a larger team and greater geographical coverage, the operation of the changeover did not seem to go well.

Susan was particularly concerned about the deputy director, who she understood was an ambitious young man who did not wish to work under her; even so, he behaved surprisingly quiescently toward her and had showed no overt hostility since the merger. At the same time, the members of the new mixed team appeared to be in constant conflict. Susan felt that communication amongst the team did not seem as good as it used to be. Recently, she had noted that some team members gathered together at work in small groups, whispering and gossiping, which she felt extremely uncomfortable with. From previous coaching, she had learned to appreciate the Chinese approach to leadership. So she approached her coach again to seek insight about the situation.

The coach suggested elements drawn from Sun Tzu's leadership approach as a way of examining the issue. According to the precepts of Sun Tzu's Essay 9 (manoeuvring the team in operation), the observed team behaviour implied that the team members were dissatisfied about their jobs or had lost confidence in their leader. The conflict in the team implied that the leader's authority was weak. When employees constantly suffered from organizational change, they would be confused and in disarray. Furthermore, the deputy director (perceived as an internal competitor) was psyching himself up toward her yet had remained inactive for a long time though without backing off; in such a situation, one must be vigilant and investigate.

Bewildered by the implication, Susan wondered if she should carry out an employee satisfaction survey to gather information from the team. The coach reminded her that this approach (which Susan had learned from the West) might not be applicable to the Chinese culture as the employees would be suspicious about the leader's intention and tend not to offer an explicit response to a questionnaire. Referring to Sun Tzu's approach, the coach suggested using a converted informant (a Class 3 spy, 'a double agent'). Susan was advised to identify a trusted team member who used to work for the deputy director but was now working for her, to act as her 'eyes and ears' and report the situation informally.

A few weeks later, during the second session, Susan reported her findings to the coach. From the informant, she had learned that the deputy director was making a lot of noise about the re-positioning of the company with the intention of taking over Susan's position. However, he was rather anxious about the probable success of his new strategy. He had become bad tempered and bullying towards the team members, setting unrealistic performance objectives and demands, but issuing the orders in Susan's name. Most employees felt angry but were too afraid of Susan to talk about it.

The coach drew on Sun Tzu's wisdom and suggested that the deputy director was not wise, and was in fact in a very vulnerable position. Susan decided to further investigate the situation and gathered evidence of his misconduct.

A month later, at the third session, Susan reported that evidence of harassment had been gathered and the deputy was being disciplined. Since then, he had been behaving extremely politely to her. The coach suggested that this behaviour meant that he wished to make peace.

The coach pointed out that according to Sun Tzu, when managing a team one should treat it as a single unity. Thus team members who have particular strengths and weaknesses should not work on their own initiative. Appropriate discipline was important. If employees were disciplined before a good working relationship had been established, they would not develop loyalty to the leader. If the employees were not loyal, then they would be difficult to employ.

The coach left Susan with the above wisdom from Sun Tzu and let her make the decision in terms of whether she should escalate the discipline and terminate the employment of the deputy director or keep him and make peace. The ethical principle (Tao) of Sun Tzu's coaching is that employees must be treated with humanity and civility, but kept under control by discipline. Then one would have a winning team.

CONCLUSIONS

In this chapter a different perspective has been offered, drawing on ancient writings but ones that still have resonance and value for leaders today. Sun Tzu's *The Art of War* succinctly offers a total leadership guide, which when translated into a model of leadership can be a powerful and interesting perspective to use in a coaching conversation.

Above all, the primacy of ethics (Tao) is made clear by Sun Tzu, when he said:

百戰百勝，非善之善也; 不戰而屈人之兵，善之善者也。

'The best leadership is not to conquer by force, but to enable people to follow without any resistance' (Essay 3).

References

Armstrong J S (2001) *Principles of Forecasting*, International Series in Operations Research & Management Science, Springer, New York

Boffey, T B and Karkazis, J (1993) Models and methods for location and routing decision, *Studies in Locational Analysis*, **5**, pp 149–66

Checkland, P (1999) *Soft Systems Methodology in Action*, NetLibrary, Inc, John Wiley, Chichester

The Economist (2009) There were a lawyer, an engineer and a politician ... *The Economist*, 18–24 April, pp 63–64

Forrester, J W, (1961) *Industrial Dynamics*, Pegasus Communications, Waltham, MA

Forrester, J W, (1968) *Principles of Systems*, 2nd edn, Pegasus Communications, Waltham, MA

Forrester, J W, (1973) *World Dynamics*, 2nd edn, Pegasus Communications, Waltham, MA

Forrester, J W (1980) Information sources for modeling the national economy, *Journal of the American Statistical Association*, **75** (371), 555–74

Forrester, J W (1985) *System Dynamics in Management Education*, (D-3721–1) System Dynamics Group, Sloan School, Massachusetts Institute of Technology, Cambridge, MA

Forrester, J W (1987) Lessons from system dynamics modeling, *System Dynamics Review*, **3** (2), 136–49

Forrester, J W (1988) *Designing Social and Managerial Systems* (D-4006–1), System Dynamics Group, Sloan School, Massachusetts Institute of Technology, Cambridge, MA

Giles, L (1910) *Sun Tzu on the Art of War*, Luzac & Co, London, http://www.chinapagecom/sunzi-ehtml#01

Griffith, S B (trans) (1963) *Sun Tzu The Art of War*, Oxford, Oxford University Press

Hakimi S L (1983) On locating new facilities in a competitive environment, *European Journal of Operational Research*, **12**, pp 29–55

Hamel, G (1996) Strategy as revolution, *Harvard Business Review*, July–August, pp 69–82

Lee, H L, So, K C and Tang, C S (2000) The value of information sharing in a two-level supply chain, *Management Science*, **46**, pp 626–43

Mintzberg, H (1994) The rise and fall of strategy, *Harvard Business Review*, January–February, pp 107–14

Mun, K C (2006) *Chinese Leadership Wisdom from The Book of Change*, The Chinese University of Hong Kong, Hong Kong

Porter, M (1996) What is strategy? *Harvard Business Review*, November–December, pp 62–78

Rosinski, P (2003) *Coaching Across Cultures*, Nicholas Brealey, London

Smith, H K, Laporte, G and Harper, P R (2009) Locational analysis: highlights of growth to maturity, *Journal of Operational Research Society*, **60**, May, pp S140–48

Syntetos, A A, Boylan, J E and Disney, S M (2009) Forecasting for inventory planning: a 50-year review, *Journal of Operational Research Society*, **60**, May, pp S149–60

Whitmore, J (1992, 2002) *Coaching for Performance*, Nicholas Brealey, London

7

Coaching for Icarus leadership
Helping leaders who can potentially derail

Professor Adrian Furnham

INTRODUCTION

This chapter will focus on the issue of coaching senior executives who may be prone to, or show early signs that they may, derail: that is significantly fail to fulfil either their promise or, more specifically, the job requirements. The 'data' on senior management failure suggests that a surprising number of carefully selected, obviously talented individuals not only don't fulfil the hopes of the organization that appoints them but can cause dramatic, permanent and swift damage to organizational morale and productivity (Babiak and Hare, 2006; Finkelstein, 2003; Kets de Vries, 2006, 2007; Hogan, 2006). There is a growing literature on bad, derailed, sick or toxic leaders.

It will be argued that the paradox of business leader success is that it is precisely those characteristics that enable people to succeed and be noticed early on in their careers that later derail them. In short, excess does not lead to long-term success (Furnham, 2008a; Furnham, 2008b; McCall,

1998). People can easily have too much of a good thing, particularly with respect to certain personality traits such as self-esteem, boldness, risk taking and a tendency to be expressive or mischievous. Equally it will be argued that those who need coaching most are least likely to benefit from it and vice versa. This is therefore a particular challenge for coaches.

The chapter will focus on how, when and whether coaching can help those prone to failure and derailment not to fall into the trap. It is quite clear that it is too tough at the top. Furthermore, it's tougher on the way up. The characteristics that lead to leadership ascent may become a liability once the top job is reached. Typical, acute and chronic sources of senior management stress include: work overload, time pressures and deadlines, driving through change, being in the media spotlight, understanding the dynamics of the board, career planning, work–life balance, keeping up with legal and technical change, strategic planning and the 'vision' thing. These can cause 'toxicity' that can lead whole groups to fail at work.

No matter how insightful and talented people are, this is a long list. The issue then is to help senior managers with the skills required for these challenges.

Derailment is different from burnout. Burnout is associated with physical exhaustion and illness, with increasing use of legal and illegal drugs, and with marital and family conflict in addition to the usual suspects associated with neuroses: anxiety, depression, hypochondria, low self-esteem. This leads to feeling that one has nothing left to give, that one has essentially achieved nothing and that somehow it is one's clients (patients/students/customers) who are the cause of the problems.

There are physical, behavioural and work-performance indicators of burnout. Those interested in burnout have usually suggested that there are three distinguishable but related factors that make up the syndrome (Furnham, 2005). The first is exhaustion. Individuals experiencing burnout report being physically and emotionally drained, feeling 'all used up' with little more to give. They feel under constant strain and always tired. We all know the feeling but for the burnt-out it is both acute and chronic.

The second symptom is cynicism. Individuals experiencing burnout express doubts as to whether they really make any contribution and are hence less interested, enthusiastic and committed to their job. They are utterly alienated, with a sense of anomie. They cannot be bothered. At work they are automata. They are cynical about management and peers, customers and subordinates, in fact about anybody and everybody with whom they come into contact.

The third symptom is a total lack of personal efficacy. Effective employees generally feel confident, competent and considerate at work. They feel they accomplish worthwhile things, making a real contribution to their employers, clients, friends and family. They can report exhilaration at work and are happy to be there. Individuals experiencing burnout do not experience any of this. Indeed their reaction is the precise opposite.

Further, not all derailing managers are toxic, though they tend to have a toxic effect on work groups. Reading the list of typical characteristics of the dysfunctional parent in the toxic family, it is not difficult to see why children from these families end up as they do. Moody, egocentric, uneducated, immoral 'caregivers' give little real care. Instead of providing a loving, stable environment, they do the opposite, which can have a disastrous long-term effect on the child.

The same can happen at work. Dysfunctional, derailing managers create toxic offices. Often in a brief period of time, they manage to create mayhem, distrust and disaffection. This can have long-term consequences even in stable adults. That perfidious issue of 'stress at work' and its more serious cousin, the nervous breakdown, are often caused by the dysfunctional manager.

Managers can have considerable influence over their employees' health, happiness and future. They can create an environment that allows employees to give their best. They can stretch staff by setting reachable, challenging goals, and they can give them support in doing so. They can be helpful, encouraging and consistent. Yet there are some poor managers who create a working environment at the precise opposite end of the spectrum. Some high-fliers derail in toxic offices: others become toxic managers.

LEADERSHIP MODEL: THE ICARUS SYNDROME

Icarus was the son of the inventor Daedulus in the Greek myth. Both were locked up by the Cretan king Minos but the talented and inventive Daedulus made them both wings of feathers and wax so that they could escape. The wise father told his son the only 'design fault' was that the wings might melt if he flew too close to the sun. (Clearly the physics of the ancient Greek storytellers was not too good, as the higher one flies the cooler (not the hotter) it gets.) But Icarus ignored the good advice of his wise father, flew too high and due to melting of his wings crashed into the sea and drowned.

It is not clear from the myth precisely why he disobeyed his father. Was he a sensation seeker prone to accidents who did it out of boredom? Was he rather a disobedient child who liked to rebel? Was he simply 'cocking a snoop' at King Minos and beguiled by his own hubris? Was he a narcissist who had passed out top of the self-esteem class of life? We do not know. Indeed it is the function both of myths and case studies that they allow for multiple interpretations. But the modern derailed high-flyer bears an uncanny resemblance to Icarus. So how and why are they chosen? What did the assessors miss? Or was the problem in the way they were managed?

The literature on management failure and derailment suggests that a very high number of people regarded as extremely talented and able derail like Icarus. There are many reasons for this, including poor selection and lack of support as well as very difficult business conditions.

However, those that have studied the area in depth suggest that there is an interesting paradox for the derailed high-flyer. Those whose special characteristics encourage them to succeed and climb the slippery ladder of success are precisely those who are prone to failure.

Many leaders are singled out as being adventurous, bold or imaginative. The question is whether those everyday, positive attributes have a clear psychological origin. And more particularly, whether it is possible that they could be too adventurous or bold. It has been suggested that the very adventurous or mischievous executive may share traits with individuals who are diagnosed as having antisocial personality disorder (Furnham, 2009). It has been suggested that certain leaders at Enron fell into this category and this may have been a significant contributory factor in the organization's collapse. Their toughness and disregard for laws and regulations, which served them well during its rise, were the very factors that ultimately led to their derailment and the business's collapse. Perhaps a more important second trait/disorder is antisocial personality disorder, also known as being a psychopath.

Perhaps the greatest elements that lead to derailment are issues around self-esteem and self-confidence. The line between quiet, self-aware self-confidence and unattractive narcissism can be a fine one. This may be considered to be a case of narcissistic personality disorder and is worth spelling out in detail.

This probably relates to a self-esteem problem or, to use another good Greek word (and legend), narcissism. Narcissism is malignant self-love, overbearing self-confidence, inexplicably high self-esteem. The problem for the high-flyer is this: you probably need a great deal of self-esteem to get to the top, but you need to lose some of it when you get the job.

The manifestation of too much, as well as too little, self-esteem can be both a cause and a consequence of management failure.

People with low self-esteem seldom get into positions of power. Low self-esteem prevents risk taking, bold decision making, opportunism and openness to excitement and challenges, which are the stuff of success in business. We all need enough self-respect for healthy day-to-day functioning. We need to be sufficiently interested in, and confident about, ourselves to function well in the cut and thrust of business life.

It is those with seeming limitless self-esteem and concomitant hubris that are the real problem. Extreme narcissists are a hazard, and not as uncommon among our captains of industry as we might want to believe. They are often people completely preoccupied with being superior, unique or special. They shamelessly exaggerate their talents and indulge in addictively boastful and pretentious self-aggrandizement. They are often mildly amusing but frequently possess extremely vindictive characteristics.

Dotlich and Cairo (2003) talk of the self-blinding brilliance of the arrogant narcissist. They list four signs and symptoms: a diminished capacity to learn, an off-putting refusal to be accountable, resistance to change and an inability to recognize one's limitations.

The psychological interpretation of unnaturally high levels of narcissism is essentially compensatory. Many business narcissists believe they have been fundamentally wronged in the past and that they are 'owed'. Their feelings of internal insecurity can be satisfied by regular adulation, affirmation and recognition. They yearn for a strong positive self-image to combat their real feeling of helplessness and low self-esteem.

One of the most frequently observed characteristics of the narcissist is capriciousness – inconsistent, erratic and unpredictable behaviour. Naturally, most psychologists see the origins of narcissistic behaviour in early childhood: the inconsistent parent (caregiver) who was attentive to all outward, public signs of achievement and success but blind to and ignorant of (or worse, disapproving of) the child's personal feelings.

This inconsistency often leads to young adults being confused and failing to develop a clear sense of who they are or establishing a coherent value system. They are 'not comfortable in their own skin'. This can and does result in a lifelong compensatory quest for full self-regard and self-assertion. The wells of the origin of the problem are both deep and murky, and the passions they engender seem remorseless.

The narcissist is quite plainly dysfunctional. He or she fails to understand or appreciate others, be they colleagues, subordinates or clients. Narcissists often see people as sort of possessions whose major function is as an accessory to their pursuit of fame and glory. People at work are used to reflect their glory. Do any of our current or past great business figures spring to mind at this point?

Narcissistic bosses are ambitious and competitive, often politically astute and identified with positions of high rank and power. Whilst they are comfortable with their strength, it is their denied shortcomings that cause problems. They are good at being loved but are less happy when dealing with criticism or hostility.

Personal and work relationships for narcissists are particularly interesting. If the narcissist's 'other half' is prepared to offer continual, unconditional, even escalatory admiration, all is well. But they have to direct all their efforts, all the time, to minister to the needs of their master to overcome the inner emptiness and worthlessness he/she is experiencing. Naturally, narcissists search them out because they are rare, probably equally dysfunctional, people, labelled appropriately as 'complementary narcissists'. They are complementary/complimentary in both senses.

Many high-flyers, like Icarus, are narcissists. Indeed they find that their narcissism serves them well. They seem confident and give others confidence.

What happens to high-flyers? Their strengths are noticed and they are fast-streamed. Whichever part of the organization they work in, they tend to excel. If they are in marketing, they tend to be ideas and action men, resourceful and imaginative. If in finance, they tend to be brilliant not only with figures but at strategic planning. They love number tumbling and 'modelling the future'.

But they tend to be forgiven in their faults, which are overlooked. The fact that the high-flying marketing executive is undisciplined, inconsistent, poor at paper work and egocentric is ignored and down-played. They can be unrealistic, impractical and spendthrift. High-flyers who are known for their integrity can suddenly be revealed as rigid, intolerant zealots. Those known for their people skills may come to be labelled soft, indecisive, too tolerant of poor performance.

The central question for this chapter is whether, when and how coaching can prevent the overconfident or over-adventurous leader/manager from being derailed by his or her dark side. But what are the general symptoms of the dysfunctional manager? These are common but not necessarily related to the Icarus syndrome because their dysfunctionality prevents them from reaching high, positions of power and influence in the organization.

Not all toxic managers could be described as suffering from traits that have a clinical dimension. Some simply display behaviours that are detrimental to their staff, their organizations and themselves, and may be simply described as dysfunctional. We have summarized some of the behaviours that such individuals can display in Table 7.1. Our view is that not all dysfunctional managers display all of these behaviours, but most display three or four that, if displayed frequently, are a major source for low staff morale and poor performance within their team or organization.

Such managers and leaders, and those with more serious behavioural problems, have over the years sought professional help from coaches, counsellors or sometimes just wise friends. In speeches and memoirs

Table 7.1 Characteristics of dysfunctional managers

Inconsistency and unpredictability	This is often the hallmark set of behaviours. Such managers are unpredictable to staff, clients and customers, even to their family. You can never be sure what they will say or do. They are fickle and capricious. They give contradictory and mixed messages that are very difficult to interpret.
Low tolerance of provocation and emotional sensitivity	They may easily fly off the handle, can be moody, or take offence and harbour grudges. Such behaviours get worse as stress levels increase.
Hedonism and self-indulgence	They are less likely to be puritans; and instead enjoy pleasure. They are often deeply selfish. There can be real problems if their pleasures are addictive, which so often they can be.
Now-ness and lack of long-term planning	They can't or won't plan for the future. They don't understand postponement of gratification. Hence they experience serious setbacks when unexpected things happen.
Restlessness and excitement seeking	They get bored easily and can't seem to pay attention. They appear to need thrills and variety to keep them going. Inevitably, they find themselves in situations that are commercially, even physically, dangerous.
Learning problems	They find it more difficult to learn from their mistakes. In fact, they don't like learning at all. The skill-based seminar is not for them. Outdoor, physical training, perhaps, but not the conference centre.
Poor emotional control	They shout, weep, sulk and gush with little embarrassment or control. They become well known for their outbursts
Placing little value on skill attainment	They place little value on upgrading their skills. They talk about gut feelings, experience or, worse still, luck.
Perpetual low-grade physical illness	They can suffer from frequent illness. They get coughs, colds and the flu, whatever is going around.

they have recorded their very deep gratitude to these individuals for helping them deal with the stresses of leadership and the negative effects that it was having on their behaviour.

THE RESEARCH

Most research in this area is still done by the case study method, particularly by those who take a more psychoanalytic approach (Kets de Vries, 2006). The problems of individual leaders are carefully described and dissected, informed by the personality disorders literature.

Another series of studies has been done around the successful psychopaths; an example is Babiak (1995), who described in detail the industrial psychopath. However the research in this area has been dramatically improved by the development of the Hogan Development Survey (HDS). Hogan and Hogan (Hogan and Hogan, 1997: 3) note that:

> when under pressure, most people will display certain counterproductive tendencies. We refer to these as 'risk factors'. Under normal conditions these characteristics may actually be strengths. However, when you are tired, pressured, bored or otherwise distracted, these risk factors may impede your effectiveness and erode the quality of your relationships with customers, colleagues and direct reports. Others may be aware of these tendencies but may not give you any feedback about them. Your boss may even ignore them.

Their taxonomy of derailment is shown in Table 7.2.

Others have taken the original model and changed the terminology. Thus Dotlich and Cairo (2003) use the following terms:

▌ Arrogance: they're right and everybody is wrong.
▌ Melodrama: they want to be the centre of attention.
▌ Volatility: their mood swings create business swings.
▌ Excessive caution: they can't make important decisions.
▌ Habitual distrust: they focus on the negative all the time.
▌ Aloofness: they disengage and disconnect from staff.
▌ Eccentricity: they think it's fun to be different just for the sake of it.
▌ Passive resistance: their silence is misinterpreted as agreement.
▌ Perfectionism: they seem to get the little things right even if the big things go wrong.
▌ Eagerness to please: being popular matters most.

These are essentially the same ideas but using more approachable terminology and one that business people can accept and understand.

Table 7.2 Hogan taxonomy of derailment

Excitable	Concerns being overly enthusiastic about people or projects and then becoming disappointed with them. Result: seems to lack persistence.
Sceptical	Concerns being socially insightful, but cynical and overly sensitive to criticism. Result: seems to lack trust.
Cautious	Concerns being overly worried about being criticized. Result: seems resistant to change and reluctant to take chances.
Reserved	Concerns lacking interest in or awareness of the feelings of others. Result: seems to be a poor communicator.
Leisurely	Concerns being independent, ignoring others' requests and becoming irritable if they persist. Result: seems stubborn, procrastinating and uncooperative.
Bold	Concerns having inflated views of one's competency and worth. Result: seems unable to admit mistakes or learn from experience.
Mischievous	Concerns being charming, risk-taking and excitement-seeking. Result: seems to have trouble maintaining commitments and learning from experience.
Colourful	Concerns being dramatic, engaging and attention-seeking. Result: seems preoccupied with being noticed and may lack sustained focus.
Imaginative	Concerns thinking and acting in interesting, unusual, and even eccentric ways. Result: seems creative but possibly lacking in judgement.
Diligent	Concerns being conscientious, perfectionistic and hard to please. Result: tends to disempower staff.
Dutiful	Concerns being eager to please and reluctant to act independently. Result: tends to be pleasant and agreeable, but reluctant to support subordinates.

Now there is also empirical evidence that high scores on this dark side (disorders) relate to poor leadership. Thus Moscoso and Salgado (2004) used a personality disorders measure to test 85 job applicants, whose job performance was rated by their direct supervisors eight months later. Three measures were obtained: task performance, contextual performance and overall job performance. The results showed that the seven dysfunctional personality styles (suspicious, shy, sad, pessimistic, sufferer, eccentric and risky) predicted the three measures of job performance. The egocentric personality style negatively predicted contextual performance.

The research is clearly very well informed by the psychiatric literature on the personality disorders that are seen to be the critical derailers. Those who come from a psychiatric, psychological, psychoanalytic and psychometric tradition all seem to agree that the personality disorders provide an excellent and useful framework around which to understand leader derailment (Hogan, Brady and Fico, 2008).

USING THE MODEL WITH COACHEES

It is argued that three characteristics (the dark side) seem to characterize the Icarus derailing manager: a poorly developed social conscience, inflated self-esteem and Machiavellian influence tactics. In many ways the best place to start is by examining popular books that seek to explain the personality disorders and how people might learn to live and work with those that have them. Arrogant, overly self-confident managers can be helped by friends and workmates. However, they are unlikely to seek out help unless it flatters them, and they need to be wary of the celebrated adage that 'pride goes before a fall'.

The Hogan HDS measure generates a rich and helpful detailed report that could be used by a coach and given to coachees. Consider the example for someone described as Mischievous: the box below contains a summary of a 'typical' report.

Hogan Report

Behavioural implications

You scored in the MODERATE RISK ZONE on this scale. Leaders with similar scores:

▌ seem clever;
▌ test the limits;
▌ are unafraid of risk;
▌ do not dwell on past mistakes;
▌ can be impatient and get bored easily.

Leadership implications

You are an engaging and somewhat unpredictable person, and others will enjoy your company. However you are unafraid of failure and tend to push the limits. Others in the organization may not have your tolerance for risk. Although you might not dwell on your mistakes, others will keep track, and this could erode your credibility over time. You are also likely to develop risky career and business strategies.

Competency analysis

▌ DECISION QUALITY: Because you are so fearless, you are likely to make decisions without consulting others.
▌ RISK TAKING: You are comfortable when confronted with challenges and choices that entail risk and uncertainty.
▌ LEARNING FROM EXPERIENCE: You may overlook or dismiss mistakes that contain important information for the development of your career.

Developmental recommendations

▌ Other people may think that you follow your own agenda and don't consider how your decisions impact on them. As a result they may be as reluctant to make commitments to you as you seem to be in return. Thus, you need to be careful to follow through on all your good-faith commitments.
▌ If you find circumstances have altered the conditions under which you made a commitment, then negotiate the changes with the persons to whom you have made the promise – rather than simply going on about your business.
▌ You tend to have a higher tolerance for risk than most people. Be aware that not everyone is as adventurous as you seem to be.
▌ You may have disappointed others by not following through. You need to acknowledge your errors and make amends – rather than trying to explain the situation away.
▌ At your best, you are charming, spontaneous and fun. You adapt quickly to changing circumstances, you handle ambiguity well, you add positive energy to social interactions, and people like being with you.

What about the narcissistic manager? Dotlich and Cairo (2003) recommend three things the narcissistic managers might do to prevent derailment. First, determine whether you fit the arrogant profile. Second, find the 'truth tellers' in your organization and ask them to 'level' with you. Third, use setbacks as an opportunity to cross back over the line before real failure hits.

Oldham and Morris (1995: 90–91,) offer four tips for working what they call self-confident 'star quality' people:

▌ Be absolutely loyal. Don't criticize or compete with them. Don't expect to share the limelight or to take credit. Be content to aspire to the number-two position.

▌ Don't expect your self-confident boss to provide direction. He or she will probably expect you to know what to do, so be sure you're clear about the objectives before you undertake any task. Don't hesitate to ask.

▌ You may be an important member of the boss's team, but don't expect your self-confident boss to be attentive to you as an individual. Don't take things personally.

▌ Self-confident bosses expect you to show interest in them, however. They may be susceptible to flattery, so if you're working on a raise or promotion or are trying to sell your point of view, a bit of buttering up may smooth the way.

They also offer helpful tips on dealing with self-confident people (pp 95–96):

▌ Self-confident individuals need to be number one. To love a self-confident person requires that you accept, admire and respect this aspect of his or her character. Appreciate the considerable strengths this person brings to the relationship. Enjoy the fruits of your partner's success and the interesting life he or she may provide.

▌ To hold this person's attention, pay a lot of attention. Your love and loyalty are very important to the self-confident person in your life. You bring to the relationship the ability to love, and your mate counts on it. Accept that you may be more capable of selfless love than is your self-confident partner. Give your love without keeping track of who's giving more. If you need to be loved more intensely and equally, however, accept that this person is not for you.

▌ Be careful not to tie your self-esteem to the amount of love and attention the self-confident person in your life spontaneously shows you, or to the extent to which he or she really understands you. Love yourself no matter what. This 'message' is especially important for children of highly self-confident parents.

▌ Many self-confident types will alternately move emotionally close and then apparently lose interest in you, especially after a relationship has become established. Be aware of this back-and-forth pattern, try to wait it out while maintaining your own emotional balance and do not jump to the conclusion that your self-confident partner no longer has feelings for you. More likely he or she has become preoccupied with other concerns. Remind the self-confident person that you exist and that you continue to care for him or her.

▌ When you need to confront your self-confident partner, simply state how you feel or what you observe without judging him or her. Remember that for all their self-esteem, self-confident people have difficulty dealing with criticism. Be sure at the same time to express your admiration and praise. Keep in mind that although the self-confident individual may not admit that you have a point, he or she will try to deal with it. Self-confident individuals can step back from themselves and correct their behaviour, even if they are not so good in the 'you're right/I'm wrong' department.

▌ Continually make your feelings known, even about apparently obvious matters; don't count on a self-confident individual to sense or keep track of them. Keeping your partner informed about your feelings and attitudes will enable him or her to understand you better and avoid conflict later.

Lambert (2008) suggests that leadership coaching can impact on four potential areas of organizational life: improving leadership in those with high potential, facilitating transitions to larger jobs, on-boarding those new to the organization, and developing a selected group of individual with specific needs. In this sense its aim is both to reduce risk and to encourage growth.

The problem for the coaching of potential derailers is that it is subtly different. This is not about coaching for confidence – indeed almost the precise opposite – but it certainly is coaching for self-awareness. It is, of necessity both directive and non-directive.

Coaching the Icarus syndrome usually means coaching top-level people who experience both unique and particular problems. Arrogant CEOs are easy targets for news-hungry media as well as investor and press criticism. The media may view their rise as a failure of corporate governance or as due to a reluctance to confront the all-powerful and all-confident leader who rejects advice. The human resources press has speculated that seeking the virtue of humility over hubris and emotional intelligence leads to poor selection decisions.

Certainly prevention is better than cure. After the appointment process however, diagnosis can be harder than cure. It can take organizations some time to realize that senior managers and leaders are driving them on the path to disaster. This is particularly the case when failing leaders have had a spectacularly 'stellar career', where they have appeared to have the Midas touch.

It is important not to fall for the classic attribution error of seeing the cause of all problems to be exclusively within the personality, values or abilities of leaders. Some leaders are set up to fail. Others have impossible tasks trying to lead corrupt, incompetent organizations that resist appropriate processes and procedures. Economic, political and social forces can conspire to ensure that in effect no leader can succeed. In fact a significant proportion of leadership failure can be attributed to systemic aspects.

However there is a difference between failed and derailed leaders. The former are usually associated with poor judgement, inexperience, inability or wider market conditions. Failure is usually associated with the absence of a quality. Derailment on the other hand, is more associated with the presence of a quality.

There are various ways to assist potentially derailing managers. Developing the manager's self-awareness can be a useful intervention for the coach, although this may be less useful when dealing with managers who suffer with an antisocial personality disorder; for them, information is just further information to use against others.

In the main derailed leaders often overestimate their abilities. Those who underestimate them tend to appear lacking in confidence and therefore are unlikely to be selected for high positions. Thus derailment-prone leaders have found it pays to overestimate their abilities.

To assist in this process the coach can use:

▌ assessment or development centres, which can be useful for adjusting self-ratings for middle managers;
▌ 360° feedback, which can provide useful anonymous feedback to the most senior leader and is even more useful when colleague ratings are compared with self-ratings;
▌ HDS or similar products that focus on dark side behaviours.

Thus classic methods such as development centres, 360° feedback, coaching and CBT counselling are available. A paradox here is that because derailed managers are by definition so often self-absorbed, eager to blame others for all their shortcomings and poor at learning from experience, they do not benefit from these interventions.

Another idea is transitioning. This is a polite term for movement – usually sideways, downwards or out. Nearly all derailed leaders have been judged to be highly effective, competent and talented, and so promoted to positions that bring more responsibility and more scrutiny. Senior jobs are more complex and call for more subtle influencing and persuading skills. Senior managers have to form strategic alliances, empower and delegate. Earlier, lower-level jobs do not call for the same skills. More is expected of senior leaders.

The coach's role may be to help in this transitioning move, offering support to the manager and helping him or her build the new networks and skills for the move into a different area, while staying within the organization.

Capretta, Clark and Dai (2008) list the things organizations should do to prevent derailment:

▌ Have systems that integrate development into managers' work.
▌ Note what each person could and should learn from each assignment.
▌ Ensure that leadership development is a lifelong not a one-off journey.
▌ Support risk taking and be tolerant of experience-giving mistakes.
▌ Ensure managers complete jobs before moving them on.
▌ Become a feedback culture with mechanisms to ensure formal and informal feedback regularly.
▌ Invest in good coaches.
▌ Empower those dedicated to talent (ie HR, specialists) to do their job better.
▌ Look for, rank, strategize and prioritize derailment factors.

Clearly derailed leaders differ from one another. It is the role of the coach to understand those differences and apply coaching techniques appropriately.

WHO LEARNS WHAT FROM COACHING?

Is there a paradox at the heart of adult executive coaching? Those who need it most sometimes benefit from it least (Furnham, 2008c). They can withdraw from coaching for various reasons. Some have little self-insight and are blinded by their arrogance and egocentricism. Others either feel threatened by a sort of 'imposter syndrome' or worry that having coaching implies there is something wrong with them. They suspect that it is remedial or really little more than a type of therapy. There may also be another reason: they are not bright enough.

The literature on intelligence at work is clear. Intelligence (or whatever 'disguised concept' or term one wants to use: cognitive ability, problem-solving capacity, business smarts) is the most powerful individual difference predictor of success at work. It means more than any other factor such as charm, educational background or personality. Further, and this is crucial, higher intelligence reflects higher trainability. Hence training increases rather than decreases differences among employees, because the brighter ones gain more and gain it more efficiently and effectively, and therefore more cheaply.

Bright people learn faster and better. To train or coach the intellectual high-flyers therefore increases the blue water between the top and the average. The good get better, the average stay that way.

CONCLUSIONS

This chapter has considered two paradoxes. First, that some of the characteristics that lead to leadership roles are precisely those that derail leaders. Second, that those who may need coaching most benefit from it least and vice versa. Thus (pathological) narcissistic bosses may choose to have a coach to feed their narcissism but gain little or nothing from the experience. The jury is still out about what type of intervention works for the personality disorders.

Coaching is a comparatively new 'intervention' although what coaches do has been done for hundreds of years. The autobiographies and biographies of many great leaders testify to the help they gained from others who gave them good advice, counsel and mentoring. The job of a good coach is just as much to bring out the best in great leaders as to save them from themselves.

References and further reading

Babiak, P (1995) When psychopaths go to work: a case study of an industrial psychopath, *Applied Psychology*, **44**, pp 171–88

Babiak, P, and Hare, R (2006) *Snakes in Suits: When psychopaths go to work*, Regan Books, New York

Capretta, C, Clark, L and Dai, G (2008) Executive derailment: three cases and how to prevent it, *Global Business and Organizational Excellence*, **3**, pp 48–56

Dotlich, D, and Cairo, R (2003) *Why CEOs Fail*, Jossey Bass, New York

Finkelstein, S (2003) *Why Smart Executives Fail*, Portfolio, New York

Furnham, A (2004) *Management and Myths*, Palgrave Macmillan, Basingstoke

Furnham, A (2005) *The People Business*, Palgrave Macmillan, Basingstoke

Furnham, A (2007) Personality disorders and derailment at work, in *Research Companion to the Dysfunctional Workplace*, ed J Langan-Fox, C Cooper and R Klimoski, pp 22–39, Edward Elgar, Cheltenham

Furnham, A (2008a) *Head and Heart Management*, Palgrave Macmillan, Basingstoke

Furnham, A (2008b) *Management Intelligence*, Palgrave Macmillan, Basingstoke

Furnham, A (2008c) *Personality and Intelligence at Work*, Routledge, London

Furnham, A (2009) *The Elephant in the Room: The psychology of leadership derailment*, Palgrave Macmillan, Basingstoke

Furnham, A and Crump, J (2005) Personality trait, types and disorders, *European Journal of Personality*, **19**, pp 167–84

Hogan, R (2006) *Personality and the Fate of Organizations*, Lawrence Erlbaum, Mahwah, NJ

Hogan, R, Brady, R and Fico, J (2008) Identifying potential derailing behaviours: Hogan Development Instrument (HDI), in *Psychometrics in Coaching*, ed J Passmore, Kogan Page, London

Hogan, R and Hogan, J (1997) *Hogan Development Survey Manual*, Hogan Assessment Systems, Tulsa, OK

Hogan, R and Hogan, J (2001) Assessment leadership: a view from the dark side, *International Journal of Selection and Assessment*, **9**, pp 40–51

Katcher, B (2007) *30 Reasons Employees Hate Their Managers*, Amacom, New York

Kellerman, D (2002) *Bad Leadership*, Harvard Business School, Boston, MA

Kets de Vries, M (2006) *The Leader on the Couch*, Jossey Bass, New York

Kets de Vries, M (2007) *Coach and Couch: The psychology of making better leaders*, Palgrave Macmillan, Basingstoke

Lambert, A (2008) *What's New in Coaching and Mentoring? An update*, Corporate Research Forum, London

Lipman-Blumen, J (2005) *The Allure of Toxic Leaders*, Oxford University Press, Oxford

Lloyd, K (1999) *Jerks at Work*, Career Press, Franklin Lakes, NJ

McCall, M (1998) *High Flyers*, Harvard University Press, Boston, MA

Miller, L (2008) *From Difficult to Disturbed*, Amacom, New York

Moscoso, S and Salgado, J (2004) 'Dark Side' personality styles as predictors of task, contextual and job performance, *International Journal of Selection and Assessment*, **12**, pp 356–62

Oldham, J and Morris, L (1995) *The Personality Self-Portrait*, Banham, New York

Pincus, M (2005) *Managing Difficult People*, Adams Media, Avon, MA

Roth, A and Fonagy, P (2005) *What Works for Whom?* Guilford Press, New York

Scott, G (2005) *A Survival Guide for Working with Bad Bosses*, Amacom, New York

Scott, G (2007) *A Survival Guide to Managing Employees from Hell*, Amacom, New York

8

Coaching for integral leadership

Martin Egan

INTRODUCTION

Raising the consciousness of organizations and their leaders creates better quality decisions, better organizational design and harmony, and an increased understanding of customers and markets. Integral thinking impacts all the functions of business in such a dramatic way because it incorporates a clear vision of the inner dimensions of subjective mindsets and organizational culture together with the outer dimensions of systems, processes and behaviour. (Forman, 2006)

- Do leadership coaches need to improve their credibility and produce reliable evidence-based data proving a respectable return on investment (ROI)?
- Would understanding the self-development levels of both coach and coachee optimize ROI?
- Are there ever shortcomings in the theoretical foundations of coaching models?
- Can we minimize blind-spots and maximize impact?

Integral philosopher Ken Wilber's theory offers us a way of examining all aspects of these questions. Applying Einstein's dictum that, 'Theory is really useful, because it determines what we can see,' integral theory enables as many perspectives as possible in order to integrate the discord among diverse leadership frameworks. Leadership authority Warren Bennis says Wilber has 'created a unifying system for this chaotic age we're living in' (Kalman, 2007a). Wilber (1996) makes the case for an integral approach to leadership and business in this way: 'If you have a partial, truncated, fragmented map of the human being, you will have a partial, truncated, fragmented approach to business.' Conversely, an integral framework offers the most comprehensive integration possible, thus reducing the potential for blind spots.

THE LEADERSHIP MODEL

The integral approach takes account of multiple perspectives at many levels of complexity to provide a 'fit-for-purpose' map of the leader's territory. 'It is committed to rightly relating all parts to one another and not leaving anything essential out. This does not mean "totalistic" or "uniformity" or ironing out differences, but unity-in-diversity, shared commonalities along with differences' (Wilber, 2000a: 2). An integral approach is about integrating, bringing together, aligning, synthesizing and completeness.

There are five fundamental elements of the integral framework (I am not using Wilber's exact terminology). First, a quadrant model divides distinct interrelated dimensions of reality from the inner subjective mindsets and organizational culture to the outer objective of systems, processes and behaviour (Figure 8.1). The irreducible dimensions of reality represented by the quadrants are inherent in all human experience, and every language recognizes them in the perspectives they contain – 'I' (first person singular), 'we' (first person plural), 'it' (third person singular) and 'they' (third person plural) (Wilber, 2006: 18–26; Wilber et al, 2004). We are aware of the difference between our interior and exterior worlds and capable of distinguishing between the individual and the collective/group.

Continuing with the remaining elements of the integral framework, the second, 'Capacities' ('Lines' in Wilber), are discrete aspects of development: for example, cognitive, emotional, interpersonal, moral, spiritual and kinaesthetic capacities (Figure 8.2, see Table 8.1 for descriptions of capacities). The third element is 'stages of expanding awareness' ('Levels' in Wilber) and accounting for evolutionary growth in each capacity (Figure 8.2) and overall identity (Figure 8.3, Table 8.1).

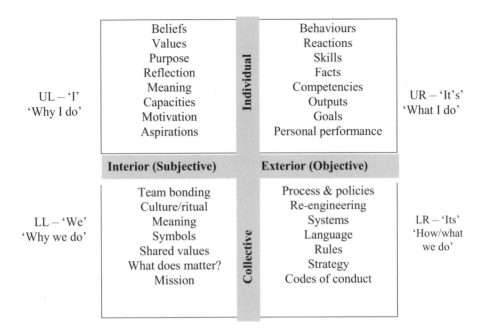

Figure 8.1 The quadrant model showing example aspects in each

Key: UL , upper left; UR, upper right; LL, lower left; LR, lower right

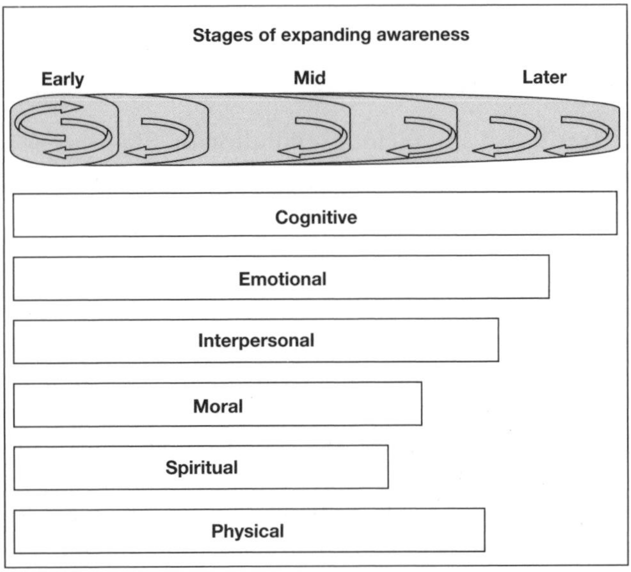

Figure 8.2 Example of relative 'Stages of Expanding Awareness' in each Capacity – the circular arrows denote a 'transcend, embrace and include' movement

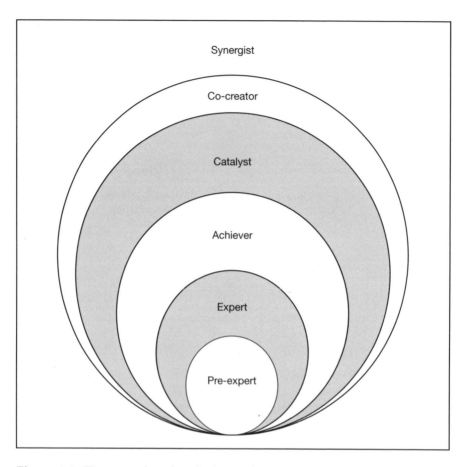

Figure 8.3 'Transcend and include' evolution of 'Stages of Awareness' in Leadership Agility (after Joiner and Josephs, 2007) as an example echoing the capacity of 'self-identity'

A fourth element brings in 'states' of consciousness – 'peak' and 'performance states'. And the fifth is 'types' as a way to include classification by type; for example, types of government, types of society and personality typologies. Implicit in these elements is a space to focus on 'shadow' aspects of self (Wilber, 1979: 80–92; 2006: 120) and there is an acknowledgment of a 'Kosmic Consciousness'– an all pervading spirit or 'oneness' in all things (Wilber, 1999b, 2003a, 2006). An integral way to address both shadow and spiritual development is the 'Big Mind Big Heart' process (Merzel, 2007).

The quadrants (Figure 8.1) can be used as a holistic lens with which we can understand the current reality of an individual or an organization.

The upper left quadrant (UL) is the realm of 'Intention', denoting the 'I' of my experience of feeling and thinking with awareness of why 'I' do things. This is where coaching that addresses the inner development of the coachee – understanding mind sets, intentions and motivations – fits. It is the quadrant of direct experience.

The lower left quadrant (LL) deals with the collective/internal – the 'we'. It is the realm of intersubjective relationships (including that between coachee and coach) and 'culture' – the myths, stories, symbols, power and team dynamics that are omnipresent. It is the interior, often unspoken, territory of shared assumptions and beliefs that shape and inform what occurs when people come together.

The upper right quadrant (UR) addresses the individual/external: actions, behaviours, processes, results and metrics – the 'it'. This is the realm of 'competences': tasks and techniques as well as the sciences such as physiology, neurology and psychology – levers of peak performance. This quadrant gets a great deal of attention from coaches and line management when working in the realm of performance coaching and in ascertaining what 'I' do or need to do to develop.

The lower right quadrant (LR) is about the collective/external. It is the 'strategic and systemic' quadrant that helps us understand environment, governance, roles and responsibilities, processes, policies and procedures as well as context, including all external relations.

Returning to the other elements of 'integral', for simplicity I write about them as they arise in the UL although they have correlates in each quadrant. I combine my treatment of capacities and stages of expanding awareness (Figure 8.3) because they are intimately linked in an individual. Turning first to capacities, Gardner (1983, 2000) is a good starting point since his multiple intelligences is a way to conceptualize them. A crucial point concerning the development of capacities is that the other capacities depend on the abilities gained via our cognitive capacity, which is 'necessary but not sufficient' for development in others (Wilber, 2000b). Cognitive capacity was researched by Piaget (Piaget and Inhelder, 1958), among others, and IQ has been a conventional (though limited) measure of this capacity. In recent years, interest has developed in emotional quotient (EQ) and interpersonal capacity, popularized by Daniel Goleman, Richard Boyatzis and Annie McKee (2004). Spiritual capacity (Benefiel, 2008; Fowler, 1987) is slowly gaining recognition too. Organization failures due to deficiencies in the moral capacity of the leaders make a compelling case to consider moral development. I will return later to 'states of consciousness' and 'types' as they are probably more familiar to readers.

Table 8.1 Summary descriptions of key capacities

Capacities	Cognitive	Emotional	Interpersonal	Moral/Ethical	Spiritual	Physical
Definition of ability	Both linguistic and logical – Analyse, interpret and decide. Ideas, concepts and mental constructs. Ability to include more wide-ranging perspectives and aspects of situations.	Awareness of one's inner 'felt-sense': the texture, quality and rhythm of an 'emotion', mood, attitude and disposition. Higher complexity includes feelings of gratitude, wonder, deep empathy as emotion.	Understanding and engaging emotional responses to relate effectively with others. Includes social awareness, empathy and relationship management competencies. Understands what motivates others and gains cooperation.	Makes decisions with consideration for what is good, right and fair. Decisions by a group creates an 'ethos' or ethics. This capacity depends on the previous three capacities.	The increasing ability to learn from and explore sources of meaning, purpose and wisdom. Intuition and connectedness to life.	Physiological abilities. Degrees of ability to deal with stress, to notice and tend to one's energy levels through appropriate hydration, diet, exercise and sleep management and rest.
Early stage	Concrete terms. Difficulty integrating information incompatible with their own views. Influenced by authority.	Feelings and states seen as externally generated. Poorly developed self-management.	Lacks trust, not team players. Competitive relating. Relies on 'argument'. Collaboration seen as trading favours. Conflict avoided or needlessly engaged.	'Right and good' determined by punishment and reward. 'Ethics' is the art of mutual 'back-scratching'.	Not usually a strong sense of purpose or contact with life beyond survival and comfort.	Emotional and physical responses distinguished. Basic attention to health and energy. Stress ignored until it incapacitates.

	Cognitive	Emotional	Interpersonal	Moral	Meaning	Energy / Health
Mid stage	Rational mind on abstract objects, eg hypothetical scenarios.	Emotional states named on basis of logical 'cause and effect' way of thinking. Strengths built on and weaknesses pursued.	Aware of emotional currents and group dynamics. Relates to others' world views. Shares success. Debate not argument. Collaboration as mutual fair exchange.	There is a 'right way'. Sense of fairness transcends individual interest and extends to the group.	Questions previously 'black and white' beliefs. Openness to cultivate a new more congruent relationship with meaning.	Good health, vigour and balance. Greater control and maintenance of energy = higher sustained longer term performance and reduced stress.
Later stage	Integrates complex reason, intuition and synthesises. Accommodates opposing views. Inquiring and generative perspectives.	Intimately understands internal states and triggers. High self-regulation. Optimistic and resilient. 'Contains' and balances others' difficult emotions without reactivity.	All perspectives valid. Adjusts communication styles. Inspires others. Seeks 'win–win'. Conflict an opportunity to understand. Open to feedback. Dialogue not debate.	Guided by social contracts and universal principles. Decisions stem from intent of fairness, kindness, beneficial practices seeking highest good.	Understanding the essence behind concepts. A felt responsibility of service to all. Love and compassion all encompassing.	Has practices to restore and renew energy. Conscious of causes of stress. Aware of nuances in self and others' energy.

Summaries based on 'Lines and levels' from Integral Institute (Integral Institute, 2006) with appreciation to Brett Thomas of Stagen

THE RESEARCH

At its simplest, integral theory makes intelligent use of others' work and finds ways to integrate and include all disciplines in interrelationship (Integral Institute, 2005). Wilber integrates the wisdom traditions of East and West, and draws on the thinkers of each era in each discipline for each quadrant and element of the integral framework (Wilber, 1996–2007).

'Hard' empirical evidence-based data belong intrinsically to UR and LR, whilst the 'soft' interior experiential evidence, requiring personal inquiry and reflection, belong to UL and LL. An integral view allows both 'hard' and 'soft' data to co-exist. I describe this as 'inner laboratory' and 'outer laboratory' collaboration similar to what Cashman's (2001) treatment of the UL provides a welcome addition to the literature for this under-represented quadrant. *Molecules of Emotion* (Pert, 1999) is a good example of the interrelationship of UL and UR quadrants. The temptation of non-integral or partial approaches to research is for researchers to reduce everything to their preferred quadrant. Each is true and partial both from a quadrant and 'stage of awareness' perspective. 'No human mind is capable of 100 per cent error' – all perspectives are true and partial (Wilber, 2000a: 51).

Experience of integral approaches to various disciplines is growing. Integral Coaching Canada (Hunt, 2009) was the first provider of government-approved coaching and training programmes embodying integral theory principles. Conventional research is rarely integral, focusing instead on isolated elements. However, the integral framework can be used to draw together disparate findings. In terms of 'stages of awareness', for example, Laske (2006) highlighted the importance of developmental research in coaching. He offered a (developmentally informed) typology of coach–client relationships and explored which are likely to be developmentally counterproductive relative to ROI. Fuhs (2008) focused on the quadrant spread in leadership literature. He found only a minority of leadership books providing an all-quadrant balance, while most were skewed towards the UR and LR. His findings give cause for concern since the implications of ignoring any quadrant seem self-evident. The most balanced among those in the study were 'Primal leadership' (Goleman, Boyatzis and McKee, 2004) and 'Action inquiry' (Torbert, 2004). Encouragingly, Fuhs also suggested 'Principle-centred leadership' (Covey, 1992), 'Integrative leadership' (Hatala and Hatala, 2004) and 'Conscious business' (Kofman, 2006) as balanced in all quadrants.

Evidence of the importance of an all-quadrant focus in leadership and corporate sustainability success showed that both interior and exterior approaches were equally important; 47 per cent of success factors were

Table 8.2a Overview of heroic levels of leadership agility – 'stages of awareness'

At each new level of agility, managers retain and go beyond leadership capacities and skills they developed at previous levels. Percentages refer to research-based estimates of the percentage of managers currently capable of operating at each agility level.

Level of agility	Assumptions about leadership	Agility in pivotal conversations	Agility in leading teams	Agility in leading organizational change
		Heroic levels		
Pre-expert (~10%)				
Expert (~45%)	*Tactical, problem-solving orientation.* Assumes that leaders are respected and followed by others because of their expertise and authority.	*Either strongly assertive or very accommodative in dealing with differences. May flip from assertive to accommodative and vice versa. Tends to avoid giving or requesting feedback.*	Supervizes more than manages. Creates a group of individuals more than a team. Primarily one-on-one with direct reports. Too caught up in own work detail to lead strategically.	Organizational change initiatives are focused primarily on incremental improvements inside unit boundaries with relatively little attention to stakeholders.
Achiever (~35%)	*Strategic, outcome orientation.* Assumes leadership is about motivating others by making it challenging and satisfying for them to contribute to achieve key outcomes.	Primarily assertive or accommodative in dealing with differences, but can compensate by using their less preferred style. Accepts or may initiate feedback, if perceived as helpful to achieve their end.	Full-fledged manager. Engages direct reports in meetings to discuss strategic or organizational issues, though these may be orchestrated to gain buy-in to their own views.	Organizational change initiatives also analyse the external environment. Seeks to gain stakeholder buy-in through strategies ranging from one-way communication to solicitation of input.

Updated overview kindly provided by Bill Joiner (January 2009) and reproduced with permission.

Table 8.2b Overview of post-heroic levels of leadership agility – 'stages of awareness'

At each new level of agility, managers retain and go beyond leadership capacities and skills they developed at previous levels. Percentages refer to research-based estimates of the percentage of managers currently capable of operating at each agility level.

Level of agility	Assumptions about leadership	Agility in pivotal conversations	Agility in leading teams	Agility in leading organizational change
Post-heroic levels				
Catalyst (~5%)	*Visionary, facilitative orientation.* Assumes leadership involves articulating an innovative, inspiring vision, then bringing the right people together to transform vision into reality. Leadership is about empowering others – facilitating their development.	Skilled in balancing assertive and accommodative styles as needed in specific situations. Likely to identify and question underlying assumptions, including their own. Genuinely interested in learning from diverse viewpoints. Proactively seeks and utilizes feedback.	Intent on creating a highly participative team. Acts as both team leader and facilitator. Models and seeks open exchange of viewpoints on challenging issues. Empowers direct reports. Team initiatives also for individual development.	Organizational change initiatives often include developing a culture promoting teamwork, participation, and empowerment. Proactive engagement with diverse stakeholders, believing this will increase the quality of decisions, not just gain buy-in.

Co-Creator (~4%)	*Oriented toward shared purpose and collaboration.* Feels that leadership is ultimately a service to others. Includes collaboration with other key leaders to develop a shared vision that gives each meaning and purpose.	Integrates and shows agility in his/her assertive and accommodative sides while engaged in pivotal conversations. Processes and seriously considers negative feedback even when it is highly charged emotionally.	Develops collaborative team leadership, where others feel full responsibility both for their own areas and also for the unit or organization they collectively manage. Prefers consensus decisions but can use authority as needed.	Develops key stakeholder relationships with deep mutual influence and genuine dedication to the common good. Creates companies or units where corporate responsibility and full collaboration are embedded.
Synergist (~1%)	*Holistic orientation.* Experiences leadership as a process of participation in a palpable life purpose that benefits others while also serving as a vehicle for personal transformation.	Centred in expressing assertive and accommodative energies, appropriately. Cultivates a present-centered awareness that augments external feedback and supports a strong, subtle connection with others, even in difficult conversations.	Capable of moving fluidly between varieties of team leadership styles that are uniquely suited to each situation. Shapes or amplifies the energy dynamics at work in particular situations, bringing mutually beneficial results.	Maintains deep, empathetic awareness of own and stakeholder conflicting views and interests. Accesses 'synergistic intuitions' to transform apparently intractable conflicts into mutually beneficial solutions.

Updated overview kindly provided by Bill Joiner (January 2009) and reproduced with permission.

UL/LL and 53 per cent were UR/LR (McEwen and Schmidt, 2007). Further, the contribution made by systems (LR) accounted for only 40 per cent, implying that using a systems approach is 'necessary but not sufficient for success'.

Let us now turn to intimately related concepts of capacities and stages of expanding awareness (Figure 8.2). It is important to note that an individual will be at varying stages in each capacity, because development in each capacity is not even. The practical implications of stages of capacity development are huge; Kegan (1995) argues that 'If a person's stage of awareness is not sufficient for the challenges they face, they will be "in over their heads" with drastic implications for business.' I believe this is a key area for competent coaches to identify and develop in their coachees to demonstrate ROI. However, for some, the concept of hierarchical stages is controversial, usually because they confuse 'evolution hierarchies' with 'dominant hierarchies' (Wilber 2000a: 25–26).

Research on adult development exposes the same trend – as one's awareness expands through progressive stages, one gains an ability to take greater and greater perspectives and to take decisions for wider time spans, influencing more of the business, workforce, competitors and society. Success is a direct reflection of interior capacities and mindsets (McEwen and Schmidt, 2007). In their acclaimed paper, 'Seven transformations of leadership', Rooke and Torbert (2005) show that levels of corporate and individual performance vary according to each individual's stage of personal development.

I use the 'five levels of leadership agility' (Joiner and Josephs, 2007) to echo a capacity related to self-identity. Joiner and Josephs make the case for the 'agility imperative', using their research and real-life stories demonstrating each of their levels (Tables 8.2a and 8.2b). In line with the findings of other developmental researchers, the distribution of agility levels is 90 per cent what they call 'heroic' levels (Table 8.2a) and 10 per cent 'post-heroic' (Table 8.2b). A comparison of the leadership characteristics, conversational skills, team leading and organizational change approaches of heroic and post-heroic types will reveal the benefits of the latter.

Thus far, I've described how both horizontal and vertical dimensions are implicit in integral theory.

USING THE INTEGRAL FRAMEWORK WITH COACHEES

What is a leader or coach who is capable of taking the multiple perspectives of an integral approach like? Kofman (2003) suggested that an integral leader (or coach) is one who resonates very powerfully with all the people he or she encounters and has the ability to touch everybody where they are. Further, such leaders awaken in others the passion for creating something that transcends each of them and involves the wider community. This is challenging to actualize and embody and requires a dedication to self-awareness. I think it is an imperative for coaches wanting to work developmentally to take leaders to these stages of awareness and to know their own limits. Jung argued that 'an analyst [a coach] can help his [coachee] just so far as he himself has gone and not a step further' (Jung, CW 16: 545). Laske (2006) warned that working with a coachee who is at a higher developmental level than the coach may be unethical. He pointed out the prevalence of 'espousal' – coaches using language from a higher level without truly 'inhabiting' it. If coaches could embrace all elements of the integral framework and apply them appropriately, the latter concerns would be eliminated.

Engaging in personal inquiry and exploration is essential if one is to experience the full potential of integral theory. Building the development of coaches, here I encourage a shift in focus from coachee to coach. As a memory aid we can use Wilber's 'AQAL' (pronounced 'ah-qwul'), referring to 'all quadrants, all levels, all lines – states and types', as a way to cover all the elements. A tour of the quadrants is a good way to begin since they are simultaneously arising as four fundamental aspects of our being in the world and four dimensions of any event or situation.

There are two possible ways to use the quadrants as a lens; one is to look from the perspective of all four quadrants (quadrant eyes) and the other is looking from the perspective of a single quadrant. I have developed a quadrant inquiry (Table 8.3) to give a flavour of what can be encountered in each quadrant and to help discover how the quadrants interrelate.

A coach would not always take a coachee through a full quadrant inquiry, but the structure should provide the critical ability to discern where the coachee is in relation to each quadrant as it exists in his or her life and work. Without necessarily revealing it to the coachee, a quadrant inquiry can be used as a template to discover the beliefs, assumptions, mindsets and mental models the coachee holds (UL). Information gathered about the UL is a foundation for examining behaviours and competencies (UR). In work or general contexts we use the information from UL and UR to examine the relationships between the coachee's mental models and his or her behaviours in relation to the organization's culture (LL), work environment and systems (LR). Volckmann (2003) stresses that when we are coaching leaders, our challenge is to help them to clarify all these variables on the basis of their own recognition of how their current perspectives can be leveraged for learning.

Table 8.3 Quadrant inquiry suggestions

UL – individual subjective	UR – individual objective
▌ Sit, stand or lie. Take a deep breath. Use your favourite relaxation or meditation method to become still. Adopt the perspective of a detached observer and check inside for sensations, feelings, thoughts, drives and impulses. Just notice them. ▌ Energy state tracking: as you go about your daily activities simultaneously notice where your attention goes. Notice your energy state – is it resourceful or unresourceful, high energy or low energy? (Loehr & Schwartz, 2005) ▌ Take an inventory of aspirations and desires. ▌ Record your remembered dreams on waking (a useful route to shadow awareness). ▌ Practice a daily or weekly review of your predominant motivations and intentions over that period. ▌ Do a decade-by-decade life review and note the memories that stand out – the events that shaped your self-image. ▌ Contemplate the question 'Who am I'? Notice your attachments to various identities. ▌ What assumptions do I automatically make? How can I check these? ▌ What does what I think and believe about others tell me about myself? (Shadow – Wilber, 1979)	▌ Slowly scan your body to notice the physical sensations at each point. ▌ Do some stretches or exercise and notice any change in the sensations. Sense the 'field' around you. Try to become aware of the subtle and causal energy in your body and around you. ▌ Familiarize yourself with your physiology and anatomy and pay attention to it. ▌ How does your body respond to stress? Notice what your body holds or carries and how it builds or clears. ▌ Review your rest, recovery and renewal, and sleep-management regimes. ▌ How hydrated are you throughout the day? Do you ensure a balance of nutrition and exercise? ▌ How do others experience your behaviour, demeanour, body language and responses to situations? ▌ Do you have the necessary practical skills for living well? ▌ What objective metrics or feedback can you acquire on body, personality traits, competencies and skills? ▌ Have a health check-up and consider using both conventional and complementary professionals.

QUADRANT INQUIRY

Becoming familiar with the territory of each quadrant is not a one-off event. It requires a form of regular reflective inquiry (see Table 8.3) as a cumulative recognisance exercise aided by quiet reflection, journalling

Table 8.3 *Continued*

LL – collective subjective	LR – collective objective
█ Consider the values of your culture, your family of origin, your community.	█ What systems do you interact with? (Legal, national, local, political etc.)
█ What collective beliefs predominate where you live and work?	█ Consider the chain of processes that provide your food, energy, transport, water, healthcare etc.
█ Listen to different broadcasting and media sources and notice the often contradictory implicit views and attitudes they hold. Notice how you identify or disidentify with them.	█ What is your relationship and involvement in your immediate community, country and globally?
█ Notice when and how the pronoun 'we' is used in groups or in conversations. .	█ How do you live and interact in your ecosystem?
█ Where do you feel you can experience belonging and membership?	█ What relationship and responsibility do you take in the systems you work with (policies, procedures, laws, regulations etc)?
█ What rituals and symbols are in your life? Do you celebrate traditions, festivals and communal events?	█ How effective is the way you organize your life, patterns of working and processes for living?
█ What is your relationship to popular culture?	█ What is your carbon footprint?
█ What visions and values do you share with others?	█ What is the impact of decisions you make and your daily actions on the wider community and planet?
█ What is your sense of sharing in collective responsibility?	█ What people networks and community links help you in your life's goals and purpose?
█ In what ways are you dependent and interdependent?	█ How do you manage and relate to your competitors or 'outsiders'?
█ How do you relate to others in groups?	█ What's your relationship with technology?

and discussion. Hence, we consciously seek to identify our unconscious values and deeply held beliefs, assumptions and automatic patterns of thinking and acting. A daily practice of as little as one minute's silence (Boroson, 2007) can yield noticeable increases in awareness.

I suggest in Table 8.3 questions for a personal 'quadrant inquiry' (Egan, 2009). Which quadrants tend to be your preferred way of perceiving the world? How does this appear in your life? I usually find, almost like a typology, that we have a dominant quadrant that attracts the lion's share of our attention. There is value in being aware which one comes naturally and in discovering the costs of not giving sufficient attention to the others. In this way, one can gradually gain more mastery of the ways an occurrence in one quadrant impacts on the others. Volckmann (2003) offers some integrating questions that build on my quadrant inquiry (Table 8.3):

▊ What are the implications for your own self-management, your own learning, the relationship between what you say is important and the actions you are taking?
▊ What are the implications for your own alignment with the culture of the organization, and of the large network it is a part of?
▊ What are the implications for how your actions integrate with those of others to foster the effectiveness of the system?
▊ What are the implications for the evolution of the system, itself?

These demanding questions are not for the coachee who seeks gentle affirmation, but when used in a safe 'holding' (Winnicott, 1972) context within a solid working alliance they can transform the leader's capacity for critical self-reflection and self-management. Applying a quadrant lens is a structured way of deepening our encounter with self, other and organization – essential territory for leadership mastery. A fruitful awareness practice during the day is to pause occasionally and notice which quadrant has your focus.

There is a simplification of the quadrant framework that gives an easily applicable in-the-moment coaching and self-management tool; it reduces the quadrants to the encounter with self, other and organization. By merging the UR and LR we get three catch-all dimensions of 'I' (self, UL), 'we' (other, LL) and 'it' (task, system, UR/LR). This can be seen as the three sides of an equilateral triangle (Figure 8.4).

Axialent Inc, co-founded by Kofman (2006) to offer integrally informed consulting, combines the 'I–we–it' framework with a 'Be–Do–Have' model (Taylor, 2005). The principle is that when we pay enough attention to our 'Being' – how we are – this informs what we Do and

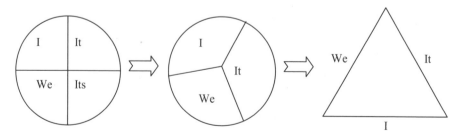

Figure 8.4 A simplified application of quadrants as 'I-we-it' and the 'equilateral triangle'

results (Have) follow. Put differently, the UL is the foundation of UR but they are interdependent. In coaching, we then seek to help coachees to give equal attention to 'I–we–it' in all their endeavours. Finding ways to keep the triangle equal-sided, to achieve balance among the 'I', 'we' and 'it' dimensions of a coachee's situation, complements the 'Be–Do–Have' philosophy. In many situations, as the case study below demonstrates, the 'I–we–it' dimensions become unbalanced, with sub-optimal consequences in all dimensions. For example, the intended outcome ('it') is compromised, the coachees' relationships ('we') may become strained or broken whilst their self-satisfaction and integrity ('I') also suffer.

Continuing to apply AQAL to the coaching process we move on to 'stages of expanding awareness'. I find that I can make a working approximation of stage through conversations within the 'I–we–it' framework. I try to notice and check to understand the coachees' primary motivations and indications of their predominant world view (Laske, 2006; Kalman, 2007b). The degrees of leadership agility (Tables 8.2a and 8.2b) that a coachee demonstrates in specific situations provide hints of the stretch into later agility levels. I try to cultivate an 'I–Thou' relationship (Buber, 1958) and my experience of relationship with a coachee also tells me about his or her capacities and relative development. Once we make a rough map of the territory we can mutually agree explicit potential development areas.

In the assessment phase, where continual mutual checking is necessary, a critical distinction has to be made between horizontal and vertical development needs. On the one hand, horizontal development is about growth within the confines and frames of reference of an existing mindset or worldview, typically gaining more knowledge or skills. Vertical development, on the other hand, is about capacity shifts from current mindsets to wider, more expanded perspectives capable of holding greater complexity. Put another way, horizontal development is all about translation and vertical development is all about transformation (Wilber, 1997). I believe that impactful leadership coaching must be more about transformation than translation. However, coaches may decide that only horizontal development is within their scope, or that coachees are not likely to want to develop vertically (Kegan and Lahey, 2009). To help leaders to work productively with their challenges, coaches need a comprehensive framework to open creativity and develop their understanding of the coachees' complexity, their motivations and relationships to their challenges.

Kegan (1995) develops what is meant by transformation by asking: 'What form is transforming? What is the form that is undergoing some gradual or dramatic reconstruction of its parts into what is really a new whole?' He goes on to say of this process that 'the great embarrassment or liberation of transformation itself is the recognition that what we have been taking as reality is actually only a construction of reality.' This is the territory of vertical development: a breaking down of the old and breaking through of the new in an unfolding cycle of transcend, embrace and include. I do not believe that it can be achieved through coaching (or therapy) alone but through a conscious engagement with living, meaning making and dedicated commitment to awareness, consciousness and purpose.

The five levels (stages) of leadership agility show both horizontal and vertical development in action for leaders (Table 8.2). With the appropriate developmental support and challenge, coaches can help leaders to transform the ways they make meaning of events and experiences and combine forces with an archetypal current to 'transcend and include'. Supporting leaders through shifts in their leadership capacity is like being a midwife to the natural unfolding of their own capacities as they progress in their lives.

An AQAL coaching experience touches both horizontal and vertical aspects of development. Following AQAL in coaching is not sequential but iterative, where we gather data, update the overall picture and re-examine. Using an AQAL inquiry also helps both coach and coachee to select which capacities they may wish to develop relative to their most developed one. The Integral Institute developed an Integral Life Practice programme with specific exercises designed to work on each capacity in a balanced AQAL way. Coaches already use tools and techniques, the precision and potency of which can be enhanced by assessing which capacities they address and which new 'stage' they develop. The summaries of low, medium and high development in each capacity (Table 8.1) indicate the developmental challenges at each stage.

In the quadrant inquiry (Table 8.3) I only touched briefly on 'states'; coaching for state management can help coachees to begin to master and take responsibility for their own states (emotional, mental, energy, alertness, physical and others). Since states are often confused with stages, there is a crucial point to stress about the difference between them. States are transitory, passing conditions that come with their own frequency or pattern, whereas a stage is the actual 'structure' of one's current stage of awareness (the mindset that interprets states). Some state experiences, for example in the spiritual capacity, can give a glimpse of a later stage of awareness but this must not be confused with a permanent stage structure (Wilber, 2003a). Increasing one's 'state' awareness and repeatedly cultivating more awakened states can eventually lead to a breakthrough to the next unfolding stage.

Having considered quadrants, capacities, stages of awareness and states, all that remains for an AQAL inquiry is 'type'. I will not expand on type here as there are many typing tools to choose from (Myers Briggs, NLP (McNab, 2005) primary rep systems, brain dominance, masculine/feminine).

CASE STUDY

A 40-year-old executive, whom I will call Brian, wanted to reach 'the next level of [his] game' because he struggled with other leaders during meetings. His circumstances are summarized in Table 8.4. We aimed to increase his self-awareness (UL) and self-management, including emotional self-control, transparency in communication and adaptability (UR). He said he wanted to develop a service orientation and resonance with team members and greater organizational awareness (LR); challenges included influencing and developing his team, change management, dispute settlement and wider company collaboration (LR). We focused on increasing alignment between inner and outer reality, between collective and individual. The aim was for Brian to recognize his own relationship between interior (his beliefs and feelings) and exterior (his behaviours and responses) and to notice if they were aligned or misaligned.

Brian had a well-developed ability for forethought, abstract thinking and using metaphor, which allowed me to appeal to his cognitive capacity to get his interest in other capacities. His cognitive capacity was less developed than his emotional capacity, while his interpersonal capacity seemed well developed in an everyday sense. Through building trust and rapport, I was able to encourage self-compassion and an attitude of self-respect for his emotional and interior world. I inferred that his moral capacity was healthy. Music and a sense of deep connectedness with nature, life-force or energy gave him a sense of transcendence and immanence – an expression of his spiritual capacity. Later we discovered that he found this too in his intimate relationships and in quiet moments.

What I have introduced so far came from one meeting based on a cursory AQAL investigation. An essential source of data was myself – I used 'self-as-instrument'. Put differently, I learned about Brian by listening compassionately and enquiring about what 'really' mattered behind what he said and did. I tried to see Brian clearly as separate and unique, with different psychology and experiences. This required me to let go my own identity whilst a part of my mind was testing what I heard but not 'doing' anything, and waiting for what wanted to emerge (Sharmer, 2007). I will now present an example where Brian found the 'I–we–it' model helped identify and achieve his goals.

The company was planning to introduce a new client management system that seemed to have popular consent from most of the executives.

Table 8.4 AQAL summary of coachee's situation

Interior Subjective		Exterior Objective	
UL quadrant	LL quadrant	UR quadrant	LR quadrant
▮ Motivated to work on self ▮ Reasonable capacity for self reflection ▮ Mood – state management challenges ▮ Reactive in some work situations ▮ Self-confident ▮ Reluctant to reveal weakness or vulnerability	▮ An achievement culture where hitting targets and 'winning' is all ▮ Regular client entertainment dinners ▮ Friday drinks a ritual ▮ Relationship with stakeholders	▮ Six-figure salary ▮ 50-hour week ▮ Postgraduate qualifications ▮ Healthy and physically fit ▮ Clear account targets ▮ 360° feedback collected – experienced as either blunt and inflexible or avoidant ▮ Effectiveness at motivating some staff? ▮ Successful track record	▮ Commute to work ▮ Comfortable office ▮ Responsible for international team ▮ Frequent travel ▮ Global clients ▮ Married with children ▮ Hierarchy/matrix organization ▮ Ability to realize his own influence in the system? ▮ Economic market
Capacities and stages (lines and levels)	Cognitive – well developed Emotional (intrapersonal) – lagging relative to cognitive Interpersonal – well developed outside 'difficult conversations' Moral – no signs of cause for concern Spiritual – not consciously focused on but a good foundation Physical (kinesthetic) – very fit but room to learn how to use sensation as an inner information source		
States	Emotional state management was a priority		
Type	Characteristics indicative of personality type A. Seemed to prefer extroverting to introverting, and was more automatically 'masculine' at work.		

Brian was not in favour since he believed he would not meet his targets as a result of disruptions. Nonetheless, he did not believe that it was possible for him to go against the CEO and the others. Although not communicating his concerns verbally, Brian's mood at work these past weeks showed all was not well.

When I asked what he really wanted to happen, Brian said he hoped the project would be postponed until he transferred to another division. I helped him to see that when he got into unresourceful states, he regressed to earlier 'stages of awareness'. I spent about 10 minutes on body-focused breath work (UR and UL) to create a 'grounded' state. My next objective was for Brian to get a detached external perspective on his mental models and mindset and to imagine how the situation might look from higher levels of leadership agility.

By applying the 'I–we–it' model and taking an expanded perspective, Brian saw potential for a positive outcome. With that in mind, we examined how Brian would like to proceed in relation to 'I–we–it'. Initially, for the 'I'-dimension, he wanted to 'tell them' how bad it was going to be; for the 'we' he wanted them to understand his concerns; and for the 'it' he wanted to delay the upgrade. Notice how each point has a personal focus – a 'me–me' perspective. It was as if his desired outcome was the only focus for 'I–we–it'!

I helped Brian to 'park' his outcome focus and to attend to the process and immediate territory of 'I–we–it'. What was it that really mattered to him? What was his personal truth here ('I')? What kind of relationship did he want to maintain with the CEO and colleagues ('we')? For the task ('it') of deciding about the upgrade, how would he like to do it justice? With a new perspective, Brian re-examined what he wanted for 'I–we–it'. For 'I', he wanted to honestly express his concern about the impact on his targets; for 'we', he wanted to maintain relationships through open mutual listening and sharing of each other's needs and concerns; and for 'it' he wanted to ensure he left 'no stone unturned' before taking the decision. This seemed a realistic, 'high-level' starting point. We then rehearsed the conversation Brian might end up having with the CEO until he felt able to do justice to his 'I–we–it' objectives. The interpersonal and emotional risks Brian was taking with me were exactly the risks he needed to take as a leader – personal disclosure, honest expression (restraint even), engagement and participation.

Brian had the conversation and negotiated a timeframe and a mutual agreement that he believed was superior for 'self, other and company'. He communicated to resolve potential conflict, exercised self-management and engagement with self, other and organization. Through integrally informed coaching, Brian learned how to develop a better quadrant balance for himself. He found synergy in listening to himself and relating more fully to others. Coaching helped achieve the comprehensive aims we set (UL, UR, LL and LR – case study, paragraph 1) at the outset. He regarded this as a significant ROI for himself. It also provided increased benefits to his company, family and community.

He continued to maintain more resourceful states and to act 'as-if' he were operating from a later level. Within a year, in leadership agility terms, Brian had 'broken through' from achiever to catalyst – a level reached by only 5 per cent of leaders (Table 8.2).

CONCLUSIONS

Wilber's work provides a map showing how all disciplines weave together to form a total tapestry. Familiarity with an integral approach will allow coaches and leaders to maximize their understanding of all elements that impact on effectiveness and leadership development. Wilber argues that fragmented, incomplete development approaches are inadequate for the 21st century (Egan, 2008). This chapter has offered one way in which leaders in business and government can engage with integral thinking and apply it to the challenges they face.

Coaching for leadership implies possible development requirements in a broad range of core capacities necessary to meet the challenges of leaders' roles (Oliver, 2009). Until both horizontal development and vertical development are considered in performance assessments and leadership coaching, the long-term effectiveness of leaders will remain compromised.

ACKNOWLEDGEMENTS

I am grateful to Billy Desmond (www.yourpotentiality.co.uk) for his input on the quadrant summary. Thanks also to Matthew Kalman (www.integralstrategies.org) and John Oliver (www.human-equity.com) for their comments on the manuscript. Special thanks go to Bill Joiner for providing the Leadership Agility data.

References

Benefiel, M (2008) *The Soul of a Leader: Finding your path to success and fulfillment*, Crossroad Publishing, New York

Boroson, M (2007) *The One Minute Master: Stillness for people on the go*, Mass Market Paperback

Buber, M (1958) *I and Thou*, translated by Ronald Gregor Smith, Charles Scribner's Sons, New York

Cashman, K (2001) *Leadership from the Inside Out: Becoming a leader for life*, Executive Excellence Publishing, Provo, UT

Covey, S R (1992) *Principle Centered Leadership*, Free Press, New York

Egan, M (2008) Integral leadership for the 21st century: a multidimensional, comprehensive, experiential approach, paper delivered at the Embracing Excellence International Conference, Association for Coaching, London

Egan, M (2009) [online] http://integrallifecom/member/martin-egan/blog

Erikson, E H (1950) *Childhood and Society*, new edn 1995, Vintage, London

Forman, J (2006) Personal communication; John is a founding member of the Integral Institute, and a founder and the Managing Partner of Integral Development Associates; for more information, see IDA's website at www. integraldevelopment.com

Fowler, J (1987) *Faith Development and Pastoral Care*, Fortress Press, Philadelphia, PA

Fuhs, C (2008) Towards a vision of integral leadership: a quadrivial analysis of eight leadership books, *Journal of Integral Theory and Practice*, **3** (1), spring, pp 139–62

Gardner, H (1983) *Frames of Mind: The theory of multiple intelligences*, Basic Books, New York

Gardner, H (2000) *Intelligence Reframed: Multiple intelligences for the 21st century*, Basic Books, New York

Goleman, D, Boyatzis, R E and McKee, A (2004) *Primal Leadership: Learning to lead with emotional intelligence*, Harvard Business School Press, Boston, MA

Hardt, J V (2005) [online] http://wwwbiocybernautcom/documentation/ spiritualSci/halohtm#nav1top

Hatala, R J and Hatala, L M (2004) *Integrative Leadership: Building a foundation for personal, interpersonal and organizational success*, Integrative Leadership Institute, Alberta, Canada

Hunt, J (2009) The spring issue of *AQAL Journal of Integral Theory and Practice* is dedicated to research from Integral Coaching Canada [online] (www. integralinstitute.org) (www.integralcoachingcanada.com)

Integral Institute (2005) *AQAL Journal of Integral Theory and Practice*, peer reviewed and published quarterly [online] www.integralinstitute.org

Integral Institute (2006) Resources are available to members: http:// multiplexintegralinstituteorg/Public/cs/files/43/business_and_leadership/ defaultaspx

Joiner, W B and Josephs, S A (2007) *Leadership Agility: Five levels of mastery for anticipating and initiating change*, Jossey-Bass, San Francisco, CA

Jung, C G (CW 16) *The Realities of Practical Psychotherapy, Collected Works 16: The practice of psychotherapy*, 1966 edition, Princeton, NJ

Kalman, M (2007a) [online] http://wwwintegralstrategiesorg/ whatisintegralhtml#leaders

Kalman, M (2007b) Kalman's kosmos, *Integral Leadership Review*, **8** (2) (March) [online] http://wwwintegralleadershipreviewcom/archives/2007-03/2007-03-kalmanphp

Kegan, R (1995) *In Over Our Heads: Mental demands of modern life*, Harvard University Press, Boston, MA

Kegan, R and Lahey, L (2009) *Immunity to Change: How to overcome it and unlock the potential in yourself and your organization*, Center of Public Leadership, Harvard Business School Press, Boston, MA

Kofman, F (2003) Interview with Russ Volckmann [online] http:// integralleadershipreviewcom/archives/2003/2003_03_kofmanhtml

Kofman, F (2006) *Conscious Business: How to build value through values*, book and abridged CD set, Sounds True, Boulder, CO

Laske, O (2006) *Measuring Hidden Dimensions: The art and science of fully engaging adults*, Interdevelomental Institute Press, Medford, MA, see also [online] http:// interdevelopmentalsorg/pubs/IDM-OLaske-Contributions-of-Evidence-based-Coachingpdf

Loehr, J and Schwartz, T (2005) *The Power of Full Engagement*, Free Press, New York

McEwen, C A and Schmidt, J D (2007) *Leadership and the Corporate Sustainability Challenge*, Mindsets in Action report [online] http:// wwwavastoneconsultingcom/MindsetsInActionReporthtml

McNab, P (2005) *Towards an Integral Vision: Using NLP and Ken Wilber's AQAL model to enhance communication*, Traford, Victoria, Canada, see also [online] www.excellenceforall.co.uk

Merzel, D G (2007) *Big Mind Big Heart: Finding your way*, Big Mind Publishing, Salt Lake City, UT

Oliver, J (2009) Has conducted organizational research on development and company performance [online] www.human-equity.com

Pert, C B (1999) *Molecules of Emotion: The science behind mind–body medicine*, Simon & Schuster, London

Piaget, J and Inhelder, B (1958) *The Growth of Logical Thinking from Childhood to Adolescence*, Basic Books, New York

Rooke, D and Torbert, W R (2005) Seven transformations of leadership, *Harvard Business Review*, **83** (4) (April), pp 66–76

Sharmer, O C (2007) *Theory U: Leading from the future as it emerges*, SoL, the Society for Organizational Learning, Cambridge, MA

Taylor, C (2005) *Walking the Talk: Building a culture for success*, Random House Business Books, London

Torbert, W (2004) *The Secret of Timely and Transforming Leadership*, Berrett-Koehler, San Francisco, CA

Volckmann, R (2003) Leadership coaching tip, *Integral Leadership Review*, **3** (3) (March), [online] http://www.leadcoach.com/archives/e-journal/2003/2003_03.html

Wilber, K (1979) *No Boundary: Eastern and Western approaches to personal growth*, Center Press, Los Angeles, CA

Wilber, K (1996–2007) For a light introduction I recommend *The Integral Vision: A very short introduction to the revolutionary integral approach to life, God, the universe, and everything*, Shambhala, 2007. Wilber (2000) focuses on what integral theory has to offer business, politics, science and spirituality. Wilber

(1996) is in a thorough and accessible Q & A format. Wilber (1999) focuses on psychology.

Wilber, K (1996) *A Brief History of Everything*, Shambhala, Boston, MA (new edn, Gateway, 2001)

Wilber, K (1997) A spirituality that transforms, *What is Enlightenment*, 12, august–winter [online] http://www.enlightennext.org/magazine/j12/wilberasp

Wilber, K (1999a) *Integral Psychology*, Shambhala, Boston, MA

Wilber, K (1999b) *One Taste: Daily reflections on integral spirituality*, Shambhala, Boston, MA

Wilber, K (2000a) *A Theory of Everything: An integral vision for business, politics, science, and spirituality*, Shambhala, Boston, MA (new edn, Gateway, 2001)

Wilber, K (2000b) A summary of my psychological model [online] http://wilber. shambhala.com/html/bookx/psych_model/psych_model10.cfm/

Wilber, K (2003a) *Kosmic Consciousness*, audio CD, Sounds True, Boulder, CO

Wilber, K (2003b) *Waves, Streams, States, and Self: A summary of my psychological model (or, outline of an integral psychology)* [online] http://wilber.shambhala. com/

Wilber, K *et al* (2004) [online] http://holons-news.com/free/whatisintegralpdf – a version of the general integral introduction

Wilber, K (2006) *Integral Spirituality: A startling new role for religion in the modern and postmodern world*, Integral Books, Boston and London

Winnicott, D (1972) *Holding and Interpretation: Fragment of an analysis*, Hogarth Press, London

9

Coaching political leaders

Professor Jean Hartley and Kate Pinder

INTRODUCTION

In this chapter we consider the coaching relationship, and its contexts, processes and outcomes when coaching takes place with elected politicians. Elected politicians undertake their roles at local, devolved, national or international level. They may be senior leaders (eg ministers, council leaders, mayors) as well as representatives of communities and constituencies. They may be in political control, in opposition or in coalition. If they hold different political roles they may experience control, opposition and coalition simultaneously, for example, if they are political representatives at county and district local authority level, whilst their political party is in opposition at national level. In whatever role, formal political authority carries with it particular responsibilities and vulnerabilities that distinguish it from managerial leadership (where most of the research and practice on coaching has taken place).

The work of the coach is therefore to be sensitive to the particular contexts, role demands and expectations (from self and a variety of publics and other stakeholders) of the elected political leader. We examine this through a leadership model that conceptualizes the contexts, the challenges and the capabilities of political leadership. In other words, our model does not focus solely on the characteristics of individuals and their self-development but places this in a socially constructed view of leadership whereby effective leadership is concerned with being able to 'read the context' (and sometimes shape it), focus on key priorities (challenges) and acquire or enhance the skills and behaviours to achieve the key tasks of leadership. The chapter illustrates key points about coaching with politicians, using a case study of political leadership in local government.

THE LEADERSHIP MODEL

Leadership is viewed in this model not solely as a set of individual skills, nor solely as a particular authority role (eg council leader, leader of the opposition) – though both of these are important. The main focus in this model is on leadership as a set of social processes of influencing and motivating individuals and groups, and of shaping goals and outcomes amongst diverse stakeholders through influence, persuasion and negotiation. A useful definition of leadership is 'the reciprocal process of mobilizing, by persons with certain motives and values, various economic, political, and other resources, in a context of competition and conflict, in order to realize goals independently or mutually held by both leaders and followers.' (Burns, 1978: 425).

The work of Heifetz (1994) is valuable for its emphasis on leadership as an active process of working with individuals, groups, communities and organizations. He makes the distinction between technical and adaptive problems or challenges, which require different approaches to the leadership task. Technical leadership is appropriate where the problem is fairly well understood and where there is an agreed course of action. Here, leadership is based on bringing together and energizing resources and people to achieve agreed goals – leadership as a type of project management. However, adaptive leadership is needed where the challenge is complex and where different individuals or groups may not agree either on what the problem is or how it can be tackled. Many of the complex cross-cutting problems of contemporary society are of this type (eg community safety, alcohol-related violence, public transport) and require the ability to lead and shape changes in attitudes, values and behaviours. A great deal of political leadership is concerned with adaptive leadership: that is, influencing individuals and groups to engage in difficult problem definition and problem-solving choices. Such choices often need the active engagement from those involved in the issue (for example, crime will not be solved solely by legislation or by more police; its reduction requires active work by citizens). This requires the management of influence beyond the organizational boundaries, influencing partnerships and alliances (Hartley and Fletcher, 2008). Nicklen (2008) builds on this in relation to coaching, arguing that the coach needs to take account of the different organizations and systems, conditions and tasks to be achieved by the leader.

Nicklen gives four different case studies to illustrate his point that leadership will vary 'depending on the organizational and broader systemic contexts'. We suggest that elected political leadership has to use all of Nicklen's types of leadership. First, what he calls managerial leadership, which is where the problem is known and is (mainly) rational – for instance, where choice has to be made between two options to achieve the same objective. Second, he introduces adaptive leadership – using the organization's (and we would add citizens' and other stakeholders') ability to learn and to address tough choices, perhaps by setting broad aims for the elected term and encouraging others to join the debate about how the matter might be addressed. Third, political leadership – he uses the case study of a failing school having to be closed and the need to mobilize support from a sufficient number of stakeholders, whatever their personal interests. Finally, he outlines emergent leadership where the precise approach to leadership may need to change as the problem changes – for example, leading in the context of budget uncertainties and changes in local authorities facing huge budget changes due to a major economic recession.

Others have pointed to the complex landscape for the leadership work of politicians (eg Morrell and Hartley, 2006; Leach *et al*, 2005; Leach and Wilson, 2000). This means that a leadership model for use in coaching has to be sufficiently complex to capture some of the tensions and paradoxes in the role, while also enabling clarity and focus to act on the part of the leader.

The leadership model has three main elements:

▌   the contexts within which leadership is exercised;
▌   the challenges that political leaders are aiming to achieve in a variety of arenas;
▌   the capabilities (sometimes called competencies, or skills, mindsets and behaviours) that are associated with effective performance.

Contexts

It is misleading and unhelpful if leadership theories are expressed as universals, appropriate in all circumstances. The context can be very important (Hartley, in press; Grint, 2005; Porter and McLaughlin, 2006) and leadership theories increasingly examine the interaction between context and leader. For political leadership, the significance of context has been emphasized by a number of writers. Leach *et al* (2005: 70) write that 'context is not immutable and there are opportunities for the role of political leadership in shaping . . . change, often over an extended period of time.'

In political leadership, there is an important skill in being able to 'read' the context appropriately, both observing and reflecting on change, and also knowing whether the degree and pace of change suggests action or inaction at this particular juncture. In this leadership model, we emphasize five key aspects of context: the political, the economic, the social, the technological and the environmental contexts, with questions about how far the political leader takes these issues into account in working as an elected politician.

Challenges

Leadership is increasingly exercised not only inside the organization but also outside it, with other groups and organizations (Hartley and Fletcher, 2008). This is particularly true for political leadership (Morrell and Hartley, 2006; Simpson, 2008). The leadership model utilizes the framework of there being four arenas of civic leadership, developed by Taylor (1993) and subsequently tested in research (Hartley, 2002). However, our work has added a fifth arena, in that most political leaders have also to pay time and attention to the political party of which they are a member. Of course some politicians, particularly in Scotland and Wales, are elected as independents but even they may have to take account of a coalition of political members' interests if they wish to effect change. These five arenas are shown in Figure 9.1.

Figure 9.1 shows the arenas as involving challenges or tasks in:

▌ shaping and supporting the development of grass-roots communities;
▌ negotiating and mobilizing effective partnerships with other public, private and voluntary agencies: in other words, lateral inter-organizational leadership;
▌ voicing the needs and interests of the local community in regional, national, European and international arenas: in other words, vertical inter-organizational leadership;
▌ governing the public service organization and giving its services clear strategic direction;
▌ working within the political party group, both locally and within the governing body, and developing political coalitions as appropriate.

The analysis of arenas is important because it suggests that political leaders have a number of tasks to undertake in a variety of settings

Arenas of Civic Leadership

Figure 9.1 Challenges of political leadership: the five arenas in which the challenges or tasks of leadership take place

(cf Leach and Wilson, 2000; Leach *et al*, 2005; Hartley, 2002). Having to balance competing priorities across a range of arenas and with different stakeholders is a key pressure for political leaders.

Capabilities

Boyatzis (1982) identified various personal qualities (competencies) such as skills, mindsets, values and behaviours that contribute to effective performance. He suggested a framework for thinking about competencies not only as capabilities of the individual but set in the context both of job demands and of the organizational environment. This reinforces our conceptual approach, which includes context and challenges. We have used the term capabilities rather than competencies as a way of looking at individual skills and mindsets that is more compatible with the cultures of political leadership. The 10 dimensions are derived from research and tested with many political leaders in local government (Hartley, Fletcher and Benington ,in press) and are shown in Table 9.1.

THE RESEARCH UNDERPINNING THE LEADERSHIP MODEL

There is a substantial research base for the leadership model, both in its conceptual components and in terms of its practical use with elected

Table 9.1 Ten capability dimensions of effective political leadership

---

▌ Public service values (the extent to which you make clear the public service values that underpin your work)

▌ Questioning thinking (the extent to which you challenge yourself and others in ideas and suggestions)

▌ Decision making (your effectiveness at making decisions)

▌ Personal effectiveness (your skills at dealing with others and in your own self-awareness and self-control)

▌ Strategic thinking and action (the extent to which you think and act strategically in your work)

▌ Advocacy and representation (your skills at representing others)

▌ Political intelligence (the degree to which you show astuteness and political awareness)

▌ Communication (your skills in listening and talking)

▌ Organisational mobilization (your ability to bring about major changes in your organization)

▌ Systems and tasks (the degree to which you are able to ensure the implementation of policies and practices)

© Hartley and Fletcher, 2005.

politicians. In conceptual terms, the literature on leadership, on political leadership development and on community leadership has been reviewed (eg Hartley, 2002; Morrell and Hartley, 2006; Hartley, in press). Second, 110 interviews with political leaders from 65 councils were conducted, and group discussions with local politicians on the national (English and Welsh) Leadership Academy for councillors. Third, effective political leadership was examined not only from the perspective of the politicians themselves but also in interviews with 21 informed senior managers from other organizations who worked closely with political leaders (Hartley and Morgan-Thomas, 2003). A review of leadership capabilities needed by Scottish local government politicians also confirmed the capabilities element of the leadership model (Hartley and Fletcher, 2007).

The political leadership model has been operationalized as a development tool in both a self-assessment and a 360° format for local government politicians, which has been extensively researched. This tool, the Warwick Political Leadership Questionnaire (Hartley and Fletcher, 2005), has been used successfully in three of the UK countries with local politicians and is being modified for use with national politicians. It is an effective adjunct to coaching. Coaching may take place with politicians preceding, following or without the use of the Warwick Political Leadership Questionnaire (WPLQ).

A political leadership booklet (Pinder and Hartley, 2005) provides a range of practical suggestions about how particular skills may be strengthened as well as short vignettes from a range of elected politicians about how they have improved their skills. It assists a politician with practical guidance on creating a personal development plan and also supports the idea that development can occur in a range of ways. The coach may refer to this in the coaching session(s).

There is a substantial research base for the WPLQ (Hartley and Morgan-Thomas, 2003; Hartley and Fletcher, 2005) in that it was piloted with 70 senior political leaders and then completed by a further 201 elected local politicians. Statistical tests on these data substantiated the model of contexts, challenges and capabilities. It has also been used in a major research project on local political leadership with 47 senior elected members from nine local authorities where interviews and case study analysis were successfully triangulated and the model tested (Leach *et al*, 2005).

USING THE MODEL WITH COACHEES

Political leadership is a serious business in numerical terms. There are about 120 ministers in the UK Government (in both Houses), 646 MPs in the House of Commons and over 700 lords in the House of Lords, and 297 elected members of the devolved parliaments and assemblies of the UK. At UK local government level, there are over 22,000 councillors in England, 1,222 in Scotland, 1,264 in Wales and 582 in Northern Ireland (according to the Electoral Commission website). There are 78 European Parliament members representing the UK regions. In the United States, at local government level alone, there are 87,000 local governments, including 3,034 counties, 19,498 municipalities, 16,500 townships, 13,500 school districts and 35,000 other special districts that deal with issues like fire protection. Adding state and federal level politicians swells those numbers further.

Furthermore, many politicians will be leading large organizations. For example, a UK secretary of state, such as the Home Secretary, has a budget of £9.2 billion (as at 2007–08). They are also responsible for a staff of many thousands. At local authority level, the largest council has a staff of about 50,000 (FTE), with a billion-pound budget, while the smallest employs in the region of 400 staff. Public sector organizations are indeed 'big business' (see also Hartley and Skelcher, 2008).

Politicians vary by demographic characteristics (age, gender, length of experience as politicians) and also by their political party and its institutional arrangements, by the characteristics of their organization (eg type and size of council or government department) and by their role (being in opposition brings a very different set of roles and tasks from being in political control). These have to be taken into account in the coaching focus and set of processes. The coach needs a reasonable understanding of, and curiosity about, the political institutions, processes, practices and cultures within which politicians operate. What is astute or effective leadership in one political institution may not be so in another. What works in England may not work in Scotland, let alone in countries with very different political institutions and processes such as the United States, Sweden, France or Germany.

LEADERSHIP DEVELOPMENT FOR POLITICIANS

Until the last decade or so, the idea of leadership development for politicians, in the sense of explicitly addressing leadership skills and needs, was rare. It was not countenanced because many politicians saw themselves as mandated by their political party, their election manifesto and the electorate so that leadership development was irrelevant (see box below).

360: What's a 360?

Transcript. Public Administration Select Committee, (PASC) of the House of Commons.

Discussion between Charles Walker, MP, member of PASC, and the Cabinet Secretary, Sir Gus O'Donnell, a witness.

Mr Walker: What is a 360 degree review?

Sir Gus O'Donnell: You have never heard of a 360 degree review?

Mr Walker: No.

Sir Gus O'Donnell: If you are, say, a middle manager in the Civil Service a 360 degree review means that all of the people who work for you, your peers at the same level and those who work above you will fill in forms about what it is like working with you and your strengths and weaknesses. That information would be passed confidentially to a third party who would put it together and say that is what the people who work with you think and identify the things that you need to improve. I can strongly recommend it.

Mr Walker: I can assure you that it will never happen in my case.

Many politicians report learning through bitter experience. In the past, a number of national politicians in the UK have reported going straight from the backbenches to being junior ministers with only a red box thrust into their hands, while those in the House of Lords are sometimes 'catapulted into politics' by becoming a peer and a minister in the same week.

On the other hand, politicians who come from a professional or managerial background may well be familiar with leadership development from their employment experience and be keen to engage with coaching and other means of improving their effectiveness. Thus, a challenge for a coach is to handle the range of understanding and acceptance of leadership development, and coaching in particular, amongst politicians.

While in the past politicians have lacked opportunities for formal leadership development, the situation is starting to change. Leading-edge practice started with some local authorities, which have analysed and developed the leadership skills of local politicians from the mid-1990s onwards. For national politicians, there is support from the National School of Government, which designs and delivers a range of leadership and learning interventions for government ministers, expanding these opportunities since 2005, some of this in partnership with the University of Warwick. The Institute for Government is also developing coaching for national politicians and many politicians have their own mentors, with some having coaches.

Political leadership is based on political authority, which has a different basis from managerial authority (Morrell and Hartley, 2006), and it is important for a coach to understand this. The initial mandate comes from the ballot box, and political leaders have to be sensitive to the concerns and aspirations of voters and interest groups if they are to be not only elected but able to get things done. In addition, their authority to lead is based on continuing, not once-off, support because legitimacy has to be won and re-won on a continual basis. The basis of power for politicians lies in their support from the electorate and from their colleagues in their political party (or coalition), whether at local or national level. As a consequence they have to address complex goals that are sometimes in conflict and that are often contested by different stakeholders. This contrasts with managerial leadership where authority comes from the initial selection and appointment process and the job role (Morrell and Hartley, 2006; Simpson, 2008).

Although political leaders receive a considerable amount of informal 'feedback' about their behaviour and performance, much of this can be described either as hostile reaction (since they address difficult problems) or sycophantic praise (since they are in positions of power and may be surrounded by courtiers). In addition, it is possible that much of the 'feedback' they get is outcome-based, and wrongly attributed (in the sense that politicians can only exert a limited amount of control on outcomes), rather than process/competency based. This can leave political leaders either feeling defensive about their competencies, or with a false sense of security. One experienced leader recalled 'feeling most insecure, especially at the beginning, with lots of noise ... but an unnerving vacuum in terms of feedback'. This presents a challenge for coaching.

In terms of its use in practice, the two authors have been working with the model in coaching with individual politicians since the year 2000, and used it on a number of national leadership development programmes for local elected politicians. Here, the opportunities for one-to-one coaching are the most difficult, both because of time constraints in, for example, a two-day workshop that covers a variety of political leadership issues, and also because of the mix of politicians is the greatest (from those who are suspicious of personal development, via those who are indifferent, to those who are strongly interested). Working with individual politicians on personal development inevitably works best. In such cases the response to the experience can be contagious, with one politician recommending it to another on a word-of-mouth basis. Coaching can then be designed to fit the rhythm and timetable of the politician to some extent. However, two problems can arise that the coach has to address. First, the demanding and unsocial hours of any politician means that the coach may need to be available in the evenings or weekends. Second, the competing demands on time and attention from a range of stakeholders means that there are sometimes postponed meetings, or meetings that take place under conditions of greater distraction than is ideal. The coach needs to be prepared to contract and re-contract; sometimes the time available seems short – 10 minutes, as that is the time and priority the politician gives it, so brief coaching is in order (Berg and Szabo, 2005); sometimes the contracted time expands, as the politician re-prioritizes or makes more time available. The political astuteness of the coach and some knowledge of the roles, the pressures and the policy contexts for elected politicians are crucial. Each political system is different, so the coach must understand the culture and context of the specific country.

In our own work, coaching has often included the use of the Warwick Political Leadership Questionnaire (the self-assessment and 360° feedback tool), based on the model, to develop self-awareness and understanding of leadership capabilities and further developmental learning from the creation of a personal development plan or developmental goals that are part of the coaching contract. It enables a conversation to take place, stories to be told of success and things that didn't go so well, and an exploration of the learning from that in a confidential environment and in a way which politicians rarely have access.

It is useful to distinguish between coaching and mentoring in this arena. Garvey, Stokes and Megginson (2009) discuss the difference and similarity between the two, in some cases the 'camps' being 'almost tribal' (see Gibb and Hill, 2006). They explore the roots and development of usage and their conclusion is that there is no 'one best way' in mentoring and coaching, and therefore no single definition; the context contributes to the practitioner and his or her positioning. The choice may be for someone neutral to offer coaching or mentoring, or for someone deeply steeped in the politics. A mentor who is a politician from one particular party is often unacceptable as a mentor to members of other parties and a mentor from another nation – whether within the UK or not – may be equally unacceptable. Issues of trust are particularly heightened in a political context. Interestingly, a mentor who is an independent (ie not affiliated to a political party) may escape this limitation.

Within this situation, therefore, we distinguish between a coach, who is working on analysis and self-development with the coachee, and a mentor, who is working on skills development from the perspective of someone who has 'been there, done that', and has experience and practical insight. In terms of their own development, coaches have leadership, and knowledge of organizational and personal development in individual and interpersonal psychological processes. The coach may also draw on a wide range of models about individual behaviour, group processes and political systems.

There can be a question of power within the dyad, where the coach is seen more as a helper and an equal with different skills, looking at development needs and/or a 360° analysis alongside the politician; rather than a mentor who may be seen as a role model and wise person who might offer advice from an experienced position as well as exploring possibilities and options. Both can be a valuable part of a personal development plan process, but the conversations and outcomes, whilst using similar skills, are likely to be different. As the professional world of both begins to merge, there is a composite coach–mentor appearing. Garvey (2004) indicates that as long as there is a 'common understanding of meaning with that setting', then that is probably sufficient. Most clients are clear, after the discussion of what the different approaches might be, which would suit them.

An issue with which the experienced coach or mentor is familiar is that of contracting. The chooser and user can be different in political systems, and the choosers may have their own agenda. In one situation the chief executive of a local authority chose a coach for the political leader but then wanted to stop the coaching because the leader was becoming too independent of the chief executive's advice! An issue for coaching for politicians relates to the public financing of such leadership development, and the perceived boundaries between the benefits that are of value to the public sphere compared with benefits solely to the individual leader.

Coachees easily grasp the 10 capability dimensions of the leadership model and work with their coach or mentor on the development opportunities that will enable them to improve. The development booklet provides ideas and practical suggestions as to where such opportunities might be found and it is for the coach or mentor to bring that to life with each individual coachee. Using an appreciative inquiry approach and telling narratives of where things went well, coachees are able to build up a picture of what they want to work towards, rather than concentrating on a deficit model to which politicians can sometimes feel susceptible (Cooperrider and Whitney, 2005; Lewis, Passmore and Cantore, 2008). Coachees are encouraged to ask for further feedback from carefully chosen and trusted significant others. This trust is crucial when working with politicians, since their context is often adversarial, seeking to differentiate the political parties and ideologies represented, to ensure votes follow. Coachees are encouraged to dream of what might be and to design a development plan for themselves and for the organization that would enable them to follow that dream. Further feedback therefore concentrates on what was good about what happened and how that can be built on.

Different views and expectations from different stakeholders may also be explored, either with the WPLQ 360° feedback or by encouraging the politicians to gather further evidence about the expectations from different groups with whom they have to work.

In the discussion of the context, coachees may explore whether and how they take into account political, economic, social, technological and environmental changes in their political work in their own locality, and to reflect on whether they might pay more attention to some changes. It allows the story of their own interests, often the initial trigger for their incursion into politics, and the interplay between that and the locality they serve to be shared with the coach. These may, for example, be stories of being unexpectedly catapulted into local politics ('they just wanted a paper candidate', 'they told me we didn't stand a chance, so I agreed to stand') or of having an interest in one area (a 'single issue' politician) then getting drawn into a much wider understanding and interest in the role. Such stories become part of the coaching, and it is for the coach to listen, draw out the learning, make the connections between different stories and different contexts and to reflect those back to the coachees whilst working further on their development with them. Coachees often are reinforced in and proud of their role as they tell their stories and reflect on their achievements. A number of such politicians on a programme in Scotland commented that they hardly ever reflected on their achievements as their constituents were always wanting more, and they were conscious of what needed to be done rather than what had been done. With the immediacy of constantly needing to prove their worth to the voters, they felt 'only as good as the last piece of good news'.

The third area of the model is looking at challenges and where the coachee's time and attention is devoted, sometimes comparing the politician's own view with that of his or her raters. Some politicians may spend only a few hours a week as part-timers, while others have a punishing schedule of commitments taking up almost every waking minute of the day. How is that time invested? Group or party issues? In the office/authority/constituency? In partnership areas where larger gains might be made, but control is far less? On community and individual case issues? Or working with other tiers of government? Reflection on these can elicit changes in terms of focus, desired outcomes and enabling explanation to stakeholders of where the politician spends his or her time.

Politicians may vary greatly in their self-confidence. One politician working at district level became inarticulate with county politicians, whose style she found much more hostile and confrontational. She felt out of control and out of her depth. Working with her on motivation, attitude and confidence restored that equanimity for which her party colleagues had promoted her.

What are the ethical issues for the coach? Coaches may have their own political preferences and find it against their own value systems to be supporting someone from a particular political party. How will they handle confidentiality, given that they work with someone in the public eye? It can be challenging to work with politicians, since they address issues of considerable public interest that involve a range of publicly expressed values. For these reasons, it is easier to coach outside the coach's own geographic area, and within a value set s/he can support.

In Dawn Chandler's chapter on a US perspective on coaching and mentoring (Garvey, Stokes and Megginson, 2009: 205), she refers to using 'coaching and mentoring as vehicles for employee and player learning, personal and team development and career advancement'. We did not find much written about the coaching of politicians; some US websites do offer consultant services in this regard but this appears not to be underpinned by theory. Mentoring does seem to be important however, for politicians both in the United States and the UK, and of course some politicians come from political families or dynasties (such as the Kennedys and the Bushes) where informal mentoring may be present.

CASE STUDY OF COACHING FOR POLITICAL LEADERSHIP

Carl is a local politician, and senior elected member in his local authority. An interesting point is that he was formerly a senior public sector manager, and is therefore receptive to and used to using management tools, exploring leadership and management issues, and sophisticated in his approach to learning.

Carl was part of a cohort who participated in a national political leadership development programme and completed a self-assessment as part of that. It was noticeable that he rated himself lower on the dimension of 'political intelligence' than any other capability. Some initial discussion took place during the workshop and this was followed up with a booked phone call to explore his self-assessment profile in relation to 'political intelligence' and his sense that his professional experience as a manager was interfering with his skill as a politician in that he still behaved more like a manager than a politician in some arenas. Sufficiently interested to pursue some of the issues from the programme, he requested participation in the 360° version of the Warwick Political Leadership Questionnaire. Further feedback was explored in a two and a half hour session with a qualified personal development coach. Feedback included some fairly clear issues about political understanding in terms of the local and national agenda as well as some behavioural issues around the boundaries between political and managerial responsibilities. Feedback around his capabilities highlighted the coachee's assessing them more highly than his respondents did, a not unusual position for someone confident in taking centre stage. Politicians have to have the conviction and self-confidence to deal with the range of issues, but often it seems this is a front that masks the constant draining of their confidence by people who want more and more from them. Those who have had a senior position elsewhere have extra experience and resources to draw on, and Carl had retired at the head of his profession. However, natural humility and the interest in further development meant that the messages were given due attention, and the rest of the coaching session was spent looking at what could be put in place in a personal development plan.

Carl and the coach agreed to have a follow-on session with some commitment for action. The coaching reinforced steps that had already been taken or planned in terms of strengthening his use of party ideology and political ideas. Previously Carl's common-sense ideas and personal values had prevailed, and new options were explored by the coach to further potential avenues to strengthen his political knowledge. Carl planned to talk to the officers who had given the hardest messages in terms of the leadership boundaries – 'more steering – less rowing' – and to the party leader as a mentor in this area. Particular arenas for practising new behaviours were agreed, such as his work in full council meetings and in certain committees. People were also identified who could give feedback as to when the new behaviours had been demonstrated. The coach took an appreciative inquiry stance, looking at when these behaviours had been done well, and encouraged Carl to ask the feedback givers to do the same. The political nuances of appointing such feedback givers were part of the discussion, as politicians often operate in a less supportive environment, where any suggestion of weakness or vulnerability can be used in the competition for political gain. In a follow-up phone conversation, Carl had talked to the appropriate director whose portfolio he led and to his political group leader. He had appointed some feedback givers to tell him when he was sufficiently forceful, and set himself a goal of developing 'a different persona for this role' (unlike when he chaired a meeting of professional staff, when he was employed as a manager, whose role was to ensure everyone contributed). He planned to be 'better prepared' and have possible 'statements ready' so that he could be 'tougher' with the more hostile and confrontational opposing party. The feedback from his officers was about dealing with the attacks from the opposition in a strong and forthright way, and he planned to equip his own political colleagues with points and action to support him. He was taking the opportunity to influence party policy at a national level and to explore the possibilities for developing that further. He had also some personal reservations as to how close he should get to 'his' director and the appropriate distance necessary between the two roles. Coaching both explored his preparations and also followed up on preliminary actions.

CONCLUSIONS

The leadership model underpinning the coaching recognizes the distinctiveness of political leadership and takes a socially constructed approach to leadership that sees effective leadership as needing to take account of context, the challenges in five arenas, and the development of capabilities. Coaching with politicians explores the elements of contexts, challenges and capabilities, with an understanding of the particular basis of political authority and the different routes that politicians take into their roles. It also has to work with the coachees to explore and shape the pressures of authority, their need to deal with a range of stakeholders with widely differing understanding, work with the paradoxes and tensions that politicians are subject to due to the varied expectations of a range of stakeholders. The coach works in the context of multiple stakeholder demands and the complexity of the issues, which often require adaptive leadership. Political coaching differs in these ways from managerial coaching and presents particular challenges to the coach or mentor.

References

Berg, I K and Szabo, P (2005) *Brief Coaching for Lasting Solutions*, WW Norton, New York

Boyatzis, R (1982) *The Competent Manager: A model for effective performance*, John Wiley, New York

Burns, J M (1978) *Leadership*, Harper Collins, New York

Cooperrider, D L and Whitney, D (2005) *Appreciative Inquiry: A positive revolution in change*, Berrett-Koehler, San Francisco, CA

Garvey, B (2004) Call a rose by any other name and perhaps it's a bramble? *Development and Learning in Organizations*, **18** (2), pp 6–8

Garvey, R, Stokes, P and Megginson, D (2009) *Coaching and Mentoring: Theory and practice*, Sage, London

Gibb, S and Hill, P (2006) From trail-blazing individualism to a social construction community: modelling knowledge construction in coaching, *International Journal of Mentoring and Coaching*, **4** (2), pp 58–77

Grint, K (2005) Problems, problems, problems: the social construction of 'leadership', *Human Relations*, **58**, pp 1467–94

Hartley, J (2002) Leading communities: capabilities and cultures, *Leadership and Organizational Development Journal*, **23**, pp 419–29

Hartley, J (in press) Political leadership, in *Public leadership*, ed S Brookes and K Grint, Routledge, London

Hartley, J and Fletcher, C (2005) *The Warwick Political Leadership Questionnaire*, Institute of Governance and Public Management, University of Warwick, Coventry

Hartley, J and Fletcher, C (2007) *Establishing a Member Development Framework for Scottish Local Authorities*, report for the Improvement Service, Scotland

Hartley, J and Fletcher, C (2008) Leadership with political awareness: leadership across diverse interests inside and outside the organization, in *Leadership Perspectives: Knowledge into action*, ed K James and J Collins, pp 157–70, Palgrave, London

Hartley J, Fletcher, C and Benington, J (in press) Look at it from my angle: The development and use of a 360 degree feedback instrument for political leaders, in A Weinberg (ed) *The Psychology of Politicians*, Cambridge University Press, Cambridge

Hartley, J and Morgan-Thomas, A (2003) The development of the Warwick Political Leadership Questionnaire: conceptual framework and measurement properties, conference paper at the International Studying Leadership Conference, Lancaster, December

Hartley, J and Skelcher, C (2008) The agenda for public service improvement, in *Managing to Improve Public Services*, ed J Hartley, C Donaldson, C Skelcher and M Wallace, pp 1–21, Cambridge University Press, Cambridge

Heifetz, R (1994) *Leadership without Easy Answers*, Harvard University Press, Cambridge, MA

Kubler-Ross, E (1973) *On Death and Dying*, Tavistock/Routledge, London

Leach, S, Hartley, J, Lowndes, V, Wilson, D and Downe, J (2005) *Local Political Leadership in England and Wales*, The Joseph Rowntree Foundation, York

Leach, S and Wilson, D (2000) *Local Political Leadership*, Policy Press, Bristol

Lewis, S, Passmore, J and Cantore, S (2008) *Appreciative Inquiry for Change Management: Using AI to facilitate organizational development*, Kogan Page, London

Morrell, K and Hartley, J (2006) A model of political leadership, *Human Relations*, **59** (4), pp 483–504

Nicklen, S (2008) Leadership development: a contextual approach, *International Journal of Mentoring and Coaching*, **6** (3)

Public Administration Select Committee (2008) Corrected transcript accessed at http://www.publications.parliament.uk/pa/cm200809/cmselect/cmpubadm/c45–i/c4502.htm on 4 February 2009

Pinder, K and Hartley, J (2005) *Political Leadership Development Booklet: A resource for elected members*, Institute of Governance and Public Management, University of Warwick, Coventry

Porter, L and McLaughlin, G (2006) Leadership and the organizational context: like the weather? *Leadership Quarterly*, **17**, pp 559–76

Simpson, J (2008) *The Politics of Leadership*, Leading Edge Publications, London

Taylor, M (1993) *The Four Axes of Civic Leadership*, Research paper, University of Warwick, Coventry

10

Leadership coaching with feedforward

Dr Marshall Goldsmith

INTRODUCTION

In this chapter I will look at the role of feedback in coaching and how the coach can act as a useful tool for senior managers, challenging the delusions that can sometimes dominate the thinking of senior people in organizations through applying a different approach. We call this feedforward. We will look at the approach and argue why coaches can apply this model to help managers make changes that otherwise can be difficult to make stick.

THE COACHING FEEDFORWARD MODEL

Little acknowledged, but well established, is the fact that any animal, including the most successful leaders, will tend to repeat a behaviour that is followed by positive reinforcement. The more we receive positive reinforcement and the more successful we become, the more likely we are to believe: 'I behave this way. I am successful. Therefore, I must be successful because I behave this way.' This is what I call the success delusion. I call it a delusion because, as we move up the organizational ladder, our employees, our teams, our followers are prone to tell us how great we are even when we aren't! Our behaviour, sometimes nonsensical, is followed by positive reinforcement, and we want to believe what we hear. It is our belief in ourselves that has helped us to be successful, and that is why it is hard for us to change. We believe that because we have behaved in a certain way and we are successful, therefore we must continue to behave in that way.

If we are willing to take a look at ourselves, we can change our behaviour. By understanding why we might need to change certain behaviours, we are far more likely to make the changes we need to make to become even more successful.

WHAT HOLDS US BACK?

For successful people, what holds us back is often not our humility or under-confidence. Rather, we are inclined to overestimate our contributions, to think we are better and/or more skilled than we really are, and to discount the real and hidden costs of a project, thus exaggerating its profitability.

These delusions come not from our failures but from our associations with our successes. We take the positive reinforcement we receive and apply it to our futures. This is not all bad. Our belief in our greatness, amplified though it may be, gives us confidence to strive to become even better. However, on the flip side, it can make it very difficult for us to change. At first, when we receive constructive negative feedback, we are likely to be convinced that the critic is confused, misinformed or ignorant. Then as it sinks in, we go into denial. Maybe the criticism is correct, but if it were that important, we wouldn't be so successful! Finally, if denial fails, we tend to lash out, attacking the messenger, concluding that to listen to this person would be a mistake – they aren't as successful as me! All of these responses add up to a successful, deluded leader who is resistant to change.

As successful people, we have four positive beliefs about ourselves that have helped us to become successful – these same beliefs can inhibit us from making the changes we need to reach the next level of success. These beliefs are:

▌ Belief 1: I have succeeded.
▌ Belief 2: I can succeed.

▌ Belief 3: I will succeed.
▌ Belief 4: I choose to succeed.

Belief 1: I have succeeded

Our strong belief in our past success gives us the confidence to take the risks needed for our future success. With this belief that we have succeeded, we don't think about our screw-ups and failures that we inevitably have experienced; we are filled with optimism and eagerness, ready to compete, focused on the positives and looking for the happy ending that we love so much.

Belief 2: I can succeed

We believe that we have the capability to positively influence the world, to make things happen. We believe that through the sheer force of our personality, talent and intelligence, we can steer the situation, organization or team to the direction we define as success. Successful people have a high 'internal locus of control' – we don't feel like victims of fate; we see our success as a function of our own motivation and ability. This belief plays a crucial role in our successes.

Belief 3: I will succeed

We are optimists. We believe we can do anything – hence the tendency for us to chronically over-commit. We believe that we will do more than we actually can do! We don't want to say 'no' to opportunities; we believe we will succeed even as we 'drown in a sea of opportunity'.

Belief 4: I choose to succeed

Finally, successful people are highly self-determined. We like to do what we choose to do because we choose to do it. When we do this, we are committed; when we do what we have to do, because someone has told us to, we become compliant. This is why, in my leadership coaching, I only work with people who choose to change. I know that I can only help people get better at what they choose to change; if they do not choose to change, they won't. This leads us back to the beginning of this article: the more we believe that our behaviour is a result of our own choices and behaviours, and the more it is positively reinforced (ie successful), the less likely we are to want to change the behaviour.

HOW THE SUCCESS DELUSION MAKES US SUPERSTITIOUS

These four beliefs often lead to superstitious behaviour. Often, the higher we climb up the organization ladder, the more superstitious we become. Superstitious behaviour is the result of the belief that specific activities that are followed by positive reinforcement are in reality the cause of the positive reinforcement, though this may not be true. We are not unlike BF Skinner's hungry pigeons, which were prone to repeat meaningless twitches and pecks because they believed these behaviours were correlated to the dropping of random small pellets of food. As successful leaders, we may repeat dysfunctional behaviour if it is followed by large pellets of praise, money or adoration – even if in reality the behaviour has no connection with the results whatsoever.

MAKING THE CHANGES WE NEED TO MAKE

Overcoming the success delusion requires a lot of hard work. As a coach, one of the greatest challenges is to help people see how 'because of behaviours' and 'in spite of behaviours' can lead to the superstition trap. Starting with yourself, pick one of your own less-than-desirable behaviours. Now consider this: Do you continue to act this way because you associate it with the happening of good things? Does it really help you to achieve results or is it an irrational belief that has controlled you for years? The former is a 'because of', the latter is an 'in spite of' behaviour.

It isn't easy to achieve positive change in your behaviour. The same beliefs that have helped you to get where you are may be the same ones that are holding you back from where you want to go. Knowing this, how can you achieve positive change? Get in the habit of asking key people in your life how you can improve – using feedforward instead of feedback as you'll read about in the next section (Goldsmith, 2002). Ask them to help you get from where you are to where you want to be, and realize that your first inclination to point out where they are wrong isn't going to help you! Accept the fact that there are areas of your life where change is likely to contribute greatly to your success, your team's success and even the success of your organization.

Finally, accept the fact that you are only going to change what you choose to change. The motivation and commitment to change has to come from inside you. Watch out for over-commitment. Keep it simple. Don't overdo it. And, you will get from here to there.

USING FEEDFORWARD WITH COACHEES

Long considered one of the essential skills for leaders, providing feed-back helps us know how we are doing in terms of achieving goals for the organization, developing people, communicating a vision and so on. We all need feedback to know if our performance is in line with expectations. We need to know what we are doing well and what we need to change.

Traditionally, this information is given 'back' and 'down' from leaders to employees; however, just as employees need feedback from their leaders, leaders can greatly benefit from feedback from their employees. This type of 'upward feedback' is becoming more common, especially with the advent of 360° multi-rater assessments.

Yet there is something inherently problematic with all types of feed-back: feedback focuses backward on what has already occurred, not on the infinite possibilities of the future. As a result, feedback can be limited and static as opposed to expansive and dynamic.

Over the years I have observed thousands of leaders participate in an experiential exercise. In this exercise, participants play two roles: in one role, they provide feedforward – they give another person suggestions for the future; in the second, they accept feedforward – they listen to suggestions for the future and learn as much as they can. This is a short 10–15 minute exercise, in which each participant has six or seven dialogues and is asked to do the following:

1. Pick one behaviour that they would like to change because it would make a significant positive difference in their life.
2. Describe the behaviour to a fellow participant in a one-on-one dialogue. The behaviour can be as simple as 'I want to be a better listener.'
3. Ask for feedforward – two suggestions for the future that may help them to achieve positive change in the selected behaviour. There is *no* feedback about the past; only ideas for the future are allowed.
4. Listen to the suggestions and take notes. The person receiving the feedforward is not allowed to comment on the suggestions; they may not critique; or even make positive judgmental statements, like 'Great idea!'
5. Thank the participants for their suggestions.
6. Then, ask the other person what they would like to change.
7. Provide feedforward to the other person, in the form of two suggestions targeted at helping the other person change.
8. Say, 'You are welcome' when thanked for the suggestions. The entire process of both giving and receiving feedforward usually takes about two minutes.

9. Find another person and repeat the process until the exercise is stopped.

ELEVEN REASONS TO TRY FEEDFORWARD

After finishing the exercise, I ask participants to describe the experience by completing the following sentence: 'This exercise was . . .' Words like 'great', 'energizing', 'useful' and 'helpful' are used frequently, but the most common? 'Fun!' This is probably the last word most of us think about when we receive feedback, coaching and development ideas.

When I ask participants why they saw the exercise as fun and helpful rather than painful, embarrassing, or uncomfortable, they have come up with the following 11 reasons:

▌ We can change the future, but we can't change the past. It helps people envision and focus on a positive future, not a failed past. By giving people ideas about how they can be even more successful, it increases their chances of achieving success in the future.

▌ It can be far more productive to help people be 'right,' than to prove how they are 'wrong'. Negative feedback often just proves people wrong and tends to produce defensiveness on the part of the receiver and discomfort on the part of the sender. Even when constructively delivered, feedback is often negative as it involves discussion of mistakes, shortfalls and problems. Feedforward focuses on solutions not problems and is therefore seen as very positive.

▌ Feedforward is especially suited to successful people. Because it is aimed at helping us achieve our goals, it is more palatable. We want it because it is going to help us be better at what we choose to be better at.

▌ Feedforward can come from anyone. It doesn't require personal experience with the individual. For instance, if you want to be a better listener, you don't have to ask someone who knows you personally. You can learn just as much about this from someone you don't even know. Feedforward just requires having good ideas for achieving the task.

▌ In theory, constructive feedback is supposed to 'focus on the performance, not the person'. However, in practice, feedback is almost always taken personally (no matter how it is delivered). Because successful people's sense of identity is highly connected to their work, and the more successful a person is the more this tends to be true, it is nearly impossible to give a dedicated professional feedback that will not be taken personally. Feedforward cannot involve a personal critique because it is about something that hasn't yet happened! In this way, positive suggestions are seen as objective advice; personal critiques are often viewed as personal attacks.

- Feedback can reinforce personal stereotyping and negative self-fulfilling prophecies. Feedforward can reinforce the possibility of change. Feedback can reinforce the feeling of failure. Feedforward is based on the assumption that the receiver of suggestions can make positive changes in the future.

- Most of us don't like getting negative feedback nor do we like to give it. In reviewing summary 360° feedback reports for more than 50 companies, I have found that the items, 'provides developmental feedback in a timely manner' and 'encourages and accepts constructive criticism' almost always score near the bottom on co-worker satisfaction with leaders. Leaders are not very good at giving or receiving negative feedback. It is unlikely that this will change in the near future.

- Feedforward can cover almost all of the same 'material' as feedback. Imagine that you have just made a terrible presentation in front of the executive committee. Your manager is in the room. Rather than make you 'relive' this humiliating experience, your manager helps you prepare for future presentations by giving you suggestions for the future. These suggestions can be very specific and still delivered in a positive way. In this way your manager 'covers the same points' without feeling embarrassed and without making you feel even more humiliated.

- Feedforward tends to be much faster and more efficient than feedback. An excellent technique for giving ideas to successful people is to say, 'Here are four ideas for the future. Please accept these in the positive spirit that they are given. If you can only use two of the ideas, you are still two ahead. Just ignore what doesn't make sense for you.' With this approach almost no time gets wasted on judging the quality of the ideas or 'proving that the ideas are wrong'. This 'debate' time is usually negative; it can take up a lot of time, and it is often not very productive. By eliminating judgment of the ideas, the process becomes much more positive for the sender, as well as the receiver. As mentioned earlier, successful people tend to have a high need for self-determination and will tend to accept ideas that they 'buy' while rejecting ideas that feel are 'forced' upon them.

- Feedforward can be a useful tool to apply with managers, peers and team members. Rightly or wrongly, feedback is associated with judgment. This can lead to very negative – or even career-limiting – unintended consequences when applied to managers or peers.

Feedforward does not imply superiority of judgment. It is more focused on being a helpful 'fellow traveller' than an 'expert'. As such it can be easier to hear from a person who is not in a position of power or authority. An excellent team-building exercise is to have each team member ask, 'How can I better help our team in the future?' and listen to feedforward from fellow team members (in one-on-one dialogues).

▌ People tend to listen more attentively to feedforward than they do to feedback. One participant in the feedforward exercise noted, 'I think that I listened more effectively in this exercise than I ever do at work!' When asked why, he responded, 'Normally, when others are speaking, I am so busy composing a reply that will make sure that I sound smart that I am not fully listening to what the other person is saying. In feedforward the only reply that I am allowed to make is "thank you". Since I don't have to worry about composing a clever reply, I can focus all of my energy on listening to the other person!'

The intent of this exercise is not to imply that leaders should never give feedback or that performance appraisals should be abandoned. The intent is to show how feedforward can often be preferable to feedback in day-to-day interactions. Aside from its effectiveness and efficiency, feedforward can make life a lot more enjoyable. When managers are asked, 'How did you feel the last time you received feedback?' their most common responses are very negative. As noted, when they are asked how they felt after receiving feedforward, the reply is often that feedforward was not only useful, it was also fun! Isn't this the way it should be?

As leaders we usually preach values involving people and teamwork, but sometimes excuse ourselves from their practice. Even more often, organizations fail to hold leaders accountable for living these values. This inconsistency invites corporate cynicism, undermines credibility, and can sap organizations of their vitality. The failure to uphold espoused values in general (and 'people' values in particular) is one of the biggest frustrations in the workplace.

CONCLUSIONS

Now with this bit of knowledge about the (un-)rewarding delusions of successful people and how to use feedforward, a fun tool that will help you to reach even the most successful person, it is possible that you can help coach someone to change their behaviour. Chances are you are even willing to take a look at some of the behaviours you participate in that could use a bit of alteration. Being willing to look at ourselves, and understanding why certain behaviours might be changed, will make it far more likely that we can make the changes necessary to become even more successful. As quality communication – between and among people at all levels and in every department and division – is the glue that holds organizations together, so understanding ourselves and using feedforward can dramatically improve the quality of communication in any organization. The result is a much more dynamic, much more open organization – one in which employees and leaders alike focus on the promise of the future, rather than dwelling on the mistakes of the past.

Reference

Goldsmith, M (2002) Try feed*forward* instead of feedback, *Leader to Leader*, **25** (Summer), [online] http://www.marshallgoldsmithlibrary.com/docs/articles/Feedforward.doc

11

Coaching from a systems perspective

Barry Oshry

INTRODUCTION

Many emotionally charged issues that arise between people in organizations feel personal when they are not. They are systemic, having less to do with the personal characteristics of the individuals involved than with the systemic contexts in which they are engaged.

The purpose of this chapter is to provide the coach with systemic lenses for seeing, understanding and intervening effectively in system life. The focus will be on two systemic contexts: systems as patterns of relationship and systems as patterns of process. We will see how these two contexts, generally without our awareness or choice, shape our interactions with one another; more importantly, we will see how blindness to context affects us personally and organizationally – causing unnecessary stress, relationship breakdowns, lost opportunities and diminished organizational effectiveness. And we will see how through systems coaching we are able to help leaders produce more positive outcomes for themselves and the systems they lead.

THE LEADERSHIP MODEL

A human system framework: from system blindness to system sight

We are social systems creatures. Much of our lives are spent in systems – the organization, the family, the team, the neighbourhood, the small business, the volunteer group, the community, and as citizens of the nation and the world. Yet, for the most part, we are blind to systems; we do not see how the structure and processes of the systems we are in shape our hearts and minds. Our reflexive mode of understanding human interaction is personal; we see individuals with their unique temperaments, values, styles, moods and quirks; so, when our relationships deteriorate or break down completely, our explanations also tend to be personal: there's some flaw with one party or the other, or maybe individually they're ok, but the chemistry between them is unfortunate. Personal explanations lead to personal solutions: fix, fire, rotate, avoid, control, keep from being controlled, separate, divorce or get into therapy. Faulty diagnoses lead to misdirected solutions. The challenge for all of us is to see the systems of which we are a part, to convert system blindness into system sight, and to master system conditions. This is the invaluable role systems coaching can play.

When systems are viewed as wholes, they can be seen as what they are and what they do. What they are, essentially, is patterns of relationship. Three that we have studied intensively are top–bottom, end–middle–end and provider–customer. We are constantly moving in and out of these relationships, sometimes on one side and sometimes on the other, sometimes as top, sometimes bottom, sometimes as end, sometimes middle, sometimes as provider and sometimes customer. When we are blind to these relationships, they take us out of the potential for partnership with one another and into patterns that are personally stressful and destructive of our relationships. We fall into becoming burdened tops and oppressed bottoms, torn middles and disappointed ends, righteously done-to customers and unfairly judged customers. And as we fall into these patterns, our potential contributions to our systems are also diminished.

What systems do is develop processes for coping with the conditions of their environments. They cope by differentiating, developing complexity in form and function that enables them to interact complexly with their environments: by homogenizing, maintaining or diffusing common information throughout the system; by individuating, allowing for the independent functioning of system parts; and by integrating, in which all parts feed and support one another and modulate their actions in the service of the whole. We are involved in these coping processes whether we aware of them or not. And, when we are blind to these systemic processes, we are vulnerable to falling into familiar dysfunctional relationships within groups – turf warfare among tops, alienated ineffective middle peers, and bottom groups in the grips of stifling pressures toward conformity. All of this results in diminished contributions to the survival and development of their systems.

The challenge is to move from system blindness to system sight, and this is both an intellectual and emotional project. It involves learning about these systemic relationships and processes, understanding how they shape our experiences of ourselves and others and our organizational effectiveness, recognizing in the moment when we are engaged in these relationships and processes, understanding how, unawares, we can reflexively fall into dysfunctional patterns, and learning strategies for managing these relationships and processes effectively. That's the work to be done on the intellectual side. On the emotional side, there is the challenge of being willing and able to give up our deeply embedded personal biases with their attending self-justifications, dramas and righteousness.

So that is the challenge of systems coaching: to help their coachees move from the destructive consequences of system blindness to the more satisfying and productive possibilities of system sight.

THE RESEARCH: LESSONS FROM THE POWER LAB AND THE ORGANIZATION WORKSHOP

The human systems framework described in this paper has been developed over 35 years, primarily through my involvement in two leadership development programmes – the Power Lab (Oshry, 1999) and the Organization Workshop (Oshry, 2007). A feature of both of these is an intense organizational experience in which participants are involved as either tops, middles or bottoms. In many of these programmes, there are two organizational experiences that allow participants to experience two different positions. The Power Lab is a total immersion multi-day experience, and the Organization Workshop is a one or two-day event. In both programmes, people are randomly assigned to their positions. These organizational experiences are not role plays, in that people are not given instructions as to how to act; they are simply placed in positions and asked to handle the situations that come up as best they can. Which is pretty much the way it is in day-to-day organizational life.

Each of these programmes has given my associates and me unprecedented opportunities to deepen our understanding of system life. In the Power Lab, in programme after programme, I have been able to function as an anthropologist observing the whole of systems, the interactions within and across top, middle and bottom lines. In the Organization Workshop we have created the TOOT (Time Out Of Time) (Oshry, 1999) in which, periodically, the organization action is stopped; tops, middles, bottoms and customers come together to describe their experiences – the issues they are dealing with and the feelings they are having. Over time, I began to see regularly repeating patterns of experience and behaviour within and across groups – the personal issues, frustrations and stresses tops, middles and bottoms were experiencing. Participants would even use identical words and phrases to describe their experiences in programme after programme. I also began to see regularly recurring relationship issues developing within top, middle and bottom groups. Participants would experience these personal and relationship issues as if they were unique to them and their situation. From my perspective it became ever clearer that these experiences were systemic.

Participants regularly remarked how struck they were by the similarity between the experiences and events in the programme and their day-to-day organizational realities, often describing them as 'another day in the office'. This congruence between experiences in the programmes and those in day-to-day organizational life confirm for us that we are dealing with more than workshop phenomena, that this human systems framework is capturing fundamental realities of organizational life.

In both the Power Lab and the Organization Workshop there are opportunities to coach people, to help them see the systemic contexts in which they are functioning. Coaching enables participants to understand how blindness to context takes them into paths that are dysfunctional for them and the system. And coaching helps them become aware of more productive alternatives. In the Organization Workshop this coaching comes in the form of conceptual presentations similar to what will be described in this chapter; in the Power Lab, coaching comes in the shape of in-the-action coaches. Coaching often produces dramatic changes in people's experiences, the quality of their relationships and their subsequent organizational effectiveness. Such changes teach us that these dysfunctional patterns may be predictable but they are not inevitable, and that systemic coaching can make a powerful contribution.

USING THE SYSTEMS MODEL WITH COACHEES: CONVERTING SYSTEM BLINDNESS TO SYSTEM SIGHT

In this section, we will describe systems as patterns of relationship and as patterns of processes. We will describe how blindness to these relationships and processes regularly has dysfunctional consequences for individuals, for their relationships with others and for their contributions to their organizations. Then we will examine the role systemic coaching can play in helping them move from system blindness to system sight, helping leaders see, understand and master the systemic contexts in which they are functioning. In Part I, the focus is on patterns of relationship, in Part II it is on patterns of processes.

Part I. Systems as shifting patterns of relationship

Human interactions are more than people meeting people; they are interactions taking place in the context of specific systemic relationships. In this section, I will describe: 1) three common systemic relationships; 2) problematic issues that develop with great regularity in these relationships; and 3) implications for systemic coaching.

The relationships

Three systemic relationships we have studied over the past 35 years are: top–bottom, end–middle–end and provider–customer. It is important to understand these as relationships and not as positions. Regardless of what organizational position we occupy, we are regularly moving in and out of these relationships, sometimes on one side and sometimes on the other.

In top–bottom relationships (Figure 11.1), we are top whenever we have designated responsibility for a system or some part of the system or for some process. In certain interactions we may be top, with designated responsibility for the organization or the department, the class, the team, the meeting, the family. In other interactions we are bottom when we are a member in a system or process for which others have designated responsibility.

In the end–middle–end relationship (Figures 11.2 and 11.3), we are sometimes middle, torn between the conflicting needs, wants, demands and priorities of two or more ends. Some end–middle–end relationships are hierarchical, in which we are torn between conflicting pressures from above and below, and some are lateral. We may be middle between our

Figure 11.1 Top–bottom relationship

manager (one end) and our team (the other end), between our managers and the board, between our spouse and a child, between the principal and our students, between our suppliers and manufacturing. In other interactions we may be one of those ends, exerting pressure on a common middle.

In the provider–customer relationship (Figure 11.4), sometimes we are the provider of products or services to our customers – as coaches, consultants, staff specialists, contractors, help desk operators; in other

Figure 11.2 End–middle–end hierarchical relationship

Figure 11.3 End–middle–end lateral relationship

Figure 11.4 Provider–customer relationship

interactions we are customers looking to providers for products or services.

Relationships are not positions

In organizational life we are constantly shifting in and out of all sides of these relationships. So, maybe even in the course of a single day, we could be top in certain interactions, bottom in others, middle between two or more ends, or one of two or more ends pressing on a common middle, provider to several customers and customer of several providers. We exist in a constantly shifting network of relationships.

Responsibility imbalance

In each of these relationships, there is a scenario that unfolds regularly – not always, not with everyone, but with great regularity, and this unfolds without awareness or choice. A responsibility imbalance develops in each relationship:

▌ Top feels responsible for the event, project or process; and bottom holds top responsible.
▌ Middle feels responsible for resolving whatever issues or conflicts ends have; and both ends hold middle responsible.
▌ Provider feels responsible for delivering a quality product or service; and customer holds provider responsible.

So long as top satisfies bottom, and middle satisfies both ends, and provider satisfies customer, there is no apparent problem. It is when top, middle and provider fail to deliver satisfactorily that fractures in the relationship develop.

Oppressed bottoms and burdened tops

Bottoms, having held tops responsible, now feel oppressed by them: angry, disappointed, resentful, trapped in a situation felt not to be of their own making. And tops, holding themselves responsible, feel that they are letting the system down, failing, not doing what they should be doing, or not doing it as well as they should.

Disappointed ends and torn middles

Ends, having held middles responsible for resolving their issues, now feel let down by their weak, ineffective, incompetent middles. And middles, holding themselves responsible for resolving ends' issues, now feel torn: confused, weak, unable to fully satisfy anyone, and in the extreme, doubting their own competence. In this torn condition, middles fall into differing patterns of coping. (These patterns will be relevant to the case study presented below.)

Some middles cope by aligning upward in the hierarchy; their bosses' priorities become their priorities. This pattern reduces the tearing with the boss while creating tensions with those below.

Other middles align downward in the hierarchy; in conflicts with above, they become the champions of their subordinates, a pattern that may leave their bosses questioning whether such middles have the right 'management stuff'.

Still other middles bureaucratize, surrounding themselves with such complex rules, procedures and barriers that others do their best to avoid dealing with them. And some middles ping-pong between the ends, carrying messages, explaining one side to the other, justifying one to the other, and in their efforts to be fair to all sides they end up fully satisfying none.

In any given middle peer group, there can be differing coping processes – some align up, some down, some bureaucratize, while others ping-pong (Oshry, 1994: 17–20). Such variations heighten the alienation among middles even though all of these differing patterns are variations on the same theme: coping with the stresses of middle tearing.

Righteously done-to customers and unfairly judged providers

Customers, having held providers responsible for delivery, now feel upset, angry, let down, mistreated by their providers for not getting the product or service they need, at the price they want or the quality they expect. And providers, having done their best to provide quality service, now feel unfairly judged by their customers.

Long-term disabling

As I said, as long as top, middle and provider deliver satisfactorily, there is no apparent short-term problem. However, there is a long-term problem. Should the responsibility imbalance persist over time, there is a gradual disabling of all parties. For example, if the long-term pattern is for top to be responsible and bottom not responsible, then two things are happening. Top is becoming increasingly burdened and bottom is becoming increasingly dependent. Should situations of complexity arise in which top needs bottom, top has developed no skills in sharing responsibility, and bottom has developed no capacity for assuming responsibility.

This same long-term incapacity develops in the end–middle–end and provider–customer relationships. When situations arise that need involvement from ends or customers, all parties may have been trained into incapacity.

In addition to the disabling of individuals, there is also a system-disabling process that develops when these responsibility imbalances persist over time. Even if top, middle and provider continue to satisfy, whatever enhancement in outcome could come from the involvement of the other is lost. How much greater could the results be if top and bottom, ends and middle, providers and customers shared responsibility for their processes and outcomes?

All of these scenarios unfold without awareness or choice. We simply fall into them blindly. They cause stress for individuals, create tensions in relationships and diminish effectiveness. The challenge for systems coaching is to prevent these scenarios from developing by helping coachees see, understand and master systemic relationships in ways that lead to more productive scenarios for themselves, their relationships and their systems.

The elements of systemic coaching

First coach yourself

The first challenge for the systems coach is to become expert in seeing, understanding and mastering one's own systemic relationships. We need to recognize our own shifting patterns of relationship in the various systems of which we are a part, recognizing in the moment: now I'm top, now I'm bottom, now provider, now customer, now middle, now end (that's a more difficult one to notice). And we need to notice in the moment where responsibility lies in each of these relationships. We also need to regularly practise shifting the balance of responsibility when doing so is in the service of more creative, productive and satisfactory outcomes. Mastering these relationships in our own lives gives us the understanding and humility needed to support the development of this mastery in others.

Develop conceptual clarity

Systems coaching is a conceptual as well as an experiential process. Systems coaches are both teachers of abstract concepts and consultants on specific concrete situations, and it helps to keep these two processes separate. One part of the work is to help coachees intellectually master the concepts – to understand the three relationships, to recognize that they at various times are on all sides of these, to understand the responsibility imbalance and the short and long-term consequences of that imbalance. It is against that conceptual base that coaches are able to work with specific situations the coachee is facing.

Working to improve the relationship

Say, for example, the coach is working with a coachee who is experiencing the consequences of an imbalanced relationship – maybe as a burdened top or oppressed bottom, torn middle or disappointed end, unfairly judged provider or righteously done-to customer. Coachees who have been educated in the framework may recognize the condition themselves; it is also possible that despite such education, coachees may still have fallen into the scenario unawares. The work of the coach involves:

▌ listening to and understanding the coachee's experience;
▌ helping the coachee recognize how this experience stems from a responsibility imbalance;
▌ assessing the coachee's interest in shifting the imbalance;
▌ working with the coachee to envision better outcomes for all parties if the imbalance were corrected – having a vision for a better outcome is a key motivator for change;
▌ clarifying how such a shift is in the interest of the other party as well as in the coachee's own interest;
▌ working with the coachee to develop a strategy for shifting the imbalance;
▌ developing approaches for dealing with the resistance to change that is likely to occur.

Dealing with resistance

It is reasonable to expect that as one party in a systemic relationship acts to shift the responsibility imbalance, the other will react, at least initially, with resistance. It is as if two dancers have been dancing for some time in a certain style, and then Dancer A suddenly changes style. A reasonable response from Dancer B is to become confused and upset by the disruption and try to bring Dancer B back in line. So, now what can Dancer A do? There are three possibilities: give up the new dance and revert to the old; separate from Dancer B and find a new, more receptive partner; or persevere with Dancer B, being patient, helping Dancer B experience the advantages and excitement of the new dance, keeping the vision in front of Dancer B of what this new dance can create for all concerned.

Part II. Systems as patterns of processes

In Part I, we described systems as patterns of relationship and the costly results of blindness to these relationships. We also explored the role of coaching in helping clients see, understand and master these systemic relationships. In Part II, we will explore systems as patterns of processes, and the negative consequences – personally and organizationally – that stem from blindness to these processes.

System processes

Examining systems as wholes, we can see four key processes that systems engage in as they attempt to cope with the conditions in their environment. The processes described below characterize all systems: the family, the team, the organization, and the nation; here our focus will be on the organization.

Systems differentiate: that is, they develop complex structures and processes enabling them to deal complexly with the complexities in their environment (Figure 11.5).

Figure 11.5 A differentiated system

And systems homogenize: that is, they maintain or diffuse commonality of information throughout the system. The more completely the system homogenizes, the more any part of the system understands and can do what any other part can do (Figure 11.6).

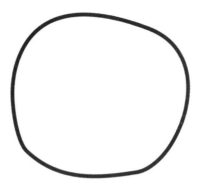

Figure 11.6 A homogenized system

Systems individuate: that is, the parts move independently of one another (Figure 11.7).

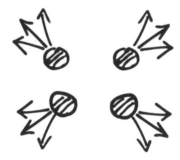

Figure 11.7 An individuated system

And systems integrate, with the parts feeding and supporting one another, modulating their separate functions in the service of the whole (Figure 11.8).

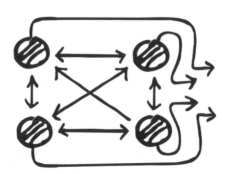

Figure 11.8 An integrated system

Healthy systems

A healthy system, one with outstanding capacity to cope with the dangers in its environment and to take advantage of the opportunities out there, performs all four functions:

▌ Differentiation allows it to cope with the complexity in its environment.
▌ Homogenization makes possible mutual understanding, respect and interchangeability throughout the system.
▌ Individuation supports freedom, uniqueness and entrepreneurism.
▌ Integration focuses energy on a common purpose.

Negative consequences of blindness

Breakdowns occur when system processes go out of balance, when systems engage in certain of these processes to the exclusion of others.

Systems within systems

Top, middle and bottom are systems within the larger system of the organization. Each of these systems-within-the-system exists in its unique environment (Figure 11.9). Breakdowns occur when these systems, in

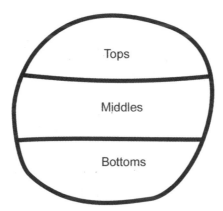

Figure 11.9 Tops, middles and bottoms

responding to the unique conditions of their environments, develop certain processes to the exclusion of others.

Top territoriality: differentiation without homogenization

The top system is that collection of people who have designated respons-ibility for the system as a whole. Examples include the top executive group, the plant management team, the parent couple in the family, the business partners. Tops exist in an environment of complexity and accountability; there are multiple difficult, complex, unpredictable issues they need to deal with, and they are collectively responsible for the system. Tops reflexively adapt to these conditions by differentiating. Differentiation is necessary for survival; without it, tops would be overwhelmed by unmanageable complexity. But there is no reflexive pull to homogenize, so a common top pattern develops: differentiation without homogenization. Tops carve out separate domains, becoming increasing knowledgeable about and responsible for their areas and decreasingly knowledgeable about and responsible for others' areas. The potential power of homogenization is lost. And, as a consequence, scenarios such as those outlined below develop with great regularity.

Top teams that begin in great promise fall into territoriality, with members becoming protective and defensive of their individual turfs. A 'mine' mentality develops – This is my territory, so don't interfere with it! There are painful interpersonal issues between top-team members around their relative importance to the system, lack of respect, lack of trust and irresolvable differences regarding what the system should be doing and what directions it should take. Once-promising relationships end in bitter and costly separation.

Top territoriality also has destructive consequences for the system, resulting in organizational silos that cause confusion throughout the system, loss of cooperation across silos, loss of potential synergies, and costly duplication of resources. And all of this develops because of tops' inability to see, understand and manage the system processes needed to cope with this world of complexity and accountability – differentiation and homogenization.

Middle alienation: individuation without integration

Middle peers – middle managers, supervisors, staff specialists – exist in a diffusing environment, one that draws them apart from one another and out toward the individuals or groups they are to lead, manage, supervise or coach. Middles reflexively adapt to these conditions by dispersing, focusing their energies away from one another and out toward these others. This individuation (dispersion) is an adaptive response; it is what middles are hired/paid to do. But there is no comparable reflexive pull to integrate, so middles grow increasingly alone and separate from one another. The potential power of integration is lost. And as a consequence, scenarios such as those described below develop with great regularity.

Middle peers are a non-team. An 'I' mentality develops in which members experience their separateness from one another, their difference and their uniqueness. Members feel competitive with one another – who am I better than, worse than, better off than, worse off than? Difference predominates so members evaluate one another on surface issues. And members see little collective power among them and little purpose in their being more closely connected. The system suffers from this lack of middle integration: tops do not get consistent information up from their middles; they can't get their initiatives consistently implemented through their middles; there is lack of coordination among system parts, less cooperation and mutual support than there could be; and bottoms are not getting consistent, system-wide information that would enable them to access what they need across boundaries. And once again, all of this develops as a consequence of middles failing to see, understand and master the system processes needed to cope with this diffusing world – individuation and integration.

Bottom groupthink: integration without individuation and differentiation
Bottoms exist in an environment of shared vulnerability, one in which they are on the receiving end of decisions and actions that affect their lives in major and minor ways. Bottoms reflexively adapt to this shared vulnerability by integrating, coalescing, becoming a collective 'We'. Integration is an adaptive response; it enables vulnerable bottoms to feel less vulnerable and, potentially, to act with greater collective influence. But the safety that comes with integration carries with it the cost of individuation and differentiation. Unauthorized individual actions and differences of opinion are experienced as dangerous, and therefore are suppressed. The potential powers of individuation and differentiation are lost. As a consequence, scenarios such as those given below develop with great regularity.

Bottom groups become systems unto themselves, with members feeling connected with one another and separate from the rest of the organization. They are a 'We', and all others are 'Them'. Along with their connectedness, there are strong pressures to conform. Difference and independence are experienced as potentially destructive to the cohesion of the 'We', so deviants are distrusted and pressured into conformity; they are cajoled into agreement with the 'We'; or they are jailed, institutionalized, or exiled. Those who disagree with the 'We' hide their disagreement from others, and sometimes from themselves. Because difference is so difficult to handle in the bottom world, because it is experienced as threatening the strength of the 'We', when differences do arise they cause painful rifts within the bottom world. Striking workers, once a cohesive entity, splinter into enemy camps because they are unable to envision and manage a differentiated strategy for coping with their vulnerability – 'We' will be the menacing force that gets 'Their' attention, and then 'They' will be eager to work with 'Us'. Similarly, workers facing change initiatives from the top splinter into those who see supporting the initiative as the only sensible strategy to follow versus those who see resisting it as the obvious path. Energy that could be integrated into coherent complex strategies is instead diverted into internal conflict. And again, all of this develops as a consequence of bottoms' inability to see, understand and manage the system processes needed to cope successfully with a world of vulnerability – integration and individuation and differentiation.

These scenarios unfold without awareness or choice. When we are blind to system processes, we simply fall into them. Put any of us together in these unique top, middle and bottom conditions, and these relational issues and their organizational consequences will develop – not always and not for everyone but with great regularity. The severity of symptoms will vary from situation to situation, but the basic pattern is consistently present. When seen through a personal lens, these issues that tops, middles and bottoms have with one another feel personal; and if issues are experienced as personal, then the usual responses follow: avoid, control, keep from being controlled, separate, divorce, fire or engage in some form of therapy for one or more of the parties. When observed through a systemic lens, we have a different understanding of these situations, and different interventions follow.

SYSTEMIC COACHING

Here again, education is a basic element of systemic coaching. One does not attempt to work these internal group relationships directly; to do so reinforces the belief that the issues are personal and specific to the coachee's situation. This is precisely what we want to avoid. The first intervention needs to make the case that the issues – territoriality, alienation or groupthink – have less to do with the people than with the systemic conditions they share. This requires some preliminary teaching about systems:

1. Identifying the basic system processes by which systems cope with the dangers in their environments and prospect among the opportunities – differentiation, homogenization, individuation and integration.
2. Presenting the image of a healthy system, one that engages in all four processes as it differentiates and homogenizes, individuates and integrates.
3. Identifying the unique environments in which tops, middles and bottoms function – the complexity and accountability at the top, the diffusion in the middle and the shared vulnerability at the bottom.

4. Demonstrating how these environments create process imbalance; eliciting certain processes will mean ignoring or suppressing others.
5. Clarifying the consequences of these imbalances for members' experiences of one another and for the system.
6. Specifying concrete strategies by which process balance can be established.

This education is best done with no reference to the clients' situations. It needs to be done in a way that supports an 'aha!' experience – This is not about us, this is about systems. That realization has the potential for depersonalizing the situation, reducing the emotionality, justification and blame, while opening the way to systemic remedies.

For all groups, the ultimate goal is the same: to create system robustness by bringing the processes into balance, but each group has different priorities in attaining this goal. The function of the coach is to help people develop and become committed to strategies aimed at developing the missing needed processes.

Tops need to differentiate, for that is the only way they can respond effectively to the complexity of their environment. However, in order to keep from falling into destructive territoriality with all its personal and organizational consequences, they need to actively work on homogenization. That is, while developing their differences, they need to simultaneously work on their commonality. Some homogenizing strategies include: sharing information with each other; letting each other in on the difficulties, issues and uncertainties they are facing; spending time walking in each other's shoes, experiencing directly each other's worlds; taking opportunities to work together in areas other than their designated responsibilities; and becoming coaches to one another. The process of mutual coaching may be the most powerful strategy tops can employ in order to simultaneously strengthen both homogenization and differentiation. As coaches, tops are committed to each other's success. Once tops are committed to pursuing homogenization as robustly as they pursue differentiation, they will find new ways to maintain their commonality while elaborating their differences.

Middles need to disperse; they need to spend the bulk of their time away from one another and out with those individuals and groups they lead, supervise, manage, coach or otherwise service. However, in order to avoid falling into the destructive alienation with all its personal and organizational consequences, middles need to work on integration. That is, they need to come together regularly – just middles, no tops (meetings with tops have other purposes). Integration involves: sharing information (thinking like intelligence officers: What clues are you picking up?); using this pooled information to diagnose system issues; sharing best practices;

using each other as resources to solve problems; becoming a collective force in the system (What is not happening? What is our vision for what can happen, and how are we going to make it happen?). Integration strengthens individuation; through integration individual middles become more informed and able to provide better service to those they lead, manage, supervise or coach, and to their tops. And individual middles are strengthened, feel less alone and more part of a powerful and supportive peer group. They become a powerful and valued force for systems change.

It is adaptive for bottoms to coalesce. Not only do they feel less vulnerable, but collectively they are less vulnerable. As a 'We', they are better positioned to avoid being exploited by the system. But, in order to avoid falling into the destructive pressures of groupthink with all its personal and organizational consequences, they need to work on individuation and integration. These need to be seen as supportive of survival rather than antithetical. 'In unity there is strength' as a motto needs to be replaced with 'In diversity there is more strength.' The challenge is to welcome independence and difference rather than fearing them, to see how these can contribute to strengthening the bottom position.

This, then, is the business of systems coaching as it relates to systems as processes: enabling coachees to see, understand and master the systemic processes in which they are functioning.

Resistance

What I have described above is the rational side of system processes coaching, yet there are also emotional factors to be considered. The longer dysfunctional relationships have been in place, the more difficulty there can be in transforming them – too much painful history to ignore or forgive, too much righteousness to surrender. Paradoxically, there is a piece of rational knowledge that may help to unlock the emotional barriers. The negative feelings that people have toward one another feel very solid, as if they reflect reality. A core piece of system knowledge is this: 'Our negative feelings are shaped by how we relate to the system conditions we are in; change how we relate and these feelings will diminish if not disappear.'

So, for example, I have at times made presentations on the power of middle integration, only to have someone come up to me at a break and say: 'Good idea, Barry, but it won't work with my group.' 'Why won't it work with your group?' 'Because we have little in common, we don't like one another, we have no collective power, so there's little point in our integrating. Maybe with another group . . .'

The piece of system knowledge this person is failing to grasp is this: We think that the reason we don't integrate is how we feel about one another, and if we felt differently then we would integrate. The reality is just the other way around. We feel the way we feel about one another because we don't integrate, and if we did integrate we would feel very differently.

This is the magic that the systems coach can bring: to demonstrate that so-called reality is the illusion of the coachee's world. Change the relationship and the illusion fades.

When tops change the way they relate to the complexity and accountability of their environment by becoming mutual coaches to one another, the tensions in their relationships disappear and they discover new power in their relationships.

When middles change the way they relate to the diffusion of their environment by integrating with one another, the indifference, competitiveness and evaluations melt away, and they discover new strength in their group.

When bottoms change the way they relate to the shared vulnerability of their environment by encouraging individual initiative and diversity, the fear of difference disappears and a new collective power emerges.

This is what it means to see, understand and master system processes.

CASE STUDY

The case of the rigid manager: is it personal or systemic?

Consider the relative power of personal versus systemic coaching in the following case. First I will describe the situation as it was presented to me; then I will examine the same situation through a systemic lens along with the implications for systemic coaching.

A change intervention that has been successful in Division A of Ace Service Co is being introduced into Division B with the help of a team of consultants/coaches. One snag: B's division head is less than enthusiastic about the project. His position is: our department managers are having enough trouble keeping up with day-to-day demands without dealing with the complexity of a whole new initiative. Still, the initiative is being undertaken and five of the six department managers seem committed to making it work despite apparent difficulties. Charles, the sixth manager, has been ignoring the initiative. The consultants/coaches have been having little success in working with him. They interpret his 'resistance' from a personal developmental framework, seeing him as being stuck at a developmental stage at which he is unable to separate himself from the demands of authority. From this framework, if Charles and the initiative are to be successful, he needs to be helped to move through that stage of development and acquire greater independence from his top.

Meanwhile, the other department managers, all operating independently of one another, are grappling with both the requirements of the new change initiative and the continuing demands of the division head, who is increasingly dissatisfied with them. His complaints: they have been lax on their paper work, reports are not timely or thorough, and there have been too many complaints from people in their operations. None of this is a problem for Charles. His paper work is fine, his reports are timely and thorough, and, as far as the division head is concerned, Charles' operation is running smoothly.

Let us assume the validity of the coaches' developmental framework: that Charles is in fact stuck at this stage of development and it would be useful to help him move through that stage. The question remains: Does a systemic lens offer a richer understanding of this situation along with more powerful intervention possibilities?

Through a systemic lens: persons and groups in the middle

The systems coach sees two familiar patterns.

Each of the department managers is attempting to cope with an end–middle–end relationship, torn between the conflicting demands and priorities of the division head on one end and the change initiative on the other. Although all suffer from the same tearing, their coping mechanisms vary, and whichever coping mechanism they fall into, the result is disappointment for one end or the other or both (Figure 11.10).

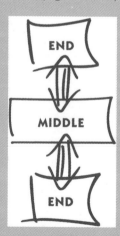

Figure 11.10 Ends and middles

Charles has resolved tearing by aligning up; the division head's priorities are his priorities. Charles is a problem to the consultants/coaches (disappointed ends), but not to his boss. The other middles are either aligning down – the change initiative being their priority – or ping-ponging, attempting to be responsive to both the priorities of the division head and the demands of the change initiative. In doing so, they have become a problem to the boss (disappointed end) while having limited success in managing the change initiative. So one challenge is to help all managers, not just Charles, find more powerful ways of coping with their middleness.

The second familiar pattern the systems coach sees is that of an alienated middle peer group: individuation without integration (Figure 11.11).

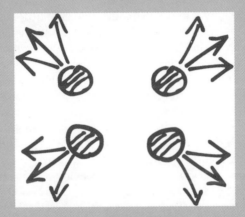

Figure 11.11 Individuals without integration

Each of these department managers is handling the stress of this situation alone. They do not function as a team nor is it likely that they even experience themselves as a potential team with any potential collective power. Each is in his and her 'I' mentality, in which their separateness from one another predominates. If they consider one another at all, they are likely to feel competitive – 'Am I handling this change initiative as well as others are handling it?' And they are likely to be evaluative of one another, with aligned-up and aligned-down managers having negative judgments of each other.

The systems coach sees this situation as one in which individuation and integration are out of balance; integration is the missing ingredient. The system coach recognizes the potential power integration has for strengthening these managers individually and for helping them develop a coherent strategy regarding the change initiative.

Integration would work by having these managers come together regularly – just them, without the division head. If the coach is present, the coach's role is to facilitate their interactions with one another, not to act as a leader. During these integration meetings managers would share information (What's working? What's not?). By pooling information they would develop a more global system picture; they would strengthen each other by sharing best practices and by coaching each other in ways to deal with difficult situations; and they would develop coherent strategies for managing both the change initiative and the relationships with the division head. Through these meetings the managers would experience the fundamental principle that integration strengthens individuation.

This is what the system coach sees as a possibility; the challenge becomes how to make this happen. The first step as usual is education. The department managers need to step away from their current situation and learn about middleness: the end–middle–end relationship with its familiar scenarios, and the middle peer relationship with its familiar scenarios. If they are caught up in the 'I' consciousness, experiencing their separateness, competitiveness and collective powerlessness, they need to see how this is a consequence of their dispersal, and that with integration and a powerful shared mission a very different experience of one another is likely to develop.

Through a personal lens, we focus on one problematic manager who needs to be helped. Through a systemic lens, we see and understand a systemic condition affecting many parties and the system as a whole. Instead of 'fixing' individuals, or in addition to such work, the business of the systems coach is to help coachees see, understand and master the systemic conditions in which they and others function.

CONCLUSIONS

Much that seems personal is not personal; many of the relationship issues people experience stem from system blindness. The goal of systems coaching is to help coachees avoid the negative consequence of system blindness, and to find the power, satisfaction and organizational effectiveness that comes with systems sight. As systems coaches, our job is to help our coachees see organizational interactions as more than people-meeting-people, but to see these as patterns of relationship – top–bottom, end–middle–end, and provider–customer – and as patterns of processes – differentiation, homogenization, individuation and integration. Our job is to help them understand how these processes shape their experiences, their relationships with others and their contributions to their systems. Overall, our goal is to develop clients who see, understand and master the system contexts in which they function, and in so doing find greater personal satisfaction, productive partnerships with others and more significant contributions to their organizations.

References

Oshry, B (1986, 1992) *The Possibilities of Organization*, Power + Systems, Boston, MA

Oshry, B (1994) *In the Middle*, Power + Systems, Boston, MA

Oshry, B (1999) *Leading Systems: Lesson from the Power Lab*, Berrett-Koehler, San Francisco, CA

Oshry, B (2007) *Seeing Systems: Unlocking the Mysteries of Organizational Life*, 2nd edn, Berrett-Koehler, San Francisco, CA

Information on the Power Lab and the Organization Workshop can be found at www.powerandsystems.com.

12

Coaching for transactional and transformational leadership

Juliette Alban-Metcalfe and Glenn Mead

INTRODUCTION

The concepts of transactional and transformational leadership were most famously described by Professor Bernard Bass in 1985. This chapter describes how this leadership model is equally, if not more, critical today for understanding organizational effectiveness and how to sustain performance as it was then. How the concepts were envisioned, particularly in relation to Bass's 'Full range of leadership' model, is outlined, as well as research underpinning the model, and recent modifications. The chapter also provides clear guidance for coaches adopting the model for leadership development, and describes a case study of its use in transforming a leader's effectiveness for the better.

THE CONCEPT OF TRANSACTIONAL AND TRANSFORMATIONAL LEADERSHIP

In the late 1970s and early 1980s, models of leadership shifted from a focus simply on balancing the need for concern for people, and the need for concern for task/production, known as the 'situational' and 'contingency' models, to the 'new paradigm' models, which sought to understand the characteristics of leadership as essentially about dealing with increasing complexity, magnitude and constant change.

The distinction between management and leadership came to the fore through the work of John Kotter at the start of the 1980s. Although he wasn't the first to stress the importance of this distinction, his book entitled *A Force for Change: How leadership differs from management* (1990) was to become a modern classic. In essence he described management as about creating order and some stability through activities such as planning and budgeting, organizing and controlling, while leadership is about motivating and inspiring individuals to energize them to overcome barriers to change, aligning them behind a clear vision, and creating productive change that enables the organization to achieve its ambitions. He regards the presence of both as essential for success.

Other models included in the 'new paradigm' category, include those of charismatic leadership (House, 1977; Conger, 1989), visionary leadership (Sashkin, 1988), and, most notably, transformational leadership (Bass, 1985; Bennis and Nanus, 1985; Tichy and Devanna, 1986). These described the notion of the leader as someone who, by defining their organization's mission and the values that will support it, defines organizational reality. Thus, in the 'new paradigm' approach, leaders are seen as managers of meaning, rather than just someone who participates in an influence process (Bryman, 1996).

The most prominent leadership scholar to contribute to the popularity of the model of transformational leadership was US Professor Bernard Bass, whose legacy continues to influence debate and practice relating to leadership. His first major publication on the subject was a book entitled *Leadership and Performance: Beyond expectations* (Bass, 1985).

BASS'S 'FULL RANGE OF LEADERSHIP' MODEL

In his model, known as the 'Full range of leadership model' (Bass, 1998), Bass asserts that all leaders display a range of styles of leadership, including 'transactional', 'transformational' and 'laissez-faire'.

Transactional leadership

In adopting a transactional style, leaders essentially exert their influence over their staff by reinforcing their behaviours either positively or negatively, depending on whether or not their staff perform according to the leader's expectations and desires. Therefore it is, in effect, a process of contingent reinforcement, which might express itself in positive contingent reward, such as when providing praise or positive feedback for good performance, or promising support for a raise or promotion in return for staff's efforts; or it might be in the form of negative reinforcement, such as an expression of dissatisfaction with the individual or the withdrawal of particular privileges.

Management by exception: active and passive

Bass also refers to a form of negative reinforcement as 'management by exception', which takes two forms of transactional corrective action, either active or passive. Active corrective action involves monitoring performance, and intervening when appropriate, whereas passive corrective action involves correcting someone only when problems emerge.

Transformational leadership

Bass maintains that the previous styles do not have the same degree of positive effect in motivating others to achieve to their highest levels of development and performance as a 'transformational' approach, something that has been supported in numerous research studies. A transformational style of leadership is named as such because of its effect to transform followers 'to perform beyond expectations', in part by 'creating an emotional bond between leader and follower and by arousing enthusiasm for a common vision' (Kearney, 2008). More specifically, transformational leaders are characterized by being able to motivate colleagues and followers to:

▌ view their work from new perspectives;
▌ be aware of their team and organization's mission or vision;
▌ attain higher levels of ability and potential;
▌ look beyond their own interests toward those that will benefit the group (Bass, 1985).

Transformational leadership is not, however, seen as being sufficient for an organization to be effective in achieving or sustaining its success. Rather, for an organization to be successful, leadership must be accompanied by transactional leadership.

Bass, identified four transformational components of leadership – idealized influence, inspirational motivation, intellectual stimulation and individualized consideration, shown in Figure 12.1.

Laissez-faire leadership

The final form of leadership style, is 'laissez-faire': a style of leadership that is, in fact, an abrogation of leadership, since there is an absence of any transaction. This style is deemed to be most ineffective (Bass, 1998).

Idealized influence
Behaving in ways that result in the leader being admired, respected and trusted, such that their followers wish to emulate them. They are extraordinarily capable, persistent, and determined.

Inspirational motivation
Behaving such that they motivate and inspire those around them by providing meaning, optimism and enthusiasm for a vision of a future state.

Intellectual stimulation
Encouraging followers to question assumptions, reframe problems and approach old solutions in new ways, and to be creative and innovative. At times, their followers' ideas may differ from those of the leader, who may solicit or encourage such responses.

Individualized consideration
Actively developing the potential of their followers by creating new opportunities for development, coaching, mentoring, and paying attention to each follower's needs and desires. They know their staff well, as a result of listening, communicating, and walking around encouraging, rather than monitoring their efforts.

Figure 12.1 The four transformational components of Bass's leadership model

RESEARCH INTO BASS'S MODEL OF TRANSFORMATIONAL LEADERSHIP USING THE MLQ

Bass's Full range model of leadership was expressed in the Multifactor Leadership Questionnaire (MLQ; Bass and Avolio, 1990a, 1990b), which has been described as the most commonly used leadership instrument (Bryman, 1996; Carless, 1998). It has been researched in numerous studies over the years by the author and other independent researchers, and has been modified to take into account new learning. For example, as a result of the analyses of 3,786 responses to the MLQ in 14 independent studies, the model was revised such that the first two transformational dimensions (idealized influence and inspirational motivation) are combined into one (Avolio, Bass and Jung, 1999). A survey conducted among US doctors who run community health centres (Xirasagar, 2008) found that three scales emerge, rather than six, namely a 'transactional', a 'transformational' (which is a combination of the four individual scales defined by Bass) and a 'laissez-faire' scale.

In his book *Transformational Leadership: Industrial, military and educational impact* (Bass, 1998), Bass refers to the fact that the MLQ has been adopted in studies that include leadership styles of secondary-school teachers, white-collar workers, priests, nuns and monks in the Catholic church, supervisors of insurance company employees, and military personnel. In reviewing the findings from these studies, Bass has concluded that, in general, transformational leadership is more effective and satisfying than transactional leadership, and he cites numerous studies that provide evidence of the superiority of the transformational approach over the transactional approach used alone (Bass, 1998).

Not all studies adopting the MLQ have provided support for the specific model. A recent research study conducted among cadets in officer training in the Israeli Defence Force sought to investigate the impact of leaders on their teams, taking account of the presence of a learning culture in the team and the degree of cohesion within it (Mannheim and Halamish, 2008). The study failed to find universal evidence of a link between ratings of the team leaders and the teams' performance for two of the tracks. In discussing their results the researchers suggest that factors such as experience of working in operational combat might moderate this relationship, as might levels of education and the specialist track in which the cadets work; in other words, contextual factors might moderate such a relationship between transformational leadership as assessed by the MLQ and team performance. Furthermore, there have been concerns about the applicability of Bass's model of leadership, given its provenance in being based on self-reports of managers, all of whom were male and in very senior positions. These concerns have centred on the fact that there might be other factors in leadership that motivate and satisfy employees in today's much more diverse organizations.

Nevertheless, without doubt Bass's contribution to our understanding of leadership has been enormous. The distinctions he highlighted between transactional and transformational leadership – emphasizing the superiority of the latter although also clearly stating that both are necessary for effective leadership – have provided hundreds of thousands of managers with invaluable support for their development. One of the most important legacies of Bass's work on leadership has been to place integrity and authenticity at its core, rather than influence and utility. He took pains to expose those who might espouse transformational leadership, or indeed superficially try to enact the style for totally self-serving reasons, referring to them as 'pseudo-transformational' while warning people of their toxicity.

TRANSACTIONAL AND TRANSFORMATIONAL LEADERSHIP IN THE 21st CENTURY

Today's organizational environment is quite different from that of 10 or 15 years ago. In both the public and private sector, organizations are increasingly asking employees to do more with the same, or less, resources than before. If they are to be sustainable, they need to be able to engage employees' discretionary effort, rather than rely on traditional methods of motivating and rewarding people. This need emphasizes the importance of a transformational approach to leadership.

At the same time, after scandals such as the collapse of Enron and WorldCom, not to mention the global financial crisis of 2009, organizations are waking up to the fact that governance is essential, and the behaviour of leaders, regardless of their seniority, must be questioned. There is some unease about the suggestion that effective leaders must be some sort of 'hero' who communicates a vision and direction for the organization to others in a one-way process, as is suggested by certain aspects of Bass's transformational factor of 'idealized influence'. This consideration for leader behaviour is further underlined by the findings of researchers such as Shamir (1995), who suggested that leadership research should distinguish between the ideal characteristics of 'nearby' leaders such as one's line manager, and 'distant' leaders such as the CEOs studied in the original studies by Bass.

A number of research studies published by Alimo-Metcalfe and colleagues (eg Alimo-Metcalfe and Alban-Metcalfe, 2008; Alimo-Metcalfe *et al*, 2008), based on a UK model of transformational leadership (ELQ™ – described in *Psychometrics in Coaching* in this book series) that has been independently validated in the United States and Australia, have re-emphasized the importance of transformational leadership behaviours, in particular in supporting positive attitudes to work and well-being at work. While this model has a great many parallels with Bass's transformational scales, there is a significant omission of any great importance of being 'heroic' or 'charismatic', and the model emphasizes the importance, for example, of building shared vision. Indeed, cross-sectional and longitudinal studies based on this model consistently show that behaviours most closely aligned with Bass's 'individualized consideration' have the greatest positive impact on employees and, as is surprisingly unusual in leadership studies, have been demonstrated to improve organizational performance (Alimo-Metcalfe *et al*, 2008).

USING THE TRANSACTIONAL AND TRANSFORMATIONAL LEADERSHIP MODEL WITH COACHEES

Although it was recognized almost 15 years ago that both transformational and transactional leadership are crucial for effectiveness, it can be argued that most organizations continue to have predominantly transactional cultures. Examination of leadership models that have been adopted nationally, competency frameworks for selection or promotion, and performance management systems reveals that what is being assessed is predominantly (and sometimes exclusively) transactional behaviour. Or at the very least, these models and frameworks tend not to focus on the transformational behaviours that are crucial for enabling the individual to be effective alongside the necessary transactional behaviours or competencies. There are of course some great exceptions, but because we are most used to transactional leadership styles, transformational leadership behaviours can be perceived as 'pink and fluffy' or unimportant.

Thus, a misperception when using transactional and transformational leadership models in leadership development coaching can be that a transformational leadership culture would be less effective in achieving and managing organizational performance. Another potential issue is the possible misperception by coachees that the prevalence of a predominantly transactional culture in their organizations will prevent the use and adoption of a more transformational approach. Therefore, an essential starting point for coaching using the transformational and transactional leadership model is for the coach to understand their complementary effectiveness and be able to explain these to the coachee.

INTRODUCING FORMAL LEADERSHIP MODELS IN COACHING

The choice of whether or not to explicitly introduce these models for discussion during the coaching sessions remains the coach's, unless he or she is part of a leadership development programme based on the use of a 360° feedback transformational and transactional leadership questionnaire, such as the MLQ™ or the ELQ™. If such an instrument is being used, the leadership model it is based on will typically form the centrepiece of the coaching conversation.

Given the choice, the coach may find it beneficial to use the models in the background to guide the coaching process, rather than to allow them to immediately become a benchmark in the coachee's mind against which his or her leadership is compared. If coachees subsequently decide that they would benefit from assessing their leadership behaviour against these models, then 360° feedback can usefully be introduced.

BACKGROUND RESEARCH ON THE ORGANIZATION'S CULTURE

Regardless of whether the coach decides to make explicit use of the models or not, some sound preparation before the coaching session ought to consider clues as to the likely attitude or position of the organization (and perhaps of the individual coachees), and therefore to the most suitable approach to use in coaching to help the coachee make sense of prevalent leadership styles in the organization. What does the coach know about the culture of the organization, either from experience of previous work with that organization, the experience and reports of other consultants, or its reputation in the eyes of the public at large? What sector is this organization in and is there a typical culture for that sector?

For example, in working with the Fire and Rescue and Ambulance Services in England and Wales, the author has not been surprised to find a generally transactional style of leadership displayed by senior executives who began their careers at the operational level, given the particularly militaristic and hierarchical culture in such organizations. Whilst this style may at times be appropriate for the operational effectiveness of sub-units such as firefighter crews and paramedic teams working in a crisis situation, it does not follow that this is the most appropriate style to be used in leading and managing people in a non-crisis situation, which is effectively most of the time. Furthermore, there is much evidence to suggest that, in fact, particularly during times of crisis, leaders can benefit from listening to the suggestions of others in their team for potential solutions. If leaders are perceived as purely transactional in their approach to others, they are much less likely to be able to benefit from the expertise and contribution of their team members when they need it most.

CONTEXTUALIZING THE MODELS

When faced with a transactional organizational culture, the coach would find it very useful to be prepared to be able to explain the difference between transactional and transformational leadership styles by providing examples to illustrate how these approaches are operationalized to best effect. For example, research conducted by Bass *et al* (2003) examined the performance of 72 infantry platoons of the US Army in real-time operational effectiveness. They found evidence to suggest that the greater the complexity of operation in hand, the more the leader relied on a transformational style of leadership to ensure effective unit performance.

In contrast to operationally focused sectors, it might be the case that many organizations in the creative and developmental sectors, such as the arts, marketing and advertising, have more laissez-faire or transformational than transactional cultures. In these cases, the coach's challenge might be identifying enough transactional interactions between leader and team members with which to work.

In addition to making an initial assessment of the organizational culture, the coach must also consider the position of the organization, be it a private or public sector body, and what effect this might have on the attitudes of its employees and the current demands on them:

▌ Is the organization in a period of growth, consolidation, stagnation or decline?
▌ What is happening in the business? Expansion leading to over-stretched staff? Cost-saving measures leading to redundancies?
▌ What are the concomitant effects on the staff and the culture?

▮ Does there seem to be enough time for anything other than getting the job done in a transactional fashion? If this seems to be the case, the coach would benefit from preparing to explain to coachees the impact their behaviour will have if they adopt a purely transactional style, with research showing that it can have a very demotivating and stressful impact (eg Alimo-Metcalfe and Alban-Metcalfe, 2008).

UNDERSTANDING THE COACHEE'S CONTEXT

The final piece of preparation is for the coach to gather some objective information about the coachee with whom he or she is working. Information such as roles and responsibilities, duration in post and track record in current and previous sectors can be useful in understanding the breadth and depth of experience of the coachee, but these do not offer much guidance for how to approach the coaching session.

It is essential to know whether the individual is being coached as part of a formal organization-wide leadership development initiative, or whether coaching has been suggested for specific individual development. For the latter, is the objective to address a shortcoming (ie a deficit approach) or to develop skills and competence required for greater effectiveness and/or responsibility (ie a talent management approach)?

The individual talent management approach and the organization-wide initiative would warrant explicit use of the transactional and transformational models in the coaching sessions, as they provide the model or exemplar against which personal development plans will be created. For the scenario where individual performance is deemed to be lacking, a less overt use of the models and a greater focus on a person-centred style of coaching would better suit coachees who need to be encouraged to make changes to their own styles and behaviours, beginning from their own point of reference and expanding their perception through skilful coaching to include a broader understanding of what behaviours are most effective.

Whilst this preparation before coaching is useful, it can only provide the coach with ideas of the range of possible attitudes that the coachee might display to coaching and to the concepts of transactional and transformational leadership. These ideas remain as hypotheses that provide the coach with information-seeking questions to ask the coachee in the initial stages of the coaching relationship. Until the first meeting with the coachee, the coach's picture will lack detail of the coachee's perception of his or her own role and performance, and of the strength of relationship with their team and line manager alike.

UNDERSTANDING LEADERSHIP STYLE IMPACT

At the heart of the coaching session must be the issue of how aware coachees are of the impact on their teams of their leadership style. Their commitment to improving their impact can also dictate the outcome, successful or otherwise, of the whole coaching relationship. The coach's objective should be to encourage coachees to think about their relationship with those they lead in terms of leadership style, and the impact of this style on the team's effectiveness. Specifically, coachees should consider the direct effect their interactions have on their staffs' motivation, enthusiasm for work, satisfaction and commitment to the organization. The components of transformational and transactional leadership have been shown to lead to increased satisfaction, motivation, job and organizational commitment and other positive outcomes in a variety of ways. Different team members will prefer to be led in different ways, and will have different needs for direction or autonomy, aspirations and motivators, so it is important for coachees to start to explore the impact they are having on the different individuals they seek to influence, and how they can test their assumptions and perceptions.

COACHING FOR LEADERSHIP DEVELOPMENT WITH 360° FEEDBACK

If the coachee's leadership development involves use of a 360° feedback instrument, the first coaching session generally involves feeding back the results of the questionnaire. This session should include a review of the model of leadership that the questionnaire measures, in order to emphasize the significance of the behaviours assessed to organizational effectiveness.

By reinforcing the reasons why a particular model of leadership is relevant, the coach should help concentrate the coachee's mind on strengthening his or her own internal locus of control and self-efficacy with the intention of taking positive steps to addressing shortcomings or to building on current leadership strengths. Coaching must be seen as an opportunity for the coachee to take charge of his or her own development, rather than a chance to hand responsibility to the coach. Focusing on the importance of the model, and emphasizing self-efficacy should also help the coachee to commit to the process, rather than wallowing in hurt and defensiveness over lower ratings.

A 360° questionnaire report offers the coach a structure to follow and to guide the coachee through, generating open questions around each

dimension or scale presented. Consideration of each item (eg 'I am sensitive to my staff's particular needs and aspirations') can offer the coach a
wide range of directions in which to explore the evidence presented. For
example:

▌ 'What are your staff's particular needs and aspirations?' A direct
question to test how much the coachee really does know. It can help
for this question to be followed up with 'How do you know you are
correct?' – which helps to test out whether such conversations have
actually taken place, or whether they should in future.

▌ 'How do you demonstrate that you are sensitive to their needs and
aspirations?' This question invites the coachee to explain what behaviours the staff might gauge as being sensitive or insensitive.

▌ 'How sensitive to their needs and aspirations do you think you are?'
While the coachee's own rating will already be on the report, the
coach prompts the coachee to give a more descriptive answer.

▌ 'What signals do you (would you) expect to see from a boss who is
sensitive to your own needs and aspirations?' This question helps to
elicit the coachee's own values, which can then be compared with his
or her own behaviour. While it could seem to be couched in accusatory
language (ie 'How would you like it if someone did this to you?'), it
provokes the coachee into thinking about leading by example, and
what sort of example he or she is setting.

▌ 'What consequences could there be if your staff continue to believe
that you are not sensitive to their needs and aspirations?' or 'What
consequences could there be if you become more sensitive to their
needs and aspirations?' The coach can continue to engage the coachee
by positing hypothetical questions to explore the outcome of the
coachee's planned inaction. Objectively, the coachee cannot deny the
data in the report (provided that the feedback was given anonym-
ously, for developmental purposes only), as they are a collection of
honest opinions about the impact of his or her leadership style; they
are the perceptions that influence their reviewers' well-being and
positive attitudes to work.

It is important to recognize that the feedback results only provide subjective opinion with little or no supporting context. What meaning does
the coachee make, and is that perception, like the self-rating and those of
the other reviewers, accurate or flawed? It is essential that, following the
instrument feedback, the coachee gathers more information to further
explore the data presented. The best way to do that is to ask the reviewers
for more specific, behavioural examples of what they would like the
coachee to:

▍ do more of;
▍ do less of;
▍ stop doing;
▍ start doing.

Encouraging reviewers' ongoing involvement in the leader's development process can be a strong indication of a leader adopting a more satisfying, transformational style.

COACHING FOR LEADERSHIP DEVELOPMENT WITHOUT 360° FEEDBACK

Coaching for leadership development without the use of a 360° questionnaire is effective when it covers the elements of transformational and transactional leadership that motivate and enable others to realize their best performance. The coach could frame questions based on Bass and Avolio's leadership model, particularly the four transformational areas of idealized influence, inspirational motivation, intellectual stimulation and individualized concern, and the transactional behaviours (Bass and Avolio, 1990a).

The coachee's immediate needs and wishes will initially drive the coaching session agenda, but the coach needs to contextualize the leadership behaviours within wider organizational objectives and explain how the leadership styles will enable the coachee to contribute more effectively. It is not necessary to particularly use the words 'transactional' and 'transformational', but this can help the explanations given. Understanding the context for leadership styles must include consideration of the other people with whom the coachee works (line manager, peers, team, etc). For example, exploration of when, and with whom, it might be appropriate to use a more or less transactional or transformational style is important.

Without 360° feedback data, there is no information from third parties included in the coaching process, at least during the initial session. The coach and coachee have only the coachee's perceptions of his or her own leadership style to work from. Given extensive research on our tendency not to be completely self-aware, and the critical importance of accurate self-awareness for effective leadership, it is important that coachees are encouraged to seek feedback from others whom they trust to be open and honest in describing their perceptions of the coachees' behaviour and its impact. These data can be very usefully introduced in follow-up coaching sessions as a basis for action.

Covering all the aspects of transformational and transactional leadership without a 360° feedback model to refer to requires thorough preparation by the coach. Questions to elicit coachees' thoughts as to what their leadership style is and what impact it has can be designed by considering the overall scales in a model such as that of Bass and Avolio, and constructing appropriate questions for individual coachees based on their circumstances and relationships.

Steering coachees towards understanding the increasingly positive impact they could have if they enhanced their transformational and transactional leadership style is also crucially important for sustaining their motivation to change. Bass (eg 1985) and Alimo-Metcalfe and Bradley (2008) have written useful articles that address the 'So what?' question.

CASE STUDY

The coaching relationship in this case study was initially intended to span around four months, being conducted in four 90-minute sessions taking place at six-week intervals. The coachee was a deputy director in a UK public sector organization, reporting to a director responsible for a key part of the administrative function of the organization.

The coachee came to coaching as part of an organization-wide initiative to offer senior managers the opportunity to develop their leadership capabilities. Without any particular leadership development model in mind or proffered by the organization, or any explicit requirement for a specified coaching approach or range of approaches to be offered, coachees were simply offered four coaching sessions in which they could address any issue regarding their working practices. When assigned to the coachee in this case study, the coach was told by the coordinating department within the organization that the coachee was considered by others to be a difficult individual, who many found to be quite aloof and uncommunicative.

The initial meeting was conducted off-site in a public meeting place. After initial introductions and explanations about the coaching process, the coachee explained his objective for the session, which was to find ways of becoming more strategic in his role rather than operational. With no knowledge of the coachee's role, this prompted the following questions and subsequent lines of exploration:

▋ What do you do/what does your role involve? What are your key responsibilities?

▐ To whom do you report? Who reports to you and how are they organized? With whom else do you work closely? (Who are your line manager/direct reports/peers?)

▐ What responsibilities require you to work at a more strategic level? What operational activities do you typically find yourself attending to? Who else in your team is involved in achieving these results?

The mood of the initial meeting was indeed downbeat and the coach felt that no emotional bond was forged. This first session had explored the coachee's immediate environment and populated the statement he had proffered (ie being more strategic than operational) with a range of reasons or potential causes that explained why this situation remained in a state of equilibrium.

The second and third sessions explored in greater detail the coachee's relationship with his line manager and peers respectively. As deputy to the director, he received his direction and objectives from his line manager invariably by e-mail, even though they occupied the same building. Face-to-face meetings did take place frequently but, according to the coachee, these involved the director running through a list of bullet-point actions on an e-mail printout that formed the agenda for the meeting. Without deviation from the agenda, the coachee found no opportunity to introduce his own issues or raise concerns.

The evidence was pointing to the coachee's line manager having a predominantly transactional style. At this stage, the coach asked how the coachee felt about this level of interaction from his line manager, as he detected a sense of unease. How would he like it to be? What could he do to effect change? The conversation evolved to explore the coachee's needs and aspirations as a direct report of his line manager: his job satisfaction and levels of confidence, his commitment and motivation to achieve beyond his expectations. This resulted in the coachee expressing his own values, which the coach compared with both transactional and transformational leadership styles. In brief, it appeared that his line manager's behaviours effectively prevented him from acting more strategically, as he needed the director to be keen to involve him in building a shared vision, to be more decisive in providing that vision and to be more open in encouraging the coachee to express his opinion and work in partnership with him. The coachee openly considered ways in which he could positively influence the relationship with his director.

The focus of coaching then turned to the coachee's peers and direct reports. Having expressed the standards by which he wanted others to treat him (ie more transformationally and less transactionally), the coachee was in the right mindset to consider how his direct reports and peers interacted with him and whether his style was considered to be satisfying and inspiring. The conversation turned to the stress levels that he and his two peers experienced as a result of the director's style and what needed to be done about it, reaching the conclusion that the coachee was the person best positioned to influence the director out of the three of them. The remaining sessions dealt with addressing the needs of his team and peers by acting in a more transformational way.

The coaching relationship was extended to six sessions in all. Eighteen months later, the coachee requested additional sessions in order to help him prepare for promotion into the director's role, upon the latter's early retirement, and explore ways to lead the department to achieving the Investors in People standard. Reports from the coordinating department stated that the coachee was 'a changed person' and that the standing of the department in the eyes of the organization was raised as a direct result of his leadership style.

Throughout the coaching relationship, neither transactional nor transformational leadership models were explicitly mentioned or discussed. The conversations covered aspects of the coachee's emotional involvement with his line manager and how the highly formal, transactional way in which business was conducted proved to be a frustration for him. The coachee's perception of his peers' abilities, needs and aspirations, and the effect on their workplace stress as a result of the departmental intransigence that they were all experiencing, caused him to consider what actions he could and should take to bring about an improvement in their collective work experience and an increase in their department's effectiveness.

CONCLUSIONS

The model of transactional and transformational leadership provides coaches with an easy to understand and explain conception of effective styles for motivating individuals in today's diverse organizations. With its emphasis on values and integrity, and on recognizing individuals' needs, aspirations and potential contributions, it is a modern approach to achieving superior, sustained performance in organizations. Most importantly, it has great face validity, and can be described as providing common-sense understanding of how to motivate and get the most out of people with mutual benefit to them.

References

Alban-Metcalfe, J and Alimo-Metcalfe, B (2009) Engaging Leadership, *International Journal of Leadership in Public Services*, **5** (1), pp 10–18

Alimo-Metcalfe, B and Alban-Metcalfe, J (2003) Stamp of greatness, *Health Service Journal*, 26 June, pp 28–32

Alimo-Metcalfe, B and Alban-Metcalfe, J (2008) *Engaging leadership: Creating organizations that maximize the potential of their people*, CIPD, London

Alimo-Metcalfe, B, Alban-Metcalfe, J, Bradley, M, Mariathasan, J and Samele, C (2008) The impact of engaging leadership on performance, attitudes to work and well-being at work: a longitudinal study, *Journal of Health Organization and Management*, **22** (6), pp 586–98

Alimo-Metcalfe, B, Alban-Metcalfe, J, Samele, C, Bradley, M and Mariathasan, J (2007) *The Impact of Leadership Factors in Implementing Change in Complex Health and Social Care Environments: NHS plan clinical priorities for mental health crisis resolution teams (CRTs)*, DOH NHS SDo, Project 22/2002

Alimo-Metcalfe, B and Bradley, M (2008) Cast in a new light, *People Management*, **24** January, pp 38–41

Avolio, B J, Bass, B M and Jung, D I (1999) Re-examining the components of transformational and transactional leadership using the Multifactor Leadership Questionnaire, *Journal of Occupational and Organizational Psychology*, **72** (4), pp 441–62

Bass, B M (1985) *Leadership and Performance: Beyond expectations*, Free Press, Oxford

Bass, B M (1997) Does the transactional–transformational leadership paradigm transcend organizational and national boundaries? *American Psychologist*, **52**, pp 130–39

Bass, B M (1998) *Transformational Leadership: Industrial, military, and educational impact*, Lawrence Erlbaum, Mahwah, NJ

Bass, B M and Avolio, B J (1990a) *Multifactor Leadership Questionnaire*, Consulting Psychologists Press, Palo Alto, CA

Bass, B M and Avolio, B J (1990b) *Transformational Leadership Development: Manual for the Multifactor Leadership Questionnaire*, Consulting Psychologists Press, Palo Alto, CA

Bass, B M, Avolio, B J and Benson, Y (2003) Predicting unit performances by assessing transformation and transactional leadership, *Journal of Applied Psychology*, **88** (2), pp 207–18

Bennis, W and Nanus, B (1985) *Leaders*, Harper & Row, New York

Bryman, A (1996) Leadership in organizations, in *Handbook of Organizational Studies*, ed S R Clegg, C Hardy and W R Nord, pp 276–92, Sage, London

Carless, S A (1998) Assessing the discriminant validity of transformational leader behaviour as measured by the MLQ, *Journal of Occupational and Organizational Psychology*, **71**, pp 353–58

Conger, J A (1989) *The Charismatic Leader: Behind the mystique of exceptional leadership*, Jossey-Bass, San Francisco, CA

Hersey, P and Blanchard, K H (1969) Life cycle theory of leadership, *Training and Development Journal*, **23**, pp 26–34

House, R J (1977) A 1976 theory of charismatic leadership, in *Leadership: The cutting edge*, ed J G Hunt and L L Larson, pp 189–207, Southern Illinois University Press, Carbondale, IL

Kearney, E (2008) Age differences between leaders and followers as a moderator of the relationship between transformational leadership and team performance, *Journal of Occupational and Organizational Psychology*, **81**, pp 803–11

Kotter, J P (1990) *A Force for Change: How leadership differs from management*, Free Press, Oxford

Mannheim, B and Halamish, H (2008) Transformational leadership as related to team outcomes and contextual moderation, *Leadership and Organization Journal*, **29**, pp 617–30

Northouse, P G (2004) *Leadership: Theory and practice*, 3rd edn, Sage, London

Sashkin, M (1988) The visionary leader, in *Charismatic Leadership: The elusive factor in organizational effectiveness*, ed J A Conger and R N Kanungo, pp 122–60, Jossey-Bass, San Francisco, CA

Shamir, B (1995) Social distance and charisma: theoretical notes and an explanatory study, *Leadership Quarterly*, **6**, 19–47

Tichy, N and Devanna, M (1986) *Transformational Leadership*, John Wiley, New York

Xirasagar, S (2008) Transformational, transactional and laissez-faire leadership among physician executives, *Journal of Health Organization and Management*, **22**, pp 599–613

13

Coaching for leadership style

Gerard Fitzsimmons and Samantha Guise

INTRODUCTION

In a recent Hay Group survey (Walker, 2007) senior managers revealed their disappointment that it takes a newly recruited or promoted middle manager an average of seven months to perform effectively, as opposed to the target of four months. Three months of lost productivity. In the same survey, 56 per cent of senior managers cited the cost of time as the major barrier to training middle managers in their organizations.

So, with increased pressures to perform but less time to learn, what happens to the journey of self-discovery that the transition to leadership could – and should – be? Can new leaders afford to engage in development that doesn't deal directly with the immediate imperative to deliver?

This will be a familiar scenario to those coaching new leaders, trying to offer a balance of challenge and support that matches these tensions. In this chapter we aim to explore how coaching may provide some answers. In particular we will explore the discipline of focusing on leadership styles – the behaviours that encourage quick wins with a team – while remaining open to the wide range of abilities, values and experiences that an individual leader draws upon.

THE HAY GROUP LEADERSHIP MODEL

We know that effective leaders create an energizing and engaging environment for the people they lead (Figure 13.1). The leader, through his or her behaviours, has the biggest impact on team climate. And team climate, in turn, affects performance. It affects the amount of effort people in a team will contribute, the motivation they feel to do their best work. The more they contribute, the more successful the team can be.

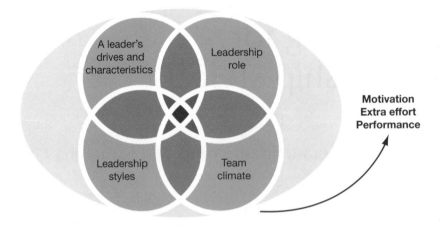

Figure 13.1 Hay Group's model of leadership effectiveness

When we look carefully at what a leader does to create team climate, six distinct patterns of behaviour emerge – six leadership styles (Goleman, 2000). Effective managers use these styles in the right measure, at just the right time, to create a positive, energizing work climate for their teams.

So what are the six leadership styles that a new leader can learn and use?

The directive style: immediate compliance

The directive style (also referred to as the coercive style) provides direct clarity about how a task needs to be completed. It raises standards in the short term by demanding compliance. It is not helpful in communicating 'the big picture' (the reason why a task needs to be performed), which means it can cause standards to drop in the long term. It is about 'how' things should be done, but it does not deal with 'what' or 'why'. When used too much or as a long-term style, it can demotivate employees.

The visionary style: long-term direction and vision

The visionary (or authoritative) style provides clarity for the short, medium and long term. It helps team members understand what they need to do, how they need to do it and, most importantly, why it matters. It provides context and paints the 'big picture'. It creates a positive team climate in which team members are able to give their best.

If there is a risk to this style, it is when team members are highly experienced and capable – when they know best. In that case the leader needs to secure their input in creating the vision and in deciding how to achieve it.

The affiliative style: creating harmony

The affiliative style can create a harmonious working atmosphere. It can make team members feel valued as individuals, not just workers. It recognizes each team member's emotional needs. Sometimes people see their managers' use of the affiliative style as avoiding the hard stuff: the stress of giving challenging feedback, the process of tackling poor performance, the recognition of the individual who has made a key contribution.

Managers using this style can feel equally disheartened if their efforts to create harmony are not responded to with equal warmth – for example, when team members just want to get the job done.

The democratic style: building commitment and consensus

The democratic (or participative) style is about gathering input. It is often characterized by a manager who holds lots of meetings. It is about building a vision and setting standards together. It is about sharing decisions and responsibility.

So what should a leader do when team members lack experience and competence – when the leader is the one who knows best? In that case team members should be involved only in those decisions where they can make a contribution safely.

The pacesetting style: accomplishing tasks to a high standard

The pacesetting style is about putting things right quickly. In situations in which team members are not delivering – they don't know what to do, they don't know how to do it, and the people or outcomes that depend on them are suffering as a result – the leader steps in to demonstrate how things need to be done.

But the pacesetting style is a quick fix; if the team lacks vision or capability, pacesetting will not help its members deliver high standards in the long term. When used too much or as a long-term style it can demotivate employees.

The coaching style: the long-term development of team members

The coaching style is used to build long-term capability. It is about understanding team members' strengths and weaknesses, and taking the time to learn about their aspirations. It is about helping each team member to be the best he or she can be.

However, we all learn from our mistakes as well as our successes, so a leader using the coaching style is prepared to trade a short-term drop in standards for the long-term increase in team capability. When people see their boss using this style they know that he or she really cares about their development.

Effective leaders

We see effective leaders doing three things. First they diagnose the demands of the situation. Then they select the right response to meet those demands – the right leadership style or styles. Finally, they keep an open mind and watch out for changes in the situation that require a different approach.

Learning to select and use the right style (or styles) in the right place, at the right time, in the right measure sounds like a tall order. Coaches can help by encouraging leaders to draw upon their own strengths and experiences:

▌ their personal characteristics (personality, motives and values);
▌ the styles that they see their bosses, mentors and colleagues use;
▌ their organization's espoused values as to the 'right way' to manage.

THE RESEARCH

The concept of organizational climate is based on work begun at Harvard University through the research of psychologists Litwin and Stringer (1968). This classic research began an ongoing process of clarifying, applying and validating the model of leadership effectiveness with leaders across different sectors and is one of the foundation stones for the leadership styles model.

A wide range of studies have demonstrated the validity of the model. A study of the leadership of a global technology company (Sala, 2002) showed that those who used a broader range of leadership styles to create high-performing climates outperformed their peers by $711 million in profit.

In a second study, a series of leadership assessments across the bottling plants of a global beverage manufacturer (Watkin, 2002) revealed a similar picture: climate correlated with productivity (increasing it by 30 per cent) and 50–70 per cent of the differences observed across leaders' climate scores was dependent on the leadership styles they chose to use.

In the public sector, where quantitative performance measures can be harder to come by, the link is maintained. In education (Sala, 2003), college principals' choice of leadership styles significantly impacted on the climate that their administrators experienced, and better climates were seen to predicate higher student retention and classroom attendance rates, higher student support ratings and higher assessments for quality of teaching and learning. Sala's work draws on earlier research in UK schools that connects Ofsted performance measures with positive climates created by headteachers using broader repertoires of styles. In the voluntary sector (Cormack and Rajendra, 2004), a development programme designed to help leaders strengthen their leadership styles and emotional intelligence competencies over two years delivered climate improvements, both for those leaders themselves and their team members. And in a study of nurse leaders (Douglas and Kenmore, 2006), those whose wards delivered lower staff turnover, absenteeism and drug errors consistently used a wide range of leadership styles.

A recent study of 3,141 leaders across a range of sectors (Malloy and Walker, 2008) rang alarm bells about the overall quality of leadership talent. The study found that 56 per cent of leaders in the survey were failing to engage those they lead, and only 26 per cent were creating an engaging climate that can encourage high performance (Figure 13.2). Further research was undertaken to understand what some leaders were doing to create high performance climates that others weren't.

The study confirmed earlier findings; leaders who used more leadership styles created better team climates than those who used fewer. The results were striking (Figure 13.3). Of those leaders creating high-performance climates, 68 per cent were using three or more leadership styles. Of those creating demotivating climates, 77 per cent were using fewer than three.

Intrigued by the clarity of this result, we looked for a distinctive pattern in the choice of leadership styles used by leaders (Figure 13.4). While leaders creating high-performance climates have more leadership styles in their toolkit, they keep the directive and pacesetting styles in

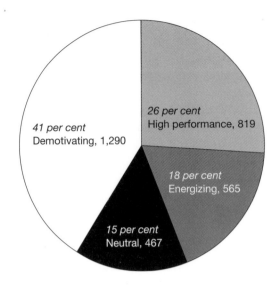

Figure 13.2 Climates created by 3,141 leaders across a range of sectors in 2007

reserve for crisis situations. These are the styles that leaders creating demotivating climates tend to rely on.

Where leaders are prepared to adapt their behaviour to the different challenges they face, we can help them focus on the leadership styles that have the most positive impact on team climate.

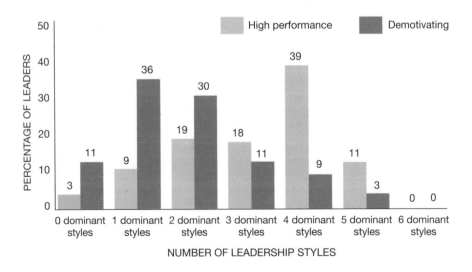

Figure 13.3 Number of styles used in different climates

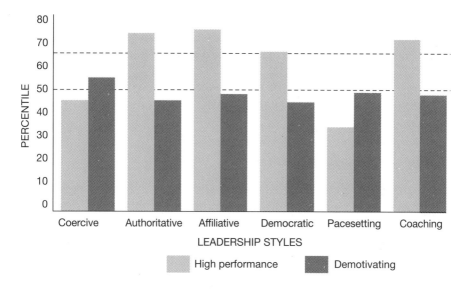

Figure 13.4 What do leaders actually do?

USING THE LEADERSHIP STYLES MODEL WITH COACHEES

Don't do that, do this!

This research reassures us that we can coach leaders effectively by getting them to first understand each distinct leadership style. We can describe the activities a leader typically engages in when using each style (eg when using the authoritative style a leader develops and articulates a clear vision and direction for the team, solicits team members' perspectives, persuades by explaining the reasons behind the vision, sets standards, monitors performance and provides balanced feedback). And we can encourage coachees to practise a wide range of styles and use them in the right measure, at just the right time with different people in different situations. We know it works, because leaders who do this create motivating climates and deliver better results. How convenient that the complexities of human behaviour can be described with such simplicity! But, of course, life's not like that.

Rather than directing an individual towards a list of ideal behaviours, we start working with whatever that individual brings to the coaching relationship: his or her strengths, preferences, self-image, aspirations, values, habits, motives and approach to learning. We make sense of these facets of each individual, and draw on them as a resource, because we know that they are the foundation upon which leadership capabilities are built. Goleman's work (2000) reveals the link between leadership styles and the emotional and social competencies that individuals develop over time. Emotionally intelligent leaders use a wider repertoire of leadership styles. They demonstrate their relationship management and social awareness in their work with their team members, and they use self-awareness and self-control to manage the potential 'derailers' that can throw them off course.

Leaders are made, not born

Goleman (1998) offers a further reassurance. Leadership can be learned. The process may be hard and take time, but the combination of motivation, extended practice and feedback breaks old behavioural habits and establishes new ones.

Goleman and Boyatzis (2008) describe it as the 'biology of leadership', proposing that the hard work of changing our behaviour actually develops our brain's social circuitry. Others present a more spiritual interpretation. In response to a temptingly neat analysis of the conditions that predicate highly effective teams, Lash (2002) offers a beautiful interpretation of the inner journey that leaders typically embark upon in order to develop the mental and emotional maturity necessary to create those conditions. Lash's description is rich with the language of transformation, even epiphany. Lash outlines a series of stages: the call, crossing the threshold, the road of trials, facing the abyss, transformation and return. These stages remind us what the transition to being a leader really feels like, at the deepest and most personal level.

The path to leadership: whose journey, is it?

As coaches we may have the opportunity to join our coachees on parts of their journey, attempting to help them strike their own pace. Many coaching models reflect the tension between the individual's growth and the organization's expectations. Boyatzis' theory of self-directed learning (2002) recognizes the freedom that adults will exercise in deciding who they are and who they want to be. The power of his model (Figure 13.5) is that it describes the journey in the coachee's terms, not the coach's (it's their journey, not ours!). But it offers us indications of the places along the way where we can be of most help.

Boyatzis' theory echoes Lash's sense of epiphany and urgency. It describes five discoveries: points of discontinuity where a moment of awareness can lead to sudden change. These are the moments a coach can look out for.

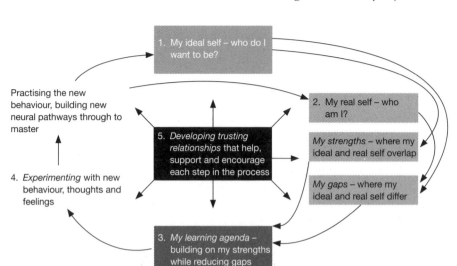

Figure 13.5 From *Primal Leadership: Realizing the power of emotional intelligence* by D Goleman, R E Boyatzis and A McKee (2002) (Copyright 2002, Harvard University Press) and Intentional change theory from a complexity perspective by R E Boyatzis (2006) (*Journal of Management Development*, **25**, pp 607–23). Adapted with permission

The first discovery: who do I want to be?

The first discontinuity, and potential starting point, is the discovery of who we want to be. Our 'ideal self', emerging from our ego, ideas, dreams and aspirations, provides a potent and imaginable state to aim for. For new leaders, picturing their ideal self requires looking beyond the new role (what I want to do) to the new person (who I want to become). For all leaders, it demands a degree of clarity about others' demands and expectations – the 'ought self' – and a determination to create a believable and desirable ideal self that is truly their own.

Clearly a coach can play a powerful role in this process: asking the questions that encourage a coachee to explore and formulate his or her ideal self, and challenging the assumptions, expectations and demands of the immediate situation. If this discovery is skipped, the learning agenda may never be fully owned by the coachee.

The second discovery: who am I right now?

The second discontinuity is the creation of an accurate self-image: a full picture of how others see us that resonates with what we know and believe about ourselves. This discovery honours the realization that the truth resides as much (if not more) in others' perceptions of us as in our own. It is the basis for acknowledging our strengths, the ways in which we are close to our ideal self, and our weaknesses, the things we want to change in order to become the person we want to be.

At its most simple level, the second discovery is about asking for feedback. Yet we know only too well the practical difficulties that can get in the way: the fear of exposure or criticism, the risk of putting others on the spot, the embarrassment of receiving praise that we feel is undeserved. All of these anxieties can be intensified for those in a leadership role, particularly when the feedback they really need is from those lower down the ranks.

Many of these difficulties are eased when a coach acts as a conduit for valuable feedback data: sharing his or her own reactions to a coachee, shadowing and observing others' reactions and using feedback tools to gather perceptions from different sources on a range of qualities.

The right tools can enlighten the right areas. Coachees need the chance to explore their inner understanding and beliefs (their values, motives, learning preferences and their own view of their capabilities). They also gain from exposure to others' views of them (how they work with others, lead, influence, handle conflict and so on). The combination of the right data at the right time provides a coachee with the raw material he or she needs to form, and own, an accurate self-image. It highlights the coachee's strengths, parts that he or she wants to keep and build upon. It demystifies weaknesses, gaps between the actual and the ideal self that can be closed. It offers choices, alternative behaviours that a coachee can adopt according to his or her preferences. And it reveals barriers that can be overcome, differences in perception that allude to a lack of self-esteem, false modesty or over-confidence.

Lash (2008) warns us that any new role, but particularly the transition into leadership, requires us to forge a new self-image, one that gives us the framework and the flexibility to break old behavioural habits and develop new ones. He outlines the key steps along the way – steps that mirror the self-directed learning model – and the questions that a coach can use to help a coachee explore his or her self-image. Most importantly he acknowledges the underlying tension inherent in 'fitting' the person to the role but reminds us of the opportunity. In his words, 'When a leader's self-image is aligned with his or her new business role, great things can happen. They are more energized and genuine, they reach out to others more to learn and seek feedback, they build support faster and they act with a greater sense of purpose and impact.'

The third discovery: what do I want to learn?

The third discontinuity is the discovery of our own personal learning agenda. Here Boyatzis is deliberately dogmatic. A learning agenda helps us focus on what we want to become. A performance agenda focuses on success, the achievement of praise and the production of proof of our capability. While increased performance may be the eventual consequence, the learning is the part that we actually own.

People only learn what they want to learn. A coach can help coachees by encouraging them to identify what that is, and by understanding the motivation behind it. Given the time and resource pressures that leaders are increasingly under, a coach can bring realism to the learning agenda (How much time can you give? What must you stop doing in order to make room for new activities? What are you doing now that you can build upon?) and, when the going gets tough, reconnect the coachee with his or her source of motivation.

The fourth discovery: how can I experiment and practise?

The fourth discontinuity is to start experimenting, to practise doing things differently. This is the point where old habits are confronted and new habits tentatively formed. New behaviours may challenge old habits of thought: assumptions and beliefs that have held a coachee back from even considering a different approach. This is the tough stuff of two steps forward and one step back, especially when the coachee is under pressure, tired or stressed.

A coach can help by creating conditions in which a coachee can experiment in relative safety. These may include the situations that the coach and coachee share together, or involve identifying work-based situations that the coachee is well placed to prepare for and manage. An insight into a coachee's learning preference (as measured by Kolb's Learning Style Inventory) is also valuable here; if a coachee is predisposed to diving in at the deep end, but less likely to reflect on what the experience has revealed, the coach can ask the questions that encourage the coachee further round the learning cycle.

The fifth discovery: who can I trust to help me?

The fifth discovery is placed, on purpose, at the centre of the self-directed learning model. When we think about a moment of discontinuity in our lives, a point of 'breakthrough' in becoming who we are now, we can usually identify the person who was there helping us through: the outstanding boss, the inspirational teacher, the colleague who challenged us, the parent who had faith in us. Our relationships are the mediators, moderators, interpreters, perceivers, providers of feedback and sources of support (or pessimism) of our learning. Relationships with those we trust, in different parts of our lives, can provide us with the ongoing encouragement we need to sustain us in our experimentation and practice.

As coaches, we hope to forge relationships that support our coachees in this way, and we manage our positioning and conduct with coachees and their organizations to uphold the trust they place in us. But we can also help by encouraging coachees to identify the network of relationships around them that provide the different forms of challenge, support and feedback that they will need. As Lash (2008) points out, for those transitioning between roles this may involve helping a coachee seek out and develop new networks.

When coaching leaders, we have a particular responsibility to model the coaching relationship in a way that encourages them to build it into their own repertoire. Their effectiveness in building the long-term capability of their team members is enhanced by their use of the coaching leadership style and their genuine interest in others' development. We can encourage them to do it well by giving them the positive experience of managing their personal learning agenda through the support of a coaching relationship.

CASE STUDY: MARIO

The call from the Director of Organizational Development at an aerospace company painted a challenging picture to us about a potential coachee. Mario was a talented physicist who had provided world-class engineering support on a number of global projects. He worked internationally and his technical expertise was not in question. His contribution to spacecraft teams had been highly valued and produced great results. So, what was the catch we wondered?

The story that unfolded described a team in meltdown: project dates missed, a lack of cooperation between members of the team, costs going out of control. What had gone wrong? When we asked the OD Director for her views, she said 'It's his personality – he has begun to lose the team; we just don't know how to handle this.' Mario had taken over the project director role, which was the biggest leadership job he had held. Far from his world-class expertise helping, it had become a huge blocker. He was fine as an expert member of a team, but now that he was leading a large international group of experts he found it very difficult to lead people from other disciplines – disciplines in which he felt much less competent. And so the coaching journey began.

After a preliminary 'let's get to know each other' session, we invited Mario to complete the Inventory of Leadership Styles. This would offer him an insight into the leadership styles being experienced by his team. At the same time we undertook an organizational climate survey, to measure the working environment that Mario's team were experiencing and to investigate the implications for the team's performance. A pattern began to emerge from the data that validated the anecdotes. Mario was technically highly competent but was struggling to manage his own behaviours in a way that would allow him to use a range of leadership styles. The working environment that was being created was deeply demotivating for his team, and so for the project. Critical intervention really was required.

Persuaded by the evidence from his team feedback, Mario agreed to take a range of psychometrics to help him understand the drivers of his behaviour and the implications for his impact on others. Using the Picture Story Exercise we were able to see that he had a very strong need for efficiency or achievement, a very low need for relationship or affiliation, and a moderate need for impact or influence. He wasn't managing these motivational drivers well. His drive for efficiency was making him hugely impatient. His low need for affiliation was getting in the way of forming a harmonious environment in the team. His moderate need for influence meant that he wasn't stepping up to being a strong and empowering leader. When Mario completed the Personal Values Questionnaire, he discovered he had high values for efficiency, high values for affiliation and low values for influence. We began to coach him around the tension between his motivational drivers and his values.

Our first area of work was around helping him to make sure that his achievement motive, backed by high values, did not go out of control and lead to the abrasive and 'in your face' kind of behaviour that the OD Director had reported. We encouraged him to experiment with some behaviours designed to create a better level of harmony in his team, along with figuring out some strategies around using more empowering behaviours.

Mario – being a scientist – of course needed more evidence before embarking on any change! So we used a 360° feedback tool, the Emotional Competency Inventory, which helps coachees explore in fine detail the relationship between their emotional intelligence and the impact they have on others' motivation and effort (Figure 13.6).

In Mario's case it was clear that there was a critical issue around a lack of self-control. He was very emotionally self-aware; if he was angry he knew he was angry. The problem was that so did everyone else, as his anger often turned into a loud tirade against them.

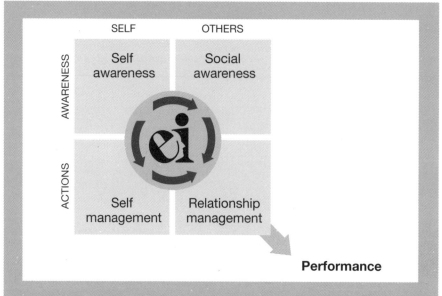

SELF   OTHERS

AWARENESS

Self awareness

Social awareness

ACTIONS

Self management

Relationship management

Performance

Figure 13.6 The emotional and social intelligence model

In a number of sessions with Mario we explored his strengths and also the critical development needs that would enhance his performance. Mario had become convinced of his need to change once he had seen all of the data – and had checked out the statistical reliability and provenance of all the tests!

But what really drove Mario's desire to change (even more than his conviction about the data) was how badly he felt about the lack of efficiency and poor standards of the team he led. Together we used this frustration as an energizer for the change.

CONCLUSIONS

Coaching around leadership styles can help leaders deliver quick wins – it focuses coachees on the behaviours that are most likely to create energizing climates and motivate team performance.

The evidence shows us that high-performance climates are created by leaders who use four or more leadership styles within their repertoire, particularly the visionary, affiliative, democratic and coaching styles. These are the obvious areas on which to focus the coaching relationship.

However, leadership development demands more than working on six groups of behaviours, not least because the complex mix of motives, values and qualities that an individual brings provides the very raw material upon which to build and sustain leadership effectiveness. Furthermore, the process of learning to be a leader takes a coachee on a journey of trials, setbacks and discoveries, during which he or she creates a new self-image that reflects changing capabilities. A coach needs to understand this complexity in order to be ready to support each discovery.

Leadership styles provide a valuable link between individual behaviour and organizational imperatives, and a potent tool for providing feedback on the impact a coachee has on his or her team. But they still allow coachees the freedom to shape a personal learning agenda – to embark on their own leadership journey – in whatever direction they wish.

References and further reading

Boyatzis, R E (2002) Unleashing the power of self-directed learning, in *Changing the Way We Manage Change: The consultants speak*, ed R Sims, pp 13–32, Quorum Books, New York

Boyatzis, R E, Goleman, D and Rhee, K (1999) Clustering competencies in emotional intelligence: insights from the Emotional Competency Inventory (ECI), in *Handbook of Emotional Intelligence*, ed R Bar-On and D A Parker, pp 343–88, Jossey-Bass, San Francisco, CA

Cormack, J and Rajendra, S (2004) *Performance Improvement through Passionate Leadership: A case study of a major UK charity*, Hay Group and Age Concern, London

Douglas, B and Kenmore, P (2006) *Nurse Leadership: Being nice is not enough*, research study, Hay Group, London

Goleman, D (1998) What makes a leader? *Harvard Business Review*, November–December, pp 93–102

Goleman, D (2000) Leadership that gets results, *Harvard Business Review*, March–April, pp 78–90

Goleman, D and Boyatzis, RE (2008) Social intelligence and the biology of leadership, *Harvard Business Review*, September, pp 74–81

Hay Group, *Emotional Competency Inventory Version 2* (ECI v2), Hay Group, Boston, MA

Hay Group, *Emotional and Social Competency Inventory* (ESCI), Hay Group, Boston, MA

Hay Group, *Influence Strategies Exercise* (ISE), Hay Group, Boston, MA

Hay Group, *Inventory of Leadership Styles* (ILS), Hay Group, Boston, MA

Hay Group, *Kolb Learning Styles Inventory* (LSI), Hay Group, Boston, MA

Hay Group, *Organizational Climate Survey* (OCS), Hay Group, Boston, MA

Hay Group, *Personal Values Questionnaire* (PVQ), Hay Group, Boston, MA

Hay Group, *Picture Story Exercise* (PSE), Hay Group, Boston, MA

Hay Group, *The Coaching Workbook*, Hay Group, Boston, MA

Lash, R (2002) Top leadership: taking the inner journey, *Ivey Business Journal*, May–June, pp 44–48

Lash, R (2008) Change from the inside, *Ivey Business Journal*, November–December, online

Litwin, G and Stringer, R (1968) *Motivation and Organizational Climate*, Harvard Business School Research Press, Boston, MA

Malloy, R and Walker, G (2008) *Managing the Downturn with Style*, Hay Group, London

Sala, F (2002) *Good Leaders = Big Profits, Research Brief*, The McClelland Center, Hay Group, Boston, MA

Sala, F (2003) Leadership in education: effective UK college principals, *Nonprofit Management and Leadership*, **14** (2) (winter), pp 171–89; also available as *Learning Leadership*, research brief, The McClelland Center, Hay Group, Boston, MA

Walker, G (2007) *Corporate Soufflé: Is the middle giving way?* Hay Group, London

Watkin, C (2002) Style Leaders, *Financial World*, July, pp 29–30

14

Leadership coaching
Strategy coaching

Declan Woods

INTRODUCTION

This chapter looks at organizational strategy and will explore the skills of coaches involved in working with leaders in this area. It will focus on the approaches of three major, and different, conceptions of organizational strategy offered by Porter, Mintzberg and Hamel before turning to look at the role of strategy coaching and coaches in theory and in practice through a case study.

Strategy typically refers to the planning, directing, organizing and controlling of a company's long-term goals, strategy-related decisions and actions. This chapter's focus is on strategy coaching: that is, coaching to support the strategy creation, development and implementation process in organizations. This is distinct from strategic coaching – coaching that benefits the organization as well as the individual. It could be argued that while all effective coaching should be strategic, not all coaching supports the strategy process.

THE STRATEGY MODELS

This section will review different authors' ideas about organizational strategy. We will first look at the ideas of Michael Porter, who suggests that an organization considers the different strategic options available and makes a clear choice between them, rather than struggling to pick the single best strategy. The second part considers the work of Henry Mintzberg, who charts the rise and fall of strategic planning and proposes that, rather than leaving it to strategic planners, managers engage in the strategy creation process. In the final part of this section we will briefly consider Gary Hamel's view that a change in mindset is needed in an organization if it is to discover radical strategies.

The work of Harvard Business School's eminent Professor of Strategy Michael Porter represented the basis for formulating a competitive strategy for much of the 1980s and 1990s. Porter (1985) proposed that organizations could adopt different generic strategies in an industry based on cost leadership, differentiation or focus. He introduced the idea of organizations having to choose to adopt a more focused approach and avoid the limitations of a diffuse strategy caused by trying to be 'all things to all people'. This process entailed the organization:

▌ clearly defining itself in terms of its basis for competing and how it would measure its success;
▌ developing policies that managers could use to communicate this critical information successfully to all parts of the firm;
▌ analysing itself and determining its strengths and weaknesses;
▌ evaluating these strengths and weaknesses in the context of external competitive forces as well as the broader environment.

Porter considered that any one of these clear positions would have been effective at the time due to the more static nature of markets. However, in a more recent (1996) article, he argued that the strategy models of the past have become outdated. Gone are the days where there was one ideal competitive position, where all of an organization's activities were benchmarked against the best practice sought, outsourcing to achieve economies of scale was the norm, and advantage was gained through focusing on core competencies and a few key success factors.

Porter further developed his arguments (1996), proposing that 'Companies must be flexible to respond rapidly to competitive and market changes.' This is as true today as it was then. Porter was an early advocate of what is known as 'positioning': that is, success in business is achieved by choosing a superior position in a given environment. Finding a position inevitably requires some difficult choices and decisions. Porter says that 'Managers have become confused about the necessity of making choices,' which has got in the way of them rediscovering a strategy. He says that in an environment where external forces militate against making clear choices and trade-offs, strong leadership is essential: 'General management is more than the stewardship of individual functions. Its core is strategy.'

However, while once central to strategy, positioning is now criticized as being too inflexible for today's fast-moving technological advances and market conditions. Furthermore, Porter says the difficulty now is that organizations do not typically differentiate between strategy and operational effectiveness. While many firms have jumped on to the bandwagons of re-engineering, outsourcing and total quality management efficiency drives and obtained operational improvements as a result, these have been insufficient to bring about lasting profitability and sustainable strategic competitive advantage. It is not surprising that managers are lured into the pursuit of operational effectiveness, however, because it is tangible and action-oriented and these are typically how managers envisage their roles.

In today's economic climate, Porter suggests that sustainable competitive advantage can only be achieved by:

▌ determining a unique competitive position for the organization;
▌ tailoring its activities to its strategy;
▌ making clear trade-off choices regarding competitors;
▌ achieving alignment or 'fit' from across its range of activities rather than over-focusing on individual parts.

In addition:

▌ Operational effectiveness is necessary but insufficient per se and there is a need to go beyond this.

While conceptions of strategy may go in and out of fashion, what appears clear is that to remain competitive a firm must both be operationally effective and also consider different strategic options and make unambiguous choices from those available. Inevitably, the process of generating and considering these choices will generate significant debate and tension and is likely to be contentious. Given this, it is critical that an organization finds a means of surfacing and managing conflict. It could be argued that if there is no controversy, the choices are not sufficiently strategic. This presents an opportunity for the strategy coach as a broker of relationships and conversations.

Moving away from Porter, Mintzberg (1994) charted the rollercoaster existence of strategic planning since its conception in the 1960s when it was seen as the panacea for organizations to improve their competitiveness through the design and implementation of strategies.

Strategic planning, drawing upon scientific management principles espoused by the likes of Taylor (1911) and Fayol (1916), split the tasks of 'thinking' about strategy from 'doing' strategy. This inevitably led to the creation of a new function within organizations – strategic planning. The reasoning behind this was that specialist strategic planners could produce the best strategies and develop detailed guidance to carry them out. Planners would hand over these instructions to managers to implement the already-agreed strategy. In this way, the managers delivering the strategy could not get it wrong. As we know, planning within organizations has not worked out this way.

Mintzberg (1994) argues that strategic planning has largely fallen into widespread disuse in companies because they confuse strategic thinking with strategic planning. Govindarajan (2005) concurs with this view, saying many senior managers suppose strategy to be planning for the coming year and spend their time on activities in the present, rather than spending most of their time divesting activities belonging to the past and creating the future.

This is not surprising since it appears there is a difference between those activities where managers think they spend their time (eg engaging in strategy formulation) and what they actually do. If we look at the latter, it appears that the typical manager is far removed from the measured, objective, rational, strategic decision maker presented in the management literature. Fores and Sorge (1981) painted a picture of time-stressed managers, heavily influenced by day-to-day problems, constantly being interrupted, unable to prioritize what they do and with little time for longer-term planning. Stewart (1984) agrees, referring to this as the grasshopper-like nature of managers' work, reporting that in a typical eight-hour working day it is not unusual for a manager to have handled over 200 different activities. In his 1973 study, Mintzberg found that more than half of CEOs' activities lasted less than nine minutes (Mintzberg, 1979). From this, one opportunity for the strategy coach could be helping managers focus their time on more value-adding strategic activities rather than fire-fighting day-to-day issues.

In practice, strategy making is a complex process and is far removed from the classical view of hard data being passed up an organization's prescribed hierarchy until it reaches its upper echelons where rational, 'economic-man' decisions are made by senior managers in a corporation's headquarters. Mintzberg tells us that 'formal procedures will never be able to forecast discontinuities' and that, while strategies can be developed by analysis, they cannot be created by it. He argues that planners should analyse data to identify genuinely new strategies and broaden consideration of the strategic choices available, rather than do this to find the one true strategy as Porter originally suggested.

Mintzberg continues: 'Three decades of experience with strategic planning have taught us about the need to loosen up the process of strategy making rather than trying to seal it off by arbitrary formalization.' Govindarajan (2005) echoes this view, reminding us that firms can only remain competitive through being innovative and adopting a creative approach to strategy formation to prevent them being easily copied and commoditized.

A reason strategic planning has fallen from grace is, as Mintzberg quoting Selznick (1957) advises, 'strategies take on value only as committed people infuse them with energy,' and planning can actively discourage the commitment of top managers. This is perhaps not surprising since planning could be seen to reduce management's power over the strategy-making process.

There are, of course, other reasons why strategic planning has fallen from prominence. There are three main, often unchallenged, assumptions on which strategic planning is based: firstly, that predicting the future is possible; secondly, that strategic planning is an objective process from which those involved in planning can remain detached; and finally, that the process of strategy making can be formalized.

As far back as 1965, Ansoff wrote about firms being able to construct accurate forecasts as the planning horizon of the firm. Over the past four decades, changes in the world's economy have challenged this notion (if the idea of being able to accurately predict the future was ever more than this). Govindarajan (2005) underlines this when he points out that a strategy starts to die from the day it is introduced. As they begin their annual strategic-planning process, many organizations are coping with the difficulties of predicting the future and its inherent uncertainty through the use of scenario planning, according to *The McKinsey Quarterly* (April 2009).

Mintzberg's work highlights tensions in managers' roles and the difficulties they face in balancing operational and strategic tasks. Opportunities for the strategy coach might lie in helping managers focus on strategic work and remain engaged with the strategy-generation process while involving others in this to help anticipate the future.

While some strategists might advocate an approach to strategy based on incremental operational improvements, Hamel (1996) says that this approach has its limits and instead he views 'Strategy as Revolution'. He argues that a change in mindset is needed within a company if it is to discover radical strategies. Rather than offering a prescription to arrive at a revolutionary strategy, he sees this as a state of mind and offers a number of ways of thinking about strategy creation.

He discusses three types of companies – 'rule makers' and 'rule takers' who are the industry, and 'rule breakers' who seek to redefine the industry. Hamel says that rule breakers are the revolutionary subversives who challenge the status quo and invent a new regime. This requires people to look at the world differently for there to be real innovation in the strategy creation process and 'without enlightenment, there can be no revolution.' He cites Anita Roddick, Body Shop founder, as an example.

Hamel believes that challenging the current paradigm is often extremely difficult for the current senior team as they are often defenders of it, saying 'you are unlikely to find a pro-change constituency among the top dozen or so officers.'

Organizations' structures are often graphically depicted as a pyramid with the CEO and senior management team positioned at the tip, as explained by Weber's rational–legal domination (1947 in Morgan, 1986). This implies that it is only those at the top that have a view about, and a valuable contribution to make to, an organization's strategy. Yet Hamel believes that strategy-making capacity is spread widely across a firm and that a broad spectrum of people should all be involved in its formation. In his experience, there are typically three important groups overlooked from this process: young people (who bring a fresh perspective on the world and emerging trends), those at the extremities of the organization (who, remote from headquarters, need to be even more resourceful as they have less access to central resources) and new hires (people who have yet to be socialized into the norms of the organization and who bring unsullied wider perspectives). Hamel says that the strategy challenge for most firms is to help this pro-change group of people find its voice. He goes further by asking CEOs if they know who and where such people are within their organization.

Turning to strategy implementation, many managers believe that it can be problematic, with this belief based on the assumption that people are against change and that only a charismatic leader can propel the organization forward to a new and better future. However, Hamel believes that while there can be challenges in executing change, they are generally not about change *per se* but its lack of engagement with people: 'That which is imposed is seldom embraced. An elitist approach to strategy creation engenders little more than compliance.' Contrary to popular opinion, he says the aim is not to get people to support the change but to give them responsibility for stimulating change and having a sense of influence over their future.

Hamel would concur with Porter that small-scale operational efficiencies are not enough to achieve the step-change in strategy required by firms in today's economic climate. Hamel believes leaders need a different way of viewing the world to both conceptualize change and engage people behind it. He reminds us that the strategy-making process should entail encouraging broader participation and participants into the process, creating an environment where those open to new ideas can express their opinions, and where unconventional views can be melded into the thinking. These are the contests that senior managers face if strategy is to be revolutionary. These issues present opportunities for the strategy coach to challenge leaders' cognitions about the past and to envisage a different and better future. Here, strategy coaching can have a powerful impact on the whole organization through influencing the behaviour and operating style of a leader.

USING THE STRATEGIC MODEL WITH SENIOR COACHEES

This section of the chapter will explore the role of strategy coaching and coaches. It will introduce a process for strategy coaching and this will be used as a structural aid for the case material that follows.

It has been assumed so far that the CEO needs a strategy coach rather than a strategy consultant, which might seem a more common choice. Given this, this section starts by differentiating the two roles by looking at what a strategy coach does not do.

What a strategy coach doesn't do

In the face of eminent strategy models and theories, it is common for a CEO to employ a strategy consultant to advise on strategy formulation. But it could be better practice to engage a strategy coach who can help the organization discover what is the right strategy for it, rather than impose one from on high (Prahalad, 2005). Strategy coaching might, therefore, prove of more value than the more traditional consulting approach to strategy.

There are a number of pitfalls for the would-be strategy coach. It is all too easy for the coach to be seduced by his or her privileged position (and that of the CEO coachee) and as a result collude due to his or her status, role or personality. An awareness of this hazard, along with coaching supervision, can prove invaluable at such times.

A common trap is the temptation to slip into consulting mode and try to solve an organization's problems for the managers or, worse still, impose generic theories and strategy models. These are risky for both parties, particularly because the coach cannot possibly know the business well enough. This is, after all, the CEO and top team's role. As Bartlett reminds us, 'coaching is much less about proving the answers than it is about asking the right questions' (Govindarajan, 2005). While there seem to be differing views about strategy creation, there is consensus around a coach's role and ability to listen and 'hold up the mirror' to help the organization evaluate its current position and develop frameworks to apply tomorrow's landscape to today's opportunities.

Instead of these, a far better contribution of the strategy coach is to encourage the coachee to consider alternative perspectives, to open up and stimulate debate on new topics and to raise the views of others in the organization likely to be affected by the strategic choices of the leadership. Tools such as De Bono's 'six hats' (1987) can be useful for helping senior leaders consider the wider risks, the full range of benefits, the process of developing change, the evidence from markets and customers, and simple 'out of the box' thinking.

Pre-coaching coachee–coach matching

Typically coaching is preceded by the matching of a coach with the coachee. While this is always important and needs to be handled sensitively, it is particularly important for strategy coaching due to the expectations the CEO and top team have of the coach and its potential impact on an organization. Business leaders expect coaches working with them to focus on issues critical to them and their organizations and to have a deep understanding of the strategy development process. It is, therefore, essential that a strategy coach demonstrates credibility, presence and impact from the first meeting with a top manager. It is also vital for the coach to demonstrate an understanding of the sector/industry as well as the organization and its challenges and how these might affect the leader. The opportunity to work with very senior leaders can be won or lost in an instant.

Senior leaders operate at speed. It can be important for credibility's sake to match this pace. However, in doing so, it can be easy to ignore the crucial early stages of developing rapport and building trust. It is time worth spending, however, as it is a crucial criterion if the coaching is to be successful.

Strategy conceptualization

Before an organization moves towards its new strategy, it can be helpful to know where it is starting from. One role the executive coach can play is to work with the CEO to conduct a diagnosis of the current organizational portfolio. Watkins (2006) tells us that 'You cannot figure out where to take a new organization if you do not understand where it has been and how it got there.' He tells us that there is a range of business situations, each presenting different challenges and opportunities and thus requiring different behaviours from leaders. He recommends understanding the stage of the organization's development first – start-up, turnaround, realignment, or sustaining success – to determine the desired leadership response and then positioning coaching to support this.

According to Prahalad (2005), it can be useful to unearth and understand the prevailing logic of the organization (why an entity believes what it does about its products/services, internal organization, competitors and sources of competitive advantage) when developing a corporate strategy. Watkins' approach can be useful for this purpose. The next step is to explore the external terrain and the future relevance of the company's logic. Barker (2005) believes many organizations overlook this critical part of the strategy-making process, jumping directly to strategic planning. This is important because past successes tend to be codified into the dominant logic. Often, there is a fine line between prevailing obsolete attitudes and beliefs and sources of future competitive advantage. One role of the coach is, therefore, to help the senior leadership develop their own understanding of the differences between the two. One of the key strengths a strategy coach brings at this stage is access to world-class practices drawn from a range of other industries (Govindarajan, 2005). After all, how many managers can claim extensive experience of global reorganizations or large-scale mergers or acquisitions that are, for most executives, once-in-a-career moments?

It is important, however, not to spend too long looking backwards. Govindarajan (2005) suggests a forward focus by encouraging the CEO to assess a firm's potential as opposed to the current performance of the portfolio.

There are two trends dictating the demand for coaching senior leaders. With higher turnover of CEOs and shorter tenure, top leaders need to develop a viewpoint on how and where the organization will compete in its industry, and then implement this point of view and produce results from it in an ever-quicker timeframe (Prahalad, 2005). Irrespective of the health of the organization, there is a need to produce value for customers and shareholders quickly. The coach needs to match this tempo because, as Peltier (2001) reminds us, 'the business world insists on results . . . soon.' While cutting costs can be quick and relatively easy to achieve, and can produce fast results, it is doubtful that this will generate value in the long term. For the coach to maintain his or her hard-won credibility, every coaching session will need to add value and provide lasting benefit well beyond the initial chemistry meeting.

Govindarajan (2005) tells us that strategy issues are far too complex for a single person to solve. As such, it might be tempting for a CEO to reach out to others within the organization for help. However, there are genuine difficulties for the CEO in being able to hold an open and frank conversation about strategy with anyone inside the organization: 'I can't talk to the chairman because in the end he's the one who is going to fire me. I can't talk to my finance director because ultimately I'm going to fire him, and I can't tell my wife because I never see her and when I do, that's the last thing she'll want to talk about' (Tappin and Cave, 2008). Lyons (2006) agrees, saying 'problems can come from talking too freely inside an organization, however flat or virtual it may be . . . Leaders need a safe and supportive theatre . . . in which to rehearse and refine their ideas.' Coaching can meet this need.

With the risks associated with seeking internal advice, it is not surprising that many leaders choose to remain silent. Given these risks, and the inherent loneliness of the CEO's position, it is not unexpected that a business leader would look outside the organization for a trusted, impartial adviser. A CEO can feel more comfortable talking to external people as they typically have nothing to gain and are detached from the internal political climate. Coaching can provide leaders with the opportunity to participate in a developmental conversation that would be all but impossible to hold internally. Here, the coach – and often only the coach – can challenge the senior leader's current wisdom and help him or her think significantly differently about the current organization's fitness for purpose. In the absence of this dialogue, there is often no reflective space or consideration and testing of a broad range of ideas.

Hamel reminds us of the advantages of including different people in the strategy creation process. One of the contributions of a strategy coach is to facilitate conversations across these groups, including the top team and senior managers, and to bring people together to talk openly about organizational imperatives that cut across organizational silos. Bartlett (2005) tells us the coach can support the CEO through accessing these diverse views by becoming a resource to the top management and, through this and by identifying blind-spots and raising levels of awareness, helping build its capability. A skilled coach is familiar with, and practised at, working with resistance to change in ways that executives often are not, and can use his or her insights on individuals and the change process to bring about cooperation and cohesion.

Strategy planning

According to de Geus (1988), 'The real purpose of effective planning is not to make plans but to change the . . . mental models that . . . decision makers carry in their heads.' To do so well, 'they may have to use provocation or shock tactics like raising difficult questions and challenging conventional assumptions.' This is a difficult role for the CEO to play, as senior leaders are both consumers and producers of that same strategy. Here again, the strategy coach can make a significant contribution.

Once a future strategic direction has been decided, the CEO must build momentum towards it without leaving casualties along the way or colluding with the prevailing logic. It is during this phase that Prahalad (2005) believes that strategy coaching and coaching for personal effectiveness can become merged. Drawing upon the strategic point of view developed earlier, the CEO can quickly ask critical questions, listen to alternative and opposing viewpoints and challenge the status quo. The aim of this stage is to develop a powerful coalition behind a particular point of view. This requires significant personal effectiveness on the part of the CEO. The coach can role-model the desired skills and behaviours and work with the CEO to develop these through preparation, rehearsal and repetition until they become fluent (Peltier, 2001).

Strategy implementation

We have all seen organizations that have implemented poor strategies well and been successful, while other firms with near-perfect strategies implemented less well have not achieved the anticipated results. The importance of the CEO's and management team's ability to execute a change in strategy should, therefore, not be underestimated. A coach tasked with helping an organization implement a chosen strategy needs to establish credibility between the leader and the team and *vice versa*. This can be particularly challenging when trying to envisage a different future for the organization that is as yet out of sight.

Davidson (2005) uses a simple three-step process – Aim, Ready, Fire – when working with entities to conceptualize and prepare for change. 'Aim' involves bringing the senior team together to assess the current situation and define a desired future state. The 'Ready' phase is about preparing the ground for the changes to come, including communicating the new-look organization and developing people strategies to align everyone's effort behind the changes. Finally, 'Fire' concentrates on launching the change, executing the strategy and delivering the results from it.

Once the corporate strategy has been agreed, it needs to be translated into business-unit-level strategies to be implemented. Coaching for change becomes the focus here to help develop the tactics for deploying the strategy and turning it into reality. Managers and individuals will need to make sense of the strategy and determine its implications for them. Canner (2005) tells us that the chosen strategy must provide meaning as well as direction and as such can be a powerful motivator for change.

CASE STUDY

Introduction

This case example demonstrates how strategy coaching was used to support a defence company making difficult strategic choices during a time of significant market-led change. It shows how I used the strategy coaching process presented above with the organization and its CEO. Details have been changed to preserve confidentiality where necessary.

The issue

A change in government policy led to a defence company having to reconsider its core markets, central strategy and core work activities. By way of background, the organization had a long history, held significant share in international markets with respected products over long lifecycles, was based across multiple sites in the UK, had a 4,000-strong workforce and generated £15 million profit from £400 million turnover in the year in which this assignment was carried out. Competitors were facing similar challenges at the same time and first-mover advantage was available since changes in legislation would have made the organization's core offerings obsolete overnight. This was the biggest challenge facing the organization in the past 75 years (almost its entire history).

On the surface, the presenting issue was straightforward: external changes required the organization to change. It needed to make some strategic choices over its future direction and respond accordingly. However, an initial hurdle was that, with the exception of the CEO and some of the non-executive directors (NEDs), the organization and its senior managers did not see the need to change and had not started to prepare for it.

The CEO had already proposed a draft strategic direction in a recently produced strategy paper but failed to obtain buy-in to it, which was delaying its sign-off and implementation. This paper had been produced largely by the CEO with the support of one or two NEDs and not actively through the rest of the corporate management team (CMT) and organization. This was partly because of time pressures but mainly due to the CEO's concerns about the CMT's effectiveness, particularly in strategic decision making.

Although there was a lead time of 18 months, gaining agreement to the new strategy did not leave long in light of the scale of the changes needed.

There were risks of loss of market share and revenues from not being ready when the new policy came into effect, which added significantly to the pressures.

In addition to achieving support for a new (still to be agreed) strategy, the CEO also wanted to repair some of the damage done by his overly directive approach to driving the initial strategy into place. He therefore wanted the strategy coaching to develop an approach to leadership for the CMT that improved its effectiveness and:

■ focused more on strategy and less on operational details;
■ developed teamworking methods to be more effective, particularly in decision making;
■ encouraged improvements in communications between the CMT and the wider organization;
■ improved working relationships and engagement within the CMT.

The strategy coaching process

Coaching for strategy conceptualization

Even though I had a track record in strategy coaching, I still needed to build my credibility and gain the confidence and trust of the CEO and top team, particularly as I had not worked with the company before. This started by exploring and agreeing how I would work with them to achieve the aim.

The first step in using the coaching model was for the CMT to develop a point of view on where, and how, to compete in the changed market. This could have stemmed from an analysis of the current performance and future potential of the portfolio. However, while this was present and future focused, the challenge here was that the prevailing logic was a barrier to change. This grew out of the organization's size ('we're enormous and have the capacity to absorb any change thrown at us – as we've done before') and a history of mergers and acquisitions (resulting in a lack of trust between divisions). This logic wasn't immediately obvious and only became apparent during individual coaching sessions with the senior managers. During this time, I found I needed to be both supportive and challenging: empathetic about their views and why they held these but especially challenging in terms of the drivers behind the need for change and the very real implications for the organization if there were no change. I found that questioning the relevance of soon-to-be outdated functions was a necessary, but difficult, way of challenging the *status quo*. I was able to reassure the CMT members that their views would be heard. It was important to gain their trust to achieve this and a useful reminder how much time (ongoing, over several coaching sessions) this could take.

In practice, the content to assess the current business portfolio (present and future) developed out of these conversations. I used the knowledge gained in my conversations with the various CMT members and division heads in my work when coaching the CEO. In turn, this enabled him to develop a more refined point of view on the new strategic direction. He valued the time and space coaching provided to think and test his ideas.

Despite the pressure to agree a new strategic direction, the CEO knew that he needed clarity of thought to generate a workable strategy and (well-thought-out, pragmatic) solutions. To achieve this, he wanted to create thinking time in an extremely busy role. In addition to the ongoing strategy creation process, I coached the CEO on his part in the CMT effectiveness issues raised previously that were having an impact on him and his work. Through a process of structured questioning, I was able to draw out his experience and abilities, enabling him to find solutions that matched his natural leadership strengths.

Coaching for strategic planning

It was not enough, however for the CEO to develop a point of view. It needed to be explored, debated and shared with the CMT and NEDs. The CEO decided to use an existing management meeting for this purpose.

Here, my role was to facilitate an open conversation between the CMT and help them reach a shared point of view. Complete consensus was neither necessary nor helpful, as a unanimous decision would probably have been a compromised strategy. Given the history, and that an impasse had been reached between CEO and CMT previously, I explored with them how they had worked successfully together before and how they could learn from those times when decisions had been reached successfully. This, and drawing on the trust earned from the individual coaching sessions, worked well in terms of facilitation style.

Specifically, this forum:

▋ established criteria by which decisions were made (eg what would a good decision look like? How will we know?);
▋ reviewed drivers for change (eg why change? why now?);
▋ explored a range of strategic options in turn and the benefits and implications of each;
▋ reviewed points of contention from the different options;
▋ worked towards an agreed solution aligned with the company's long-term vision and mission.

Outcomes and benefits

It was during the facilitated board meeting that agreement was reached on a new strategic direction. This joint consultative forum proved to be an effective setting to create a powerful alliance behind the chosen strategic direction. It created a climate that allowed the CMT to plan to implement the strategy.

In addition to achieving this, there were further benefits in terms of the CMT's development in improved effectiveness, decision making and communication, as well as an appreciation of different operating styles and individual strengths and contributions.

This process is very different from that typically used by an external strategy consultant, who might try to push a particular strategy from a box of models and tools. Using an inside-out approach, the strategy was designed by the organization and was distinctive to it. The challenge for me was to work closely with the CEO, CMT and NEDs throughout the different phases of strategy creation without becoming overly involved in it. Not surprisingly, I found this a difficult role to balance. Equally, it was not surprising that the company found creating a new strategy difficult because, ultimately, many of the answers to these questions were about its central purpose and ethos as an organization.

The company agreed a new strategic direction and plans to implement it. It executed the changes in good time and subsequently achieved the benefits from having done so, including gains in market share and operating profits.

CONCLUSIONS

The economic world has changed, and in response organizations have had to change too. Leaders are facing new competitive rules and must find an appropriate strategy with which to contend in changing markets. Today's strategies are dynamic, ever-changing and ubiquitous. Leaders must follow suit. Anixter (2005) reminds us, 'The days of the lone executive preparing a five-year strategy are over. Strategy today is a fluid, complex, and collaborative process, more so than it historically ever has been.'

To keep up will inevitably require a significant shift in mindset on the part of the leader. This is an area where a strategy coach can challenge and corroborate clients and their thinking, and make a real difference to leaders and their organizations.

Let the final word go to Lyons (2006):

Coaching is not simply a passing fad; it offers a pragmatic supporting context in which modern strategy flourishes. In today's turbulent world, strategy has developed into something that emerges, always tracking a moving target. And the preferred vehicle – responsive enough to reduce the risk in successfully travelling toward that ever-changing destination – is to be found in the dialogue of coaching.

References and further readings

Anixter, J (2005) Strategy coaching, in *The Art and Practice of Leadership Coaching: 50 top executive coaches reveal their secrets*, ed H Morgan, P Harkins, and M Goldsmith, pp 216–18, John Wiley, New Jersey

Ansoff, H I (1965) *Corporate Strategy: An analytic approach to business policy for growth and expansion*, McGraw-Hill, New York

Barker, J (2005) Strategic exploration, strategy coaching, in *The Art and Practice of Leadership Coaching: 50 top executive coaches reveal their secrets*, ed H Morgan, P Harkins, and M Goldsmith, pp 210–12, John Wiley, New Jersey

Bartlett, C A (2005) Coaching the top team, strategy coaching, in *The Art and Practice of Leadership Coaching: 50 top executive coaches reveal their secrets*, ed H Morgan, P Harkins, and M Goldsmith, pp 199–202, John Wiley, New Jersey

Canner, N (2005) Strategy coaching, in *The Art and Practice of Leadership Coaching: 50 top executive coaches reveal their secrets*, ed H Morgan, P Harkins, and M Goldsmith, pp 213–16, John Wiley, New Jersey

Davidson, W (2005) Strategy coaching, in *The Art and Practice of Leadership Coaching: 50 top executive coaches reveal their secrets*, ed H Morgan, P Harkins, and M Goldsmith, pp 219–20, John Wiley, New Jersey

De Bono, E (1987) *Six Thinking Hats*, Pelican, London

De Geus, A P (1988) Planning as learning, *Harvard Business Review*, **66** (2), pp 70–74

Fayol, H (1916) Administration industrielle et générale, *Bulletin de la Société de l'Industrie Minérale*, **10**, pp 5–164, Réédité 13 fois chez Dunod

Fores, M and Sorge, A (1981) The decline of the management ethic, *Journal of General Management*, **6** (3), pp 36–50

Ghadar, F (2005) Strategy implementation: where the fun begins, strategy coaching, in *The Art and Practice of Leadership Coaching: 50 top executive coaches reveal their secrets*, ed H Morgan, P Harkins, and M Goldsmith, pp 203–06, John Wiley, New Jersey

Goldsmith, M and Lyons, L (eds) (2006) *Coaching for Leadership*, John Wiley/ Pfeiffer, San Francisco, CA

Govindarajan, V (2005) Coaching for strategic thinking capability, strategy coaching, in *The Art and Practice of Leadership Coaching: 50 top executive coaches reveal their secrets*, ed H Morgan, P Harkins, and M Goldsmith, pp 196–99, John Wiley, New Jersey

Hamel, G (1996) Strategy as revolution, *Harvard Business Review*, July–August, pp 68–82

Lyons, L (2006) Coaching at the heart of strategy, in *Coaching for Leadership*, ed M Goldsmith and L Lyons, pp 87–99, John Wiley/Pfeiffer, San Francisco, CA

McKinsey Quarterly (2008) A fresh look at strategy under uncertainty: an interview, December

McKinsey Quarterly (2008) Leading through uncertainty, December

McKinsey Quarterly (2009) Strategic planning: three tips for 2009, April

Mintzberg, H (1979) An emerging strategy of 'direct' research, *Administrative Science Quarterly*, **24** (4), *Qualitative Methodology* (December), pp 582–89 (based on PhD thesis, 1973)

Mintzberg, H (1994) The fall and rise of strategic planning, *Harvard Business Review,* January–February, pp 107–14

Morgan, G (1986) *Images of Organisations*, Sage, London

Morgan, H, Harkins, P and Goldsmith, M (eds) (2005) *The Art and Practice of Leadership Coaching: 50 top executive coaches reveal their secrets,* John Wiley, New Jersey

Peltier B (2001) *The Psychology of Executive Coaching: Theory and application,* Brunner-Routledge, New York

Porter, M E (1985) *Generic Competitive Strategies, Competitive Advantage: Creating and sustaining superior performance,* Free Press, New York

Porter, M E (1996) What is strategy? *Harvard Business Review,* November–December, pp 59–78

Prahalad, C K (2005) The competitive demands on today's leaders, strategy coaching, in *The Art and Practice of Leadership Coaching: 50 top executive coaches reveal their secrets,* ed H Morgan, P Harkins, and M Goldsmith, pp 190–95, John Wiley, New Jersey

Selznick, P (1957) *Leadership in Administration: A sociological interpretation,* Harper & Row, New York

Steiner, G (1979) *Strategic Planning: What every manager must know,* Free Press, New York

Stewart, R (1984) Developing managers by radical job moves, *Journal of Management Development,* **3** (2), pp 48–55

Tappin, S and Cave, A (2008) *The Secrets of CEOs*, Nicholas Brearley, London

Taylor, F W (1911) *The Principles of Scientific Management*, Harper Bros, New York

Watkins, M (2003) *The First 90 Days: Critical success strategies for new leaders at all levels,* Harvard Business School Press, Boston, MA

Weber, M (1947) *The Theory of Social and Economic Organisation*, Oxford University Press, London

15

Coaching global top teams

Katharine Tulpa and Georgina Woudstra

INTRODUCTION

Leaders in the 21st century are faced with unprecedented challenges – a complex, highly networked trading environment; an aging population; a war for talent; increasing stress and mental illness in the workplace; a trend for people seeking greater meaning and purpose in their lives and work; a demand, in particular from the younger generations, for 'green' employers that have a strong culture around sustainability; and keeping up with technology, the third wave of the web and other innovations to meet market pressures.

Furthermore, there are even higher expectations than before for the leaders sitting on the top team to not only keep the company afloat, but do this ethically and responsibly. There is more scrutiny and less tolerance for egos or solo players looking after their own interests. This is creating a need for more self-aware and competent leaders who are willing to work together and put the needs of the business first, while equally being able to perform well within multicultural, virtual teams, which are often spread across remote parts of the globe.

For these reasons, we write this chapter, as effectively coaching the top team for elite performance can provide a huge support mechanism to help these leaders work through some of these challenges. In our view, there is no better time than now to be making the business case for coaching the global top team – to have a part in helping them grow, stretch and play an even bigger game, so they can make a positive impact in the world.

WHAT IS DIFFERENT ABOUT TEAMS AT THE TOP?

At the top of organizations all around the world you will find a group operating under names like – the 'executive team', the 'c-suite' the 'board', the 'operational board', the 'strategic leadership team', the 'senior leadership team', the group of 'managing partners' or simply, the 'top team'. Ask about the 'top team' and you may well hear comments like 'well, they're not really a team, but . . .' as simply labelling a group a team doesn't make it one. So, you may ask yourself, do they really need to operate as a team?

From our experience of coaching a number of global leaders and multicultural top teams, most do see the necessity to work as 'one team', yet initially can find it a challenge to do so in practice. As Stoneman (2009) summarizes:

> Many top teams do not make nearly as much as they could from the assets they have because they leave important contributions unheard because unasked for, unseen because no-one was looking for them, or frozen before birth because the chill of negativity killed the vital creative thinking that they needed.

The above we believe illustrates the particular challenges that top teams face, with the section below highlighting some differences found with senior executive teams. While it's useful to be aware of these, our overall focus for the majority this chapter is to take a more appreciative approach and identify 'what works' when coaching a top team.

Top teams focus on performance

A real team (Katzenbach, 1997) is 'a small number of people with complementary skills who are committed to a common purpose, performance goals and an approach for which they hold themselves mutually accountable'. A real top team is a tightly focused performance unit, with a high level of trust and with members who are not afraid to challenge each other.

Performance is a key issue, and when strategies for growth are based on integrated value creation, today's top teams need to assume collective responsibility for corporate performance. Jarkko Sairanen, Nokia's Head of Corporate Strategy confirms this: 'Having a corporate-wide agenda makes top-team members focus on common challenges instead of specific sub-unit agendas' (Doz and Kosonen, 2007); this is the work of a real top team.

Responses from McKinsey's (2008) global survey indicate that highly influential boards focus on the long-term strategy, encourage healthy, open debate, decide on value creation together with management, put a high priority on talent and performance management, and have unlimited access to information and executives beyond the most senior level.

Top teams deal with complexities

Many of today's global organizations are structured around product groupings, functions or service lines, yet the organizations' major strategic growth opportunities lie across market domains. Leveraging this potential calls for an integrated strategy across business units; for those that are still run as fiefdoms, delivering on this is virtually impossible.

Clutterbuck (2007) refers to a 'self-governing team', which is typical of a board of directors. These are teams who take responsibility for the organizational context. Advantages a team of this type have are its independence, while disadvantages are that the team may become self-perpetuating, with a lack of checks and balances.

Further complexities are the diverse challenges of global leaders working as part of a virtual team, whose main form of communication relies heavily on video, telephone, e-mail or web conferencing. Equally, non-verbal as well as informal modes of communication can be lost, and these are even more critical in certain cultures for building trusting relationships. There is also a learning curve of understanding cultural distinctions, as well as practical matters such a time zone differences, which make the workday even longer.

Frank Brown, Dean of Insead in Singapore, refers to 'trans-cultural leadership' or the need for today's global leaders to 'combine the best practices of traditional leadership with an understanding and sensitivity of the world's many cultures' (Davie, 2009). A global top team that can both appreciate and adapt to this way of working is better equipped for success.

Top teams share the load

Within global organizations, the context is different, the stakes are higher, and the potential is far-reaching. For those reasons, many successful top teams working within these environments recognize that shared perspectives and decision making, as well as shared risk, can help equip them to meet the demands, and ensure the survival, of the business. These are senior leaders who are willing to go beyond working as a group of individuals, to 'doing together what we can't do alone' (Lipnack and Stamps, 2000).

In *The Handbook of High Performance Top Teams* (Nemiro *et al*, 2008), collaboration, with the ability to challenge and break down traditional walls, borders, or 'membership requirements' is identified as an essential ingredient. In other words, crossing traditional boundaries, while sharing each other's knowledge and expertise, is a way for a top team to perform effectively.

RESEARCHING ELITE PERFORMANCE IN TOP TEAMS

The Hay Group conducted research across more than 120 top teams around the world (Wageman *et al*, 2008) to determine what effective senior leadership teams did to set themselves apart from others. The results of their research pointed to six conditions for creating an effective senior leadership team – three essential and three enabling (Figure 15.1).

The essentials are:

▌ Real team: this has clear boundaries and high interdependency between members.
▌ Compelling direction: this must be challenging, consequential and clear.
▌ Right people: these are selected on both their unique contribution and their ability to collaborate.

The enablers are:

▌ Sound structure: the team should be small enough to make decisions and work on vital issues and tasks and to establish norms for how the team works together.
▌ Supportive context: this ensures they have the information, materials and resources they need for tasks.
▌ Team coaching: this helps ensure the long-term success of the team.

Elite team performance relies on collective accountability. At the heart of team accountability is commitment and trust, both of which develop naturally when a team shares a defining purpose, goals and approach. Accountability grows from the time and energy a top team invests in committing fully to what needs to be accomplished and working out how best to get it done.

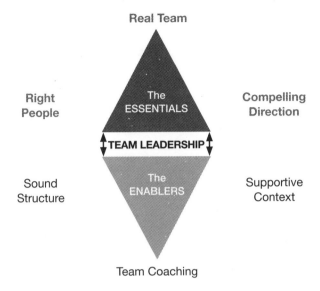

Figure 15.1 The six conditions to create an effective top team

Elite performance requires trust

> Real teams do not emerge unless the individuals on them take risks involving conflict, trust, interdependence and hard work. Of the risks required, the most formidable involve building the trust and interdependence necessary to move from individual accountability to mutual accountability. Trust must be earned and demonstrated repeatedly if it is to change behaviour. (Katzenbach and Smith, 1999)

Larsen (2008), of Futureworks Consulting, defines professional trust as follows:

▌ Trust is the confident expectations of team members (and leaders) about each other's behaviours and intentions.
▌ Trust is a quality that team members extend to others who offer them basic support and value their ways of contributing to the team's effectiveness.
▌ Trust is comfort with being as open to one another about failures, weaknesses and fears as about competencies, strength and achievements.

In *The Speed of Trust*, Covey (2006) takes the significance of trust to another level, emphasizing that trust is the hidden variable in the formula for organizational success. This is particularly so in today's global, knowledge-worker economy where partnering and building strong relationships is such a key part of doing business. He identifies the traditional business formula shown in Figure 15.2.

(Strategy × Execution) = Results

There is also a hidden variable, which equates to:

(Strategy × Execution) × Trust = Results

Figure 15.2 Covey's 'hidden variable'

Using this model, a top team can have a brilliant strategy and a solid execution plan, but it can get derailed if the trust isn't there. Equally, trust can act as a multiplier for accelerated performance, 'creating synergy where the whole is more than the sum of its parts' (Covey, 2006).

Top teams with high levels of trust engage in passionate dialogue and debate around issues and decisions that are critical for the organization's success. Individuals challenge each other in the spirit of finding the best answers and making great decisions.

ELITE PERFORMANCE REQUIRES POSITIVE CONFLICT

In our experience, a great number of top teams have difficulty challenging each other effectively. This is due to a number of reasons, including new members joining/leaving the group, a lack of trust, cultural differences, politics, an autocratic leader, insecurities in role or having a more collegiate style.

When a team is driven by a desire to preserve artificial harmony, it builds stifled resentment over a period of time, manifested in backbiting and 'briefing against' adversaries. On the other hand, some top teams are well used to battles and sometimes even explosions of frustration and emotion (although this can have more damaging repercussions, in particular with diverse global teams where there are distinct cultural differences). As Patrick Lencioni (2002) notes: 'That's not to say that some teams that lack trust don't argue. It's just that their arguments are often destructive because they are laced with politics, pride and competition rather than humble pursuit of truth.'

The most effective top teams have created a culture of 'positive conflict', in which people are encouraged to challenge each other in an appropriate way. This gets real issues that are impeding performance out in the open (naming the 'elephant in the room') where they can be addressed rather than incubated in silence. Conflict is needed to select the best actions and strategies based on an understanding of the reality of a changing environment. When politics smooth over conflict or obscure the facts of a business situation, decision making is distorted.

Elite performance requires diversity

In the context of working with global top teams, we often see a diversity of cultures, philosophies and approaches to business. While this is not unique to a multicultural team, we also find wide variations in communication styles, attitudes and behaviours. These multiple perspectives can add a tremendous amount to a top-performing team, presuming they learn to appreciate these differences, understand their own biases, and find a way to adapt or work through these challenges.

Another benefit of having a more diverse top team, from different cultures and backgrounds, or with different genders and age, is the avoidance of 'group think'. Group think is a type of thought exhibited by group members who try to minimize conflict and reach consensus without critically testing, analysing and evaluating ideas. Individual creativity, uniqueness and independent thinking are lost in the pursuit of group cohesiveness, as are the advantages of reasonable balance in choice and thought that might normally be obtained by making decisions as a group (Janis, 1972).

Clutterbuck (2007) has highlighted what makes teams effective: 'several studies have found that top management teams that have diverse backgrounds and capabilities make more innovative, higher quality decisions than those that are relatively homogeneous.' He also points out that, so long as the right processes and conditions for learning are met, the net gains of having a diverse team can lead to wider choices, more robust decision making and greater creativity, amongst other advantages. Team coaching can help in drawing this out, and to establish a collective identity that is useful for the team.

Where there is more complexity in the task, this also requires different forms of teamwork in different situations. More effective executive teams are those that focus their time and coordination efforts on the appropriate core processes given the strategic context of the team (Nadler and Spencer, 1998). This focus is a key driver for elite performance, and having a more diverse, well-rounded team can add greater bandwidth while equally providing a deeper level of value, challenge and healthy debate necessary to produce longer-term results.

WORKING WITH TOP-TEAM COACHES

Some argue that coaching the top team is the CEO's role, but the Human Capital Institute argues that CEOs are not ideal coaches due to the size and scope of the CEO role, and a lack of understanding and skill to coach a senior leadership team (HCI, 2008).The top team's performance is vital for the success of the organization, and it is therefore critical that top teams are effectively coached. An external coach whose area of expertise is coaching senior leadership teams enables the CEO/leader to be a participant in the team, as opposed to being the facilitator of the team.

Identify what the top team wants

What constitutes a highly effective top-team coach who can deliver results with the most demanding senior leadership teams? Perhaps a good place to start is to identify what we often hear from executives about what they don't want in their programme, based on many of their experiences from other forms of team or leadership development. Some of these are shown in Figure 15.3. Conversely, we have highlighted in Figure 15.4 what they often say they do want in a top-team coaching programme.

- Too much structure
- Political agendas
- Team 'bonding' sessions
- Business school or consultancy jargon
- Evaluation without context
- Irrelevant case studies
- Process without end game in mind
- Being psychoanalyzed
- Egos rammed down their throats
- Simulated tasks & role plays
- Inconsistent behaviours
- Being 'done to'

Figure 15.3 What executives *don't* want

We've found having one-to-one conversations with each team member, including the CEO, an essential component of any top-team coaching programme. As part of this, asking them what they do and don't want is a good way to manage expectations and start the dialogue around the most suitable approach for them – both individually and for the team.

- Flexibility
- Time out to think
- A shared or agreed purpose
- Credible, experienced coaches
- Real business issues
- A platform for honest dialogue
- Guidance and interpretation
- Light-bulb moments
- Get the 'elephant on the table'
- Regular performance check-ins
- Mutual respect
- Challenge

Figure 15.4 What executives *do* want

Establish credibility and trust

In order to meet the unique challenges and needs of top teams, and as demand for global coaches who are adept at working at the most senior levels continues, it will be vital for those operating in this area to be able to establish credibility and earn the trust of this group.

Whilst it is understood that 'every coach accepts the need to enhance their experience, knowledge, capability, and competence on a continuous basis, as defined by the Statement of Shared Coaching Values' (UK Coaching Roundtable, 2008), we advocate that a top-team coach needs to develop a wider set of coach and business competencies to have credibility.

To do this, it's essential for the coach to understand the strategy, the marketplace and the core issues of the organization. Coaches need the robustness to intervene whilst the team is at work, the clarity to manage multiple boundaries and not 'get in the soup', as well as the integrity to maintain a strong, supportive relationship with the team as a whole without favouring any one individual. They also need to hold the focus throughout, to enable the team to deliver its purpose and achieve results.

For a top-team coach to earn trust, which in turn can influence the whole team, one way to start is to role-model the behaviours for building relationship trust, as illustrated in Figure 15.5, Covey's (2006) 13 behaviours for building relationship.

Whilst they're all relevant, we find behaviours 1, 2, 3, 9, 10, 11 and 13 the key ingredients for establishing trust, in particular when working with multicultural top teams where listening, demonstrating respect and extending trust are paramount.

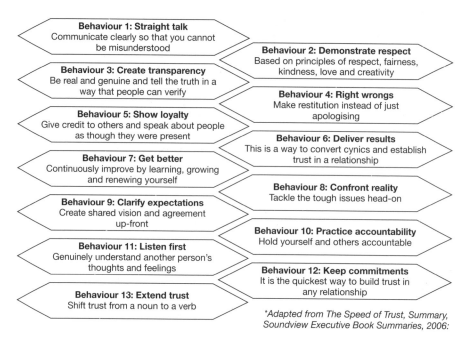

Behaviour 1: Straight talk
Communicate clearly so that you cannot be misunderstood

Behaviour 2: Demonstrate respect
Based on principles of respect, fairness, kindness, love and creativity

Behaviour 3: Create transparency
Be real and genuine and tell the truth in a way that people can verify

Behaviour 4: Right wrongs
Make restitution instead of just apologising

Behaviour 5: Show loyalty
Give credit to others and speak about people as though they were present

Behaviour 6: Deliver results
This is a way to convert cynics and establish trust in a relationship

Behaviour 7: Get better
Continuously improve by learning, growing and renewing yourself

Behaviour 8: Confront reality
Tackle the tough issues head-on

Behaviour 9: Clarify expectations
Create shared vision and agreement up-front

Behaviour 10: Practice accountability
Hold yourself and others accountable

Behaviour 11: Listen first
Genuinely understand another person's thoughts and feelings

Behaviour 12: Keep commitments
It is the quickest way to build trust in any relationship

Behaviour 13: Extend trust
Shift trust from a noun to a verb

Adapted from The Speed of Trust, Summary, Soundview Executive Book Summaries, 2006:

Figure 15.5 Building relationship trust

Focus on the right areas

Senior leadership teams have different needs, and in many cases traditional forms of leadership development are not suitable for effective top-team coaching.

In Figure 15.6, we illustrate the key domains where we find we work with senior leadership teams the most. We have captured these in 10 key areas, or domains. These areas are less about team building and delivering 'content', and more about harnessing some of the top-team requirements we highlighted previously.

Typically, identifying the right areas to focus on is derived from the initial scoping meetings, one-to-one individual interviews with each team member, and discerning the themes that emerge when the team is together. A key ingredient for effectively coaching the top team is to be willing to adapt throughout the programme according to what is most important for the team, in other words not to get locked into process or content – team coaching is not team training!

In the last section, discussing tools and techniques for coaching global top teams, we will work through how we apply aspects of this approach.

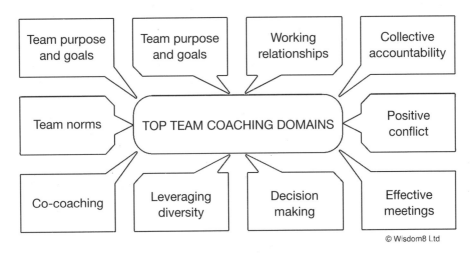

Figure 15.6 Top-team coaching domains

TOP-TEAM INTERVENTIONS

To start off, we think it's useful to define team coaching and what it aims to address:

> Team coaching is directly intervening in the process that the team members use to interact in order to improve team effectiveness. It is focused on coaching the team as an entity about task focused interventions. It also seeks to help the team discover its own lessons based on experience, reflecting back to team members the collective behaviors that hinder and advance teamwork. (HCI, 2008)

> Effective team coaching addresses the task-related behavior of the team with the intent of helping it develop and sustain three things: 1) high levels of motivation for the team's collaborative work; 2) effective collective approaches to team tasks; and 3) the ability to identify and deploy all the considerable talent that team members bring to the table. (Wageman et al, 2008)

When coaching top teams, there is often a greater need for challenge than when coaching other types of corporate teams. Highly successful, independent leaders can be stunningly quick minded, dynamic, articulate, energetic and passionate. At their worst they can be overly convinced of their own rightness, competitive, political, stubborn and self-serving. This is many times compounded by their dual role, often having a functional or divisional accountability as well as responsibility for company-wide results.

Furthermore, the global components add in another layer of complexity, which can create both opportunities and tensions. There is an even higher need for greater levels of awareness, understanding and appreciation of each team member's strengths and views.

A top-team coaching or development programme usually involves an array of different interventions; however the heartbeat of the coaches' work is coaching the team whilst members are actually doing their collaborative work, in order to improve team performance and impact. As a matter of illustration, below we have detailed interventions that we have found to be useful when working with global top teams (UK Coaching Roundtable, 2008).

▌ **Scoping meeting**
Getting clarity with the CEO/leader around the type of team they need and for what purpose. To fully understand the key business drivers, aims and market challenges the business and team is facing. Also, what shifts will be required to accelerate the team's performance (both the leader and the team) and are they prepared for this? Exploring where authority sits in the team and outside the team, the types of intervention, feedback loops, confidentiality, and the impact of the leader's engagement.

▌ **Individual interviews**
Conducting one-to-one interviews with each member of the team, using questions specifically tailored to understand the context of the team, and the areas they believe the team will need to develop further. To fully understand their role within the team, key personal and business challenges, and how they measure success. It may also be appropriate to interview broader stakeholder groups (unity board members, key customers, major shareholders, alliance partners, key customers, direct reports etc) to gather various perspectives on team brand and effectiveness.

▌ **Team assessment**
Running some form of team diagnostic for the purpose of getting a benchmark of the team's current performance. This is also a useful way for the executive team to understand a 'desired state' – a clear picture of 'what good looks like' – and what qualities or skills make up a high-performing top team. It is helpful for top-team coaches to have or develop a model, as a basis for dialogue, based on research and their own experience. The model we often use is shown in Figure 15.7.

It is important to establish a framework that best fits the context, culture and remit of the team being coached. See the 'leveraging diversity' section in the tools and techniques section for further team assessments.

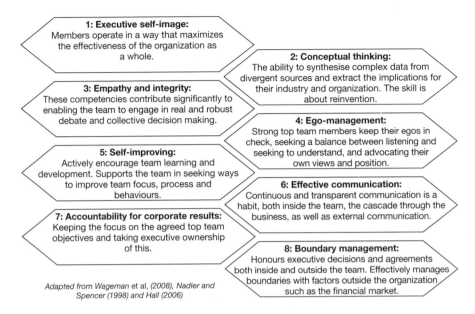

Figure 15.7 Benchmarking top team performance

▌ **One-to-one coaching**

Typically, this includes one-to-one coaching sessions with each member of the team to focus on his or her key development areas as a leader, and ways to contribute more fully as a team member and achieve maximum shareholder value for the business. In these confidential sessions, we find it useful to work holistically (including personal life as well as the work context), to help executives understand themselves better, to align their personal vision and goals with the business, and how their drivers, motives and behaviours can impact on the collective team.

At a minimum, we recommend no fewer than three coaching sessions throughout a top-team programme, with one or two sessions at the onset prior to the first team coaching session. This benefits both the executive and the coach, as a way to gain clarity and trust. Equally, having one-to-one coaching sessions with each team member enables the coach to draw out any underlying themes or concerns, which is invaluable for guiding the overall outcomes.

▌ **Team coaching**

Embarking on a series of team sessions, to include the CEO/leader, with the initial session typically run for one to two days, ideally in person (although this can be a challenge for top teams spread throughout the world). Following on from the initial kick-off meetings, we find it helpful to take a staggered approach, or work with a team over time, in order for the team to evolve and get wins that translate to real business terms along the way.

Coaching a global top team can cover many areas (some of which are highlighted in Figure 15.6). Team coaching is no different from one-to-one coaching – changing leadership behaviours to achieve a desired outcome requires time, focus and review. An effective top-team coach has learned the art of keeping the team's agenda on the radar while staying agile enough to cope with the reality of coaching a global team, often with conflicting diaries and commitments. Therefore, it's also helpful for the coach to have agreed a workable communications plan with the team, to help maintain this focus and drive.

Shadow coaching

Observing the team in action, to help members understand the gap between what they think or say they do and what they really do on a day-to-day basis. A powerful and effective tool for any top team striving for excellence as the coach – acting as an unbiased, independent observer – provides real-time, first-hand feedback on the executive or team in action, and can suggest shifts to increase their effectiveness.

As Wageman *et al* (2008) assert: 'A good team coach holds up the mirror to reflect back to the team members the collective behaviours that hinder and advance teamwork. In this way the team can discuss team processes and agree on a new path forward. Very few teams are able to decode their successes and failures and learn from them without intervention from the leader or team coach.'

CASE STUDY

A CEO, as one of the aims of a team coaching programme, wanted his senior executive team to hold more of the corporate-wide focus and accountability. He brought in a team coach to shadow the weekly senior leadership team meetings to identify current team behaviours and areas where he or the team could improve to obtain the objectives.

One observation made by the coach was that when the team members spoke they addressed the CEO rather than the team. The coach reflected this to the team and suggested a possible shift to members addressing the team as a whole.

The team had been oblivious to this engrained behaviour, and agreed that an effective senior leadership team would see all its members as accountable, and they would therefore 'speak to' each other. In addition, the CEO confessed that this team behaviour left him feeling singularly responsible for the difficult decisions and company direction. Making a relatively small shift in behaviour also shifted the team's identity as a whole and made a significant contribution to increasing both the level of collective accountability held by the team.

Shadow coaching requires the highest level of wisdom and integrity as coaches must be sure of not misusing their influence, of over-intervention or holding too tightly their own model of team effectiveness, and instead be guided by the team's development objectives.

▌ **Peer coaching**

Working with the team to have members coach and mentor each other. This form of coaching can be very powerful on a number of levels, as co-learning occurs between team members, many of whom have similar issues and challenges. We've found it works best to introduce peer coaching once a coaching ethos is established – for example, the members demonstrate an openness and collaborative way of working, with the intention of helping their colleagues succeed. Developing coaching skills within the top team can also help them momentarily 'step out' of the content of any debate and intervene in the team's process in a constructive way.

▌ **Off-site facilitation**

Running tailored off-site meetings with the team. Typically, these arise out of a specific need that arises during team coaching sessions or a change in the business (eg a need to focus on innovation, a merger or acquisition). The yearly strategy and planning process can be another trigger. We believe that experienced top-team coaches are well equipped to facilitate this level of dialogue, while also integrating it within the overall programme. If they are not comfortable with a specific topic, then it's helpful to partner or liaise with other consultancies that can bring this element of competence into the team.

USING TOOLS AND TECHNIQUES WITH THE TOP TEAM

Using our model illustrated in Figure 15.6, 'Top-team coaching domains', in this section we identify different tools and techniques that are used when working with global top teams.

The business agenda

This domain is about coaching the team around establishing and gaining commitment to what they need to prioritize and focus on the most to achieve the business results. This means working with them to establish a framework, structure and, if necessary, processes (such as revised meeting agenda formats) to ensure the team keep these priorities on the radar, as daily operational issues have a tendency to command the most attention.

Team purpose

Team purpose is about a crystal-clear sense of the team's unique added-value in advancing the organization's strategy. This is not the sum of the individual members' contributions, but the interdependencies among team members. Work in this area is to orient, focus and engage the team towards their objectives. There are many ways to coach a team to clarity; here's one from *Senior Leadership Teams* (Wageman *et al*, 2008):

1. Identify the interdependencies among team members that move the strategy forward. What leadership functions require that all the leaders be at the table?
2. Create a short list of decisions and actions that the team needs to achieve. What are the mission-critical things that can be done only by this team?
3. Raise that list to a thematic and compelling level so that it guides team decisions and actions.
4. Articulate this as a 'team purpose'.

Working relationships

This is about coaching the team to develop strong and trusted working relationships. We find it useful to generate a discussion around trust – what builds and what destroys trust. Just having this dialogue can create a shift in a team as individuals generally reflect on how they have/have not been building trust!

We have discussed the elements that go into building trust earlier in this chapter – integrity, courage and honesty all play a part. People believing that they will not get hurt when they are vulnerable is the key. This understanding is generated more when we see the human behind the 'work mask'.

Tools and techniques for developing trust are essential for top-team coaches. We recommend using ones that are an authentic fit for them and the organization's culture.

Collective accountability

When it comes to teamwork, accountability is the willingness of team members to hold themselves and each other to account both for their actions towards their goals and also on behavioural issues.

Once the team's purpose is established, collective goals can be set. Huszczo (1996) suggests doing this as part of a strategic planning session, getting the team to identify goals to resolve current problems and goals to create the ideal future (see his five steps of strategic planning).

For behavioural issues, we like Lencioni's team effectiveness exercise where team members provide one another with focused, direct and actionable feedback about how their individual behaviour can improve team performance (Lencioni, 2005). It can also be useful to work with the team around assertiveness (versus aggression or passivity) by encouraging them to use 'I' statements, instead of accusatory 'you' statements.

Positive conflict

Coach the team to speak the unspoken – as *Good to Great* author Jim Collins says, 'face the brutal truth' to allow resolution to follow. Supporting the team to create a climate of 'positive conflict' where members speak openly, where they don't hold back but share their honest point of view and name the issue, can yield great dividends. Ultimately, this not only builds trust but creates greater degrees of buy-in and commitment, which directly impact on ownership and accountability for results!

Also, 'putting the elephant on the table' is not permission to verbally slap someone around the head! Coach the team to use effective communication techniques and to look for win–win situations. Good resources on this are Kohlrieser's *Hostage at the Table* (2006) and Runde and Flanagan's *Building Conflict Competent Teams* (2008). Tools like the Thomas–Kilmann Conflict Mode Instrument (TKI) are useful for understanding how different conflict-handling modes, or styles, affect interpersonal and group dynamics and for learning how to select the most appropriate style for a given situation.

Effective meetings

This domain is about coaching the team to run effective meetings, getting the maximum contribution from all participants. Effective meetings need to be crisp, with definite start/stop times and an agenda that is pre-announced and focused, be open to constructive conflict, have commitment to outcomes and provide timely communication of results to all employees. We suggest that coaches begin by helping the team to identify what is currently working and what isn't in relation to team meetings. One resource for this is Huszczo's Team Meeting Questionnaire (1996). The results can then be used to coach the team to identify shifts to raise their game.

Decision making

Coach the team to make well-rounded decisions that benefit the higher team purpose or outcomes. One tool that is useful is the MBTI® Team Report, which looks at the different ways individual team members prefer to solve problems, which can also apply to decision making. What comes out from the team sharing their report with others, mapped against the team preference, is that some 'modes' can get overlooked. Facilitated discussions and sharing a suggested framework, getting everyone on board, using the same modes at the same time, can both speed up decisions and identify the necessary elements for making a well-rounded decision.

Leveraging diversity

This domain is about coaching the team to embrace strengths and difference within the team so as to drive performance. This starts with developing a greater level of awareness of what these are, which is shared within the team. The second part is helping them identify ways to leverage their strengths and difference in practice. There are a number of tools that can be used to facilitate dialogue and create higher levels of self and cultural awareness.

For looking at team strengths, one of our favourites is StrengthsFinder 2.0® (Gallup, 2008). Backed by a number of years of research by the Gallup organization, this instrument reveals an executive's 'top five' strengths, with strategies on how to lead with these strengths (useful to do as a collective group exercise). For multicultural teams, there is the COF, or Cultural Orientations Framework™ (Rosinski, 2003), which looks at cultural difference in areas such as communication patterns, modes of thinking, time management approaches, and sense of power and responsibility. It's particularly useful when you have a diverse team, so that you can test out the theory with them in real conversations!

Both of these tools can be accessed online and used throughout a top-team programme in both one-to-one and team coaching sessions. As with any tool, use the right one, and apply your coaching skills to encourage respectful listening, sharing and straight-talking.

Co-coaching

This domain is about coaching team members to coach and mentor each other so that they continue to grow as leaders, achieve their goals and deliver the business results. The key in this area, once the foundation skills such as deep listening, powerful questioning, observational feedback and 'getting out of the way' are covered, is to get them into coaching each other as quickly as possible. In this mode, it's about using real personal and business challenges that have been brought into the session earlier. It's also useful at this point to have worked the team around their purpose or team goals, as we've found this useful before having them work on their individual areas. The co-coaching itself can take many forms – in pairs, in triads, as an entire group.

A number of coaching techniques that work well for the coach can be used with the team. From our experience, and when they are coaching each other as a team, we find that systemic coaching principles work well with executives (and can also be used for strategic or breakthrough thinking), as well as Nancy Kline's 'Time to think' (1999), to name just a few.

Team norms

Team norms (otherwise called 'working agreements') are social contracts that support the team in having productive, effective conversations. Rather than conceptual statements like 'we value all people equally', they are real agreements that help people to do real work and to talk about tough issues. They are often a clue to what people are worried about!

An exercise that we like to use to develop team norms is:

1. In pairs, develop between three and five working agreements that, if followed, would help the team have even more productive discussions and meetings (these aren't for business as usual; they're for new behaviours or ones that aren't yet normal behaviour for the group).
2. Each pair report their two most important agreements.
3. Ask clarifying questions.
4. Reduce to around five to seven behavioural norms overall.

Working agreements belong to the team. Coach the team to monitor them during the meeting.

What coaches need to learn

Through defining some of the unique characteristics and attributes of what is required when working with a global top team, by now we hope readers will already have defined for themselves what they need to learn to coach effectively in this area.

A good place to start is to look at what's already working well when coaching executives at this level during one-to-one coaching. We've already emphasized the importance of being able to challenge clients, to stretch them and give them honest feedback (as this seems to diminish the higher one goes in an organization). Also don't underestimate the benefits of helping them find the space and time to think, as well as the opportunity to explore personal areas, which can impact on their leadership capability in different forms.

Much the same can be said about coaching a top team. For the coach, don't hold back, don't just sit on the sidelines facilitating a process, but equally don't get mixed up in the soup, or attached to content. It's also important, especially when working with multicultural teams, to be aware of your own cultural biases, and how these can be affecting your behaviours and guidance within the coaching.

Although not an exhaustive list, below we have put together '10 key success factors', or what coaches need to focus on and learn, when coaching a top global team.

Ten key success factors

1. Understand the context within which the team exists (eg type of organization, strategy, major stakeholders, the phase the company is in).
2. Ensure that the team is clear about why it exists as a team, and establish collective accountability for team goals.
3. Ensure the CEO or team leader is on board, and is well versed in your approach.
4. Contract with the leader around how you will behave, including boundaries, authority and accountability for team performance.
5. Coach the team as a team; this adds the greatest value.
6. Coach individual team members to be more effective members of the top team and to identify with the top team as their 'A team'.
7. Tailor the coaching approach to each team, and gauge it appropriately to the phase of the team's lifecycle – namely, beginning, midpoint and end.

8.   Coach the team as a system, rather than selecting one or two difficult team members to coach.
9.   Continually monitor team performance, and adjust your approach accordingly.
10. Leverage team member's skills as often as possible, and develop their ability to coach each other.

One final piece of advice we would give is to remember take a 'coach approach'. As part of this system, we are both influencing and role modelling new behaviours. Having ongoing coach supervision, too, can make a difference in the quality of both the coach's and the team's performance, as well as sustaining our energy levels over the course of the journey!

CONCLUSIONS

Throughout this chapter, our intention was to provide readers with a higher level of context, including some of the challenges, characteristics and qualities that can influence top-team performance. We also shared success criteria and typical interventions, as well as some models and techniques that have been useful for us when coaching global leadership teams.

Key themes that emerge, both from our own experience and some of the published work in this area, is that there is an increasing demand for teams at the top of global organizations to work more collaboratively – especially as traditional boundaries and borders shift in the new economy – to establish greater levels of trust throughout a now wider stakeholder group (eg government in banking), and to have collective accountability.

As top-team coaches, this gives us a platform to work from while also using this as an opportunity to stretch ourselves even further – to learn, to challenge, to up our own game. To work collaboratively, earn trust and have collective accountability as a profession, so that we can make a positive impact in the world.

ACKNOWLEDGEMENT

Thanks go to Phillip V Cornwall, who kindly contributed the diagrams for the chapter.

References

Clutterbuck, D (2007) *Coaching the Team at Work*, Nicholas Brealey International, London

Covey, S (2006) *The Speed of Trust*, Simon & Schuster, London

Covey, S and Merrill, R (2006) *The Speed of Trust: The complete summary*, Soundview Executive Book Summaries, Concordville, PA

Davie, S (2009) Know when your time is up, *The Straits Times* [online] www.straitstimes.com

Doz, Y and Kosonen, M (2007) A new deal at the top, *Harvard Business Review*, June

Gallup, Inc (2008) StrengthsFinder 2.0, www.gallup.com

Goleman, D (1996) *Emotional Intelligence*, Bloomsbury, London

Hall, M (2006) *Developing Executive Teams*, Peak Development Consulting LLC

HCI Analyst (2008) *Coaching a Top Team*, HCI white paper, Hay Group and Human Capital Institute [online] www.haygroup.com

Huszczo, G (1996) *Tools for Team Excellence*, Davies-Black, Mountain View

Janis, I (1972) *Victims of groupthink*, Houghton Mifflin, Boston, MA

Katzenbach, J (1997) The myth of the top management team, *Harvard Business Review*, November–December, pp 83–91

Katzenbach, J and Smith, D (1999) *The Wisdom of Teams*, McGraw-Hill, Boston, MA

Kline, N (1999) *Time to Think*, Cassell Illustrated, London

Kohlrieser, G (2006) *Hostage at the Table*, Jossey-Bass, San Francisco, CA

Larsen, D (2008) *Futureworks Consulting* [online] www.futureworksconsulting.com

Lencioni, P (2002) *The Five Dysfunctions of a Team*, Jossey-Bass, San Francisco, CA

Lencioni, P (2005) *Overcoming The Five Dysfunctions of a Team*, Jossey-Bass, San Francisco, CA

Lipnack, J and Stamps, J (2000) *Virtual Teams*, Chapter 1, NetAge Inc [online] www.netage.com/pub/books/VirtualTeams2.html

McKinsey Survey (2008) *Making the Board More Strategic*, McKinsey, New York

Nadler, D and Spencer, J (1998) *Executive Teams*, Jossey-Bass, San Francisco, CA

Nemiro, J, Beyerlein, M, Bradley, L and Beyerlein, S (2008) *The Handbook of High Performance Top Teams*, John Wiley, San Francisco, CA

Palifka, S (2007) *What every CEO wants to Know: Six conditions to create an effective top team*, HCI white paper, Hay Group and Human Capital Institute

Rosinski, P (2003) *Coaching Across Cultures*, Nicholas Brealey, London

Runde, C E and Flanagan, T A (2008) *Building Conflict Competent Teams*, Jossey-Bass, San Fancisco, CA

Stoneman, J (2009) *Extract from Association for Coaching Executive Forum* [online] www.associationforcoaching.com/dir/ind/am34.htm

UK Coaching Roundtable (2008) *Statement of Shared Values* [online] www.associationforcoaching.com/news/M80221.htm

Wageman, R, Nunes, D, Burruss, J and Hackman, R (2008) *Senior Leadership Teams*, Harvard Business School Press, Boston, MA

Wikipedia (2009) [online] http://en.wikipedia.org/wiki/Elephant_in_the_room

Wisdom8 Ltd (2008) [online] www.wisdom8.com, London

16

Coaching using leadership myths and stories
An African perspective

Judith Okonkwo

INTRODUCTION

This chapter will explore coaching for leadership development and the role of cultural myths and stories in facilitating the process. We will maintain a transformational perspective of leadership as it recognizes the ability for development through a variety of individualized talents, drawing on the unique and diverse gifts that each individual brings to leadership. In celebrating the diversity of the individual, we are confronted by a plethora of issues for possible consideration – age, gender, orientation, personality and national culture for example. It is the last of these, national culture, that is potently drawn on by this take on coaching.

Schein (2004) describes leadership as a 'frustrating diffusion of concepts and ideas', a view that is easily shared when one considers the wealth of literature available on the topic. The debate starts with the question 'What is leadership?' Is it a capability, a competence, a concept, or simply the ability to lead people? For some, leadership is all these things, for others there is a focus on particular aspects, primarily determined by the context within which it is being considered. These differences in leadership views have contributed in no small measure to the proliferation of leadership theories, frameworks, styles and types both in academia and in the business world (Benton *et al*, 2008a, b).

Although several studies have been conducted on the various aspects of leadership and many books have been written on exemplary leaders, a number of key questions still remain: What accounts for the observed differences in leadership styles? To what extent does the environment play a part in how leadership is expressed? Can leadership capabilities be developed? It is this final question, the development of leadership that brings us to coaching. Coaching is described as 'an activity where an individual meets with a coach on a one to one basis to work on a range of work-related issues, some of which may also include personal factors' (Knight and Poppleton, 2008). Leadership coaching in particular can be approached from a number of perspectives; individuals may be coached within a situational context, that is, depending on where they exercise leadership. Leadership coaching could also be primarily focused on what stage of leadership people are at, with the aim of progressing significantly from that – an emerging leaders coaching programme for example. Regardless of the theme of the leadership coaching, the 'quality of the coaching relationship is the single most important determinant of success in coaching' (Knight and Poppleton, 2008), and is the inspiration for the creative connections between the coach and coachee that can be fostered by coaching with leadership myths and stories.

UBUNTU: A LEADERSHIP MODEL

Leadership is typically considered from the perspective of Western academics. They have provided us with concepts and terms such as situational leadership, transactional leadership and – the term we centre on here – transformational leadership. However, all these theories draw on aspects of civilization that are not unique to a particular region or locale – we are able to define the development of the transformational leader in a variety of cultural contexts. As a foundation for leadership in this chapter, we base our thoughts and perspectives on the South African philosophy of Ubuntu (Figure 16.1). Defined in a one-line sentence, it can read 'We are, therefore I am,' a literal translation of a tenet of this philosophy. The adaptation of this concept for use among business people is not new. Kamwangamalu (2007) describes the growing use of the concept of Ubuntu in business, stating that 'it is intended to enable business leaders to understand the cultural and behavioural context in which they are developing their approach to business.' Further descriptions indicate its routine use for government programmes and as a national philosophy.

Figure 16.1 Ubuntu

Definitions of Ubuntu vary; in Kamwangamalu's (2007) review of current literature it is described as a process and philosophy, humanness, the key to all African values, the 'collective unconscious' of the African people, a collective solidarity and a statement of being. The case for a collective unconscious of the African people is supported by the prevalence of variations of Ubuntu across cultures on the continent. In Zimbabwe, Rwanda, Burundi, Uganda and a host of other nations slight variations in spelling, Obuntu for example, result in the same meaning. In other regions of Africa, the concept appears under different names, reflecting ethno-linguistic differences. This is perhaps best summed up by Forster (2006) who uses a quote from Makhudu's 1993 work that explains the pervasive effect of Ubuntu in South African life: 'every facet of African life is shaped to embrace Ubuntu as a process and philosophy that reflects the African heritage, traditions, culture, customs, beliefs, value system and the extended family structures.' In a leadership context Ubuntu's core aspect of interdependence is the focus. The sense of communalism that it defines is inextricable from the workplace, and can be seen in modern theories like 'systems thinking'. It is particularly apt for a discourse on coaching that focuses on leadership, as elements of Ubuntu form the basis for the relationship between all individuals, the coach and coachee, the leader and the led.

A leader by definition exists in relation to other people. It is this essence of community and non-isolation that Ubuntu so ably captures as a way of life. With this acknowledged relationship comes the responsibility to develop and support others. Translated into attributes for the modern leader, we see individuals in the workplace called upon to facilitate development and foster teamwork within the larger organization or their immediate team, depending on the scope of their responsibility (Benton *et al*, 2008a, b). To expand this leadership concept, consider Ubuntu in practice. All within the organization would, in the first instance, recognize their reliance on others for the continued existence of the organization. These interdependencies would result in a web of interrelationships, for which leaders at various levels would assume considerable responsibility. Exploring this further, we easily see the need for success and efficiency individually, which would translate to organizational competence. The creation of means to encourage individual success and effectiveness is an important aspect of a leader's role. To fulfil this role, the leader would in turn require a true sense of self and the support of others.

The African continent provides a wealth of history and experience that can equip the coach with a host of diversity-conscious coaching techniques. Specifically, we look to the Oriki, a form of praise poetry, often accompanied by the talking drum (see Figure 16.2), native to the Yoruba

Figure 16.2 The talking drum

people of south-western Nigeria; it is a staple of the oral storytelling traditions found on the continent. It can take one of two forms, either as the name given to a child (its short form), which is believed to be symbolic of the child's birth circumstance, heritage or future, or as a retrospective cataloguing of the positive attributes of a clan, family or individual. It is the latter form that can be adopted to enable personal storytelling as a technique for diversity-conscious coaching. The importance of naming an individual in Yoruba culture is described by Gbadegesin (1998) who explains that the name 'given will guide and control the child by being a constant reminder to him/her of his/her membership of the family and the circumstance of his/her birth'. As Coker (2008) describes it, the 'Oriki addresses itself directly to an individual, touching on all his or her essential aspects, foregrounding socio-cultural, historical and idiosyncratic realities'.

Ubuntu demands an integrative approach to life and leadership; it lends itself not only to a leadership concept, but also to the notions of coaching and storytelling. In traditional African societies, the sense of community depicted by this philosophy led to the evening gatherings where local stories and myths would be told.

THE RESEARCH

Recognition of the importance of the coach–coachee relationship is a coaching norm; alongside that reality we contend with an increasingly diverse workforce that may present additional challenges to coaches as they seek to establish this relationship. Inclusiveness as a technique in coaching enables coaches to transcend the initially apparent layers of diversity – gender, age and race. However in establishing lasting interventions for coachees tailored to their peculiar situations, the consideration of culture is critical. Setiloane (1998) points out that 'every people has its library of stories, which we have come to call "its mythology" ... Over the ages, across the whole world, every culture, every human dispensation has had its heritage of myths and depository of ancient legends and stories ... Among [the African] people there too are stories (myths) passed on for generations as an account of how people came to be.' The importance of myths in the understanding of a people is further emphasized in modern psychology and anthropology. 'By studying the myths of a culture, Jung suggested, we study that culture's psyche' (Leeming, 2005).

If comparing these myths of the world can inform us about the human psyche, and drawing further on Jung's concept of the collective unconscious – that reservoir of human experience that is common to all people – can we not then presume that the secret to leadership, or various aspects of leadership, can similarly be found in these stories, archetypes or personas of the hero? And if each culture has its own interpretation, then does that not provide a direct route to overcome the barriers that might occur as a result of cultural misunderstanding? Researchers have shown the importance of language and communication in human re-lationships. In a relationship as critical as the one between coach and coachee, the importance of 'getting the message across' is even more pronounced. In these tales we can find a solution. The use of stories in leadership coaching is recognized (Goldsmith, Lyons and Freas, 2000; Allan, 2004) and the use of myths and legends can be categorized under this. Having settled on a technique that is appropriate for our needs, we require a framework within which to conceptualize leadership; this is provided by considering Ubuntu in the context of a transformational leadership model.

A leadership model is frequently used as a framework in coaching as shown in Goldsmith, Lyons and Freas (2000) work. Combining such models with various techniques such as storytelling allows learning to be tailored to the coachee, enabling the coach to modify it as required to suit the needs of that particular session. The combination recommended here, specifically that of using culturally relevant myths and legends, is evolving and the assessment of its impact is ongoing. However, the favourable feedback received by the author to date, and supporting research for the use of culturally relevant metaphors to build rapport and establish connections, all provide a good foundation for its success.

Rollinson (2005) examines the idea 'that national cultures can influ-ence patterns of leadership behaviour within organizations'; he contrasts leadership styles and expectations in the United States and UK with what might be more appropriate in Latin American or some continental European cultures. This in turn is further considered alongside a Japanese approach to leadership. The differences are striking enough to hint at the various misunderstandings of behaviour that may be perceived in others of a different culture. Against this backdrop, there is no denying the importance of equipping leaders to be culturally aware as they embark on their respective leadership journeys. However, in preparation for the journey, the leader must be coached in a manner appropriate to his or her situation. As Mintzberg's (2006) research in Ghana shows, models of leadership vary across cultures. He talks of 'organizations that can likewise stand on their own feet and find their own way of doing things, building on the best of their own cultural traditions'. We can offer this same opportunity to leaders as we develop and coach them by using topical myths and stories.

As Hiebert and Klatt (2001) note, 'with organizations becoming increasingly global and workforces becoming more culturally diverse, leaders often find themselves dealing with unfamiliar values, attitudes, and behaviours.' The same can certainly be said of the leadership coach; globalization is a phenomenon that has far-reaching effects through all levels of the organization, resulting in increasingly diverse executive teams. The transcultural concept of archetypes, as depicted by world myths and legends, provides a ready entry into the collective unconscious of all, enabling ready associations to be found across themes and ideologies. It is the acknowledged 'similarity of myths and mythic structures throughout history and across the cultures of the world' (Jarnagin and Slocum, 2007) that propels this coaching technique to the forefront of enabling diversity-conscious coaching.

USING UBUNTU-INSPIRED LEADERSHIP TECHNIQUES WITH COACHEES

Coaching is a confidential, results oriented, highly personal learning process in which executives, with the assistance of a professional coach, build on their talents and enhance their professional effectiveness. (The Canadian Centre for Management Development)

Coaching models for leadership development typically require a number of steps; for example Goldsmith, Lyons and Freas (2000) recommend the following: assessment, developmental plan, public announcement and implementation. The first of these steps, the assessment of leadership skills, is a requisite for effective coaching regardless of the techniques to be employed. Within the interrelational framework stipulated in Ubuntu, the coach and coachee are equipped to obtain this assessment as feedback from several sources. It is the next step, creating a developmental plan, that builds on the output of the assessment and requires the coach's skill to adapt the intervention to take heed of diversity needs. The coach might have little or no knowledge of the coachee's culture; to help, tools like Argonaut for coaching across cultures have been developed, which allow coaches to understand how a culture is perceived based on research and popular literature. However, as we will demonstrate using Ubuntu as a foundation, when using myths and stories it is possible to adapt appropriate leadership models to any culture if you have a suitable metaphor that can connect the underlying principles to the current realities of the coach and coachee.

The importance and effects of culture and background on the way people believe, think and behave cannot be overestimated. Given this and the vast differences we see in different cultures and their attitude to and manner of work (Hofstede, 1997), it is crucial to incorporate some aspect of this into coaching. There are coaching tools and techniques that can transcend cultures and national boundaries. However, to do this effectively they must be presented within a suitable context. This is echoed by Zeus and Skiffington (2003), who state that the understanding of 'verbal and non-verbal signals, recognizing what is not said and appreciating preferred individual and cultural methods of learning are critical if coaching is to be successfully adapted or "transplanted"'.

Julie Allan's (2004) work on the use of stories in coaching recognizes the intention to encourage some playful and creative thought about a situation, using metaphor and analogy as a bridge that can:

▌ help connect aspects of the current situation with existing experiences and understanding;
▌ help people to step out of the situation and take a 'view from the side';
▌ engage creative thought and new connections.

The use of stories in leadership coaching is an important aspect of bridging the cultural gap that can be found in global coaching contexts. Not only does it provide an appreciable connection to cultural and perhaps societal norms, it also often has links and ties to the developmental realities of the leader in question. In a similar vein, Megginson and Clutterbuck (2004) refer to the use of metaphors and stories in their work. They recommend that the coach select the metaphor, embed it in reality, and finally ask the learner to extract lessons from it.

Exploring the use of myths and stories in leadership development further, we shall consider the practice of exhibiting the authentic leadership required for Ubuntu. By creating a suitable technique using elements of Nigerian culture, it is possible to empower coachees to tell and adhere to their personal story.

The Oriki enjoys particularly widespread appreciation as a result of the spread of Yoruba language and culture through migration, trade and slave routes. As an art it is passed from one generation to the next by the elders in the family. It is these Yoruba elders, Agbaje (2002) points out, who 'constitute the repository of the traditional intelligence, logic and verbal or oral wit' within their communities. The Oriki, as an integral part of Yoruba culture, contributes to the education and development of its people. Akinyemi (2003) explains that the principles of Yoruba traditional education are based on 'the concept of Omoluabi', the archetype of the ideal being. Thus the goal of Yoruba traditional education is to make an individual an Omoluabi – a person who is of good character in all its aspects. To the Yoruba, good character includes respect for old age, loyalty to one's parents and local traditions, honesty in public and private dealings, devotion to duty, readiness to assist the needy and the infirm, sympathy, sociability, courage and an intense eagerness to work, among many other desirable qualities.

'An important foundation of leadership is for leaders to settle on their own story' (Denning, 2007). In determining this story leaders must assess their readiness for the challenges of leadership and their willingness to commit to this worthwhile goal. In a sense these very concerns are at the heart of the leader's ability to exhibit a balanced synergy within the workplace. As stated previously, here the focus is on the authenticity of the individual as a leader, an exhibited congruence between beliefs, words and action. Building on this need, the Yoruba people offer a powerful tool to enable a leader to create his or her own story. Within the context of a situation where there is previous familiarity with the Oriki and its import in life, this technique can provide a bridge across cultures. However, it is not limited to this usage as the creation of a personal story is espoused severally across the management and coaching world.

A typical Oriki is translated below:

Adeyemi Atanda
A gbo sa ma sa
A gbo ya-ya ma ya
Ti n ba wo su u
Bi eru to ko gbon
Ogbon n b ninu
Bi omo Babalawo
Adeyemi Atanda.

The one who is indifferent to alarm
The one who is indifferent to stampede
His calm looks may be misinterpreted as folly
Whereas he is as wise as a Diviner's child.
(Coker, 2008)

The use of a personal 'praise song' as epitomized by the Oriki incorporates aspects of appreciative questioning or inquiry. The coachees contribute to the creation of their story, a story that consists of personal attributes and traits that are worthy of recognition, have contributed to previous successes and are central to who they are as individuals. Here there are evident links with the requisite elements of an individual's ability to recognize and live up to his or her 'true self' – self-awareness, self-esteem and authenticity. The Oriki thus created is a powerful tool for the individual to utilize when drawing on the subconscious not only for positive stories but for a raft of talents that can be brought to any given situation. Additionally the Oriki, which is easy to recall, will serve to promote self-coaching, allowing the coachee to build on the gains realized from coaching sessions within the workplace by having ready access to constant prompts for use in upholding the goals and actions agreed (if they tally with the Oriki). In practice use of the Oriki for individual leadership coaching would include the following steps:

▌ An assessment of the coachee's current situation within the workplace. For this step it is essential that a full picture of the coachee's current workplace realities is explored. In keeping with the philosophy of Ubuntu, all workplace relationships must be considered in their entirety. To the extent that the coachee is comfortable with doing so, the influence of significant external relationships may also be considered.

▌ A self-assessment by the coachee recounting his or her qualities. Here coachees are required to go through an intensive introspective process to assess their negative and positive qualities. This should be supported by feedback from key stakeholders in their workplace relationships; this is necessary to obtain the most objective perspective possible.

▌ Affirmation. The coachee owns and acknowledges his or her qualities, appreciating the positive and coming to terms with what may seem negative. This step is particularly important as it typically results in increased self-awareness and self-esteem for the coachee.

▌ Creating the Oriki. The coachee now dips into his or her bag of creativity and creates a personal Oriki. There are no particular restrictions on style and length, the main guidelines being the creation of something positive and memorable. A diversity-conscious approach allows for a host of poetry styles, including limericks, haikus or sonnets among others.

▌ Celebration. The Oriki is traditionally recited in celebration to honour an individual. For the coachee this should also be established through his or her own recitation and commitment to share within their network.

The Oriki that has been developed and deployed now serves as an anchor point for the coachees, an instant and commonly acknowledged reminder of their best, as well as a standard and set of values to uphold. Frequent reinforcement is achievable through the network; a greater understanding of the coachees and potentially more scope for them to 'be themselves' as a result of that are possible. The Oriki is not restricted to individual use. Following its adaptation for coaching, it is a tool that the leader can utilize at the team and organizational levels.

The emphasis here has been on the practice of praise poetry in south-western Nigeria, but the concepts and values espoused transcend cultural boundaries and can be found in myths and legends from a variety of cultures including those of the Ancient Greeks, Asians, Europeans and Native Americans. There is evidence that every gathering of humans in times past is associated with the telling of stories – folktales, myths and legends. To every story there is a point, plot, objective, a *raison d'être* if you will – something to learn.

As noted by Zeus and Skiffington (2002), potential barriers to listening include cultural and language differences. Recalling Hofstede's (1997) work and the differences seen in his dimensions across cultures, even within the same continent, it is not farfetched to imagine the significant impact related issues would have on the perception and interpretation of information conveyed between the coach and coachee. The value of the coaching experience is considerably enhanced if it is cross-culturally relevant. Benefits to the coachee are evident in the first instance in terms of assimilating the information; in addition however there is the potential for the transference of knowledge as the coachee translates this newfound means of transcultural communication within the workplace. The following case study is an example of this in practice.

CASE STUDY

The coachee, a high-achieving employee named Derin Adams, was recently promoted to a new post as the project manager for an organization in the UK. This new position brought him significant leadership responsibility as he now led a multicultural team of five people in three countries. He has been challenged by the differing needs of the team members, and has had difficulty driving them to achieve previous achievement levels. Almost resigned to pigeonholing his staff as incompetent, he has been called to assess his leadership style and its current impact, as part of the organization's leadership development programme. The programme involves an assessment and an initial one-month run of weekly one-hour sessions with a coach. As part of this intervention the coachee completed a leadership assessment tool. Along with his self-ratings, he also had a feedback group of nine, consisting of one line manager, three peers and his five team members.

His leadership assessment results highlighted the following dimensions as his top three areas of development:

- fostering teamwork;
- facilitating development;
- leading from within.

The ratings of both the coachee and his feedback group correlated positively, confirming the awareness by all stakeholders of the need to further develop these attributes.

In dialogue with the coachee, the coach determined a starting point for the intervention focused on the 'leading from within' dimension. This was driven by Derin's feelings of having been overwhelmed and the consequent compromising of self in order to cope at work. Having explored the issues surrounding the self-rating and feedback that resulted in the relatively low scores for this dimension, Derin was invited to focus on his positive attributes in a value-affirming manner. The coach followed this up by working with him to create an archetype; the suggested use of an Oriki to facilitate this was positively received and the coach mandated Derin to develop his own Oriki, drawing on his personal strengths and how best they could be applied to the situation. The resulting long-form Oriki was a celebration of Derin's work-related strengths; the process incorporated the strengths highlighted in his leadership profile such as delivering results, as well as more subtle qualities that were a feature of his personal life and endured in his self-image.

Derin, who is also a committed journal writer, went through the process of owning the image conjured by the Oriki and spending time in reflection each day on the extent to which he had been true to himself.

Three months after the intervention, a period during which Derin's commitment was simply to personify his Oriki, he had this to say: 'I was initially sceptical about the ability of the Oriki to transfer itself from the coaching sessions to my daily life as a useful tool for self-development. However, I have found it to be a simple and effective means of living consciously, of being aware of my capabilities and being influenced to act on them.'

CONCLUSIONS

The growing importance of coaching in organizations is no longer in question. With this new responsibility, and given the need to address the leadership gap and succession within organizations, it stands to reason that diversity-conscious coaching aimed at leadership development will become a major force within the workplace. This need exists against the current backdrop of an increasingly globalized workforce where employers are called on to accommodate a host of cultures. To support this, coaches need to draw on techniques that reflect the myriad values of this increasingly diverse workforce. In myths and stories, we find a vehicle for transporting the various contributions of cultures to concepts that occupy a prime place in the world today, not the least of which is leadership. From Asia to Africa, the Americas to Australia, myths and stories have guided the way people learned and developed. Often in informal settings we have relied on the knowledge of ages past; in coaching with myths and stories we have the opportunity to transfer that learning to the modern workplace.

References and further reading

Agbaje, J B (2002) Proverbs: a strategy for resolving conflict in Yoruba society, *Journal of African Cultural Studies*, **15** (2), pp 237–42

Akinyemi, A (2003) Yoruba oral literature and indigenous education, *Journal of African Cultural Studies*, **16** (2), pp 161–79

Allan, J (2004) Using fictional stories in coaching, in *Techniques for Coaching and Mentoring*, ed D Megginson and D Clutterbuck, pp 82–84, Elsevier Amsterdam, Boston

Benton, S, Brenstein, E, Desson, S and Okonkwo, J (2008a) *Development and Validity of the Insights Transformational Leadership Model*, Insights Learning and Development Limited, Dundee

Benton, S, Brenstein, E, Desson, S, van Erkom Schurink, C and Okonkwo, J (2008b) *The Insights Discovery Preference Evaluator Technical Manual*, Insights Learning and Development Limited, Dundee

Briggs, K M (1970) *A Dictionary of British Folk-Tales in the English Language*, Routledge and Kegan Paul, London

Coker, O (2008) Tradition dies hard: the contemporary relevance of Yoruba Oriki, *Wandering Scholars* (online journal), **2** (1) (January), pp 1–10 [online] http://www.wanderingscholars.org.uk/2.1.Coker_article.pdf

Denning, S (2007) *How Leaders Inspire Action Through Narrative: The secret language of leadership*, John Wiley, San Francisco, CA

Forster, DA (2006) *Validation of Individual Consciousness in Strong Artificial Intelligence: An African theological contribution*, doctoral thesis submitted to the University of South Africa

Gabriel, Y (2004) *Myths, Stories, and Organisations*, Oxford University Press, Oxford

Gbadegesin, S (1998) Individuality, community and the moral order, in *The African Philosophy Reader*, ed P H Coetzee and A P J Roux, pp 292–305, Routledge, London

Gladwell, M (2008) *Outliers: The story of success*, Little Brown, New York

Goldsmith, M, Lyons, L and Freas, A (eds) (2000) *Coaching for Leadership: How the world's greatest coaches help leaders learn*, Pfeiffer, San Francisco, CA

Hiebert, M and Klatt, B (2001) *The Encyclopedia of Leadership: A practical guide to popular leadership theories and techniques*, McGraw Hill, New York

Hofstede, G (1997) *Cultures Consequences: International differences in work-related values (cross cultural research and methodology)*, Sage, Beverley Hills, CA

Ives, Y (2008) What is 'coaching'? An exploration of conflicting paradigms, *International Journal of Evidence Based Coaching and Mentoring*, **6** (2) (August), p 100

Jarnagin, C and Slocum, J W, Jr (2007) Creating corporate cultures through mythopoetic leadership, *Organizational Dynamics*, **36** (3), pp 288–302

Kamwangamalu, N M (2007) Ubuntu in South Africa: A sociolinguistic perspective to a pan-African concept, in *The Global Intercultural Communication Reader*, ed M F Asante, Y Miike and J Yin, pp 113–22, Routledge, London

Kaschula, R H (1999) Imbongi and Griot: toward a comparative analysis of oral poetics in southern and west Africa, *Journal of African Cultural Studies*, **12** (1), pp 55–76

Knight, A and Poppleton, A (2008) *Coaching in Organisations*, CIPD Research Insights

Leeming, D (2005) *The Oxford Companion to World Mythology*, Oxford University Press, Oxford

Littleton, C S (ed) (2002) *Mythology: The illustrated anthology of world myth and storytelling*, Duncan Baird Press

Lothian, A, Hudson, L and Desson, S (2008) *The Insights Transformational Leadership Reference Book*, Insights Learning and Development Limited, Dundee

Megginson, D and Clutterbuck, D (2004) *Techniques for Coaching and Mentoring*, Elsevier Amsterdam, Boston

Mintzberg, H (2006) Developing leaders? Developing countries? Learning from another place, *Development in Practice*, **16** (1) (February), pp 4–14

Rollinson, D (2005) *Organisational Behaviour and Analysis*, 3rd edn, Pearson Education, Harlow, UK

Schein, E (2004) *Organizational Culture and Leadership*, 3rd edn, Jossey-Bass, San Francisco, CA

Setiloane, G M (1998) How African (Bantu) mythology has anticipated Darwin and Professor Philip Tobias, in *Faith Science and African Culture: African cosmology and Africa's contribution to Science*, ed C W du Toit, Research Institute for Theology and Religion, University of South Africa

Wilson, C (2007) *Best Practice in Performance Coaching: A handbook for leaders, coaches, HR professionals and organizations*, Kogan Page, London

Zeus, P and Skiffington, S (2002) *The Coaching at Work Toolkit: A complete guide to techniques and practices*, McGraw Hill, Australia

Zeus, P and Skiffington, S (2003) *Behavioural Coaching: How to build sustainable personal and organisational strength*, McGraw Hill, Australia

Summary of benefits: Association for Coaching

The Association for Coaching® (AC) is one of the leading independent and non-profit-making professional bodies aimed at promoting best practice and raising the awareness and standards of coaching, while providing support for its members.

Established in 2002, AC has experienced rapid growth, with now over 3,000 members in over 42 countries. The AC has become known for its leadership within the market and being responsive to both market and members' needs. Becoming a member gives the opportunity to be involved in an established, yet dynamic, membership organization dedicated to excellence and coaching best practice.

The Association for Coaching is a membership organization for professional coaches, training/service providers and organizations involved in building coaching capability in *executive, business, personal, speciality* and *team coaching*.

OUR VISION

To be one of the leading worldwide professional coaching bodies for coaches, organizations and sponsors of coaching, to enable individuals, businesses and in turn society to develop and achieve greater levels of fulfilment and success.

OUR CORE OBJECTIVES

- ▌ to actively advance education and best practice in coaching;
- ▌ to promote and support development of accountability, ethical practice and credibility across the profession;
- ▌ to encourage and provide opportunities for an open exchange of views, experiences and consultations;
- ▌ to develop and implement targeted marketing initiatives to encourage the growth of the profession;
- ▌ to build a network of strategic alliances and relationships to promote coaching excellence worldwide.

Below are just some of the many benefits coaches and companies can access by joining the Association for Coaching:

- ▌ **Gain new customers and referrals*** – through your dedicated web page profile on the AC online membership directory.
- ▌ **Regular seminars and events** – monthly workshops and forums across the UK on current relevant topics. This provides an opportunity to network, compare notes and gain knowledge from industry experts and colleagues. Members are entitled to discounts on attendance fees.
- ▌ **Accreditation**** – eligible to *apply* for AC individual coach accreditation after being approved as a full AC Member for at least three months.
- ▌ **International AC conference** – attend the AC's international conference at discounted rates, with speakers drawn from top coaching experts worldwide.
- ▌ **Press/VIP contacts** – raise the profile of coaching through PR activities, through the influential honorary board and contacts across the AC.
- ▌ **Member newsletters** – increase knowledge through sharing best practice and keeping abreast of the latest thinking and learning in the *Quarterly AC Bulletin* and *AC Update*.
- ▌ **Co-coaching** – Practise your coaching skills and learn through experience and observation at any of our many regional co-coaching forum groups.
- ▌ **AC forums** – an opportunity to participate in the AC online forum – a networking and discussion group for members to share their news and views and receive advice and support from others.
- ▌ **Industry/market research** – gain first-hand knowledge of latest industry trends via the AC's market research reports.
- ▌ **Dedicated AC website** – gain access to up-to-date AC activities, members' events, reference materials and members-only section.

- **AC logo/letters*** – add value to your service offering and build credibility through use of AC logo/letters in marketing materials.
- **Ongoing professional development** – acquire CPD certificates through attendance at development forums, workshops and events, and gain access to Organizational Development Guidelines.
- **Improve coaching skills** – through special invitations to professional coaching courses and participation in workshops.
- **Social responsibility forums** – join a dedicated special-interest group related to the areas of making a difference in the community and areas of sustainability.
- **Networking opportunities** – enjoy networking opportunities to draw on the advice and experience of leading edge organizations that are also passionate about ethics, best practice and standards in the coaching profession.
- **Strategic partnerships** – receive member discounts, discounted training offers, and product and service deals through strategic partnerships.
- **The AC journal** – receive twice a year by post a copy of *Coaching: an international journal of theory, research & practice*, the AC's international coaching journal, published in collaboration with Routledge.

* Associate level and above only   ** Member level only

Each approved individual member will receive a member's certificate with embossed seal.

For booking, the dedicated conference website will be up in October 2009 at www.acconference.com

Join the mailing list

To join the overall AC mailing list, register on the home page of the AC website www.associationforcoaching.com

For further information on the AC or joining, please visit the membership section of the website or e-mail members@associationforcoaching.com

Useful contacts

For general information: enquiries@associationforcoaching.com
For membership: members@associationforcoaching.com

'promoting excellence & ethics in coaching'
www.associationforcoaching.com
www.acconference.com

Index

NB: page numbers in *italic* indicate figures or tables